ROUTLEDGE LIBRARY EDITIONS:
ETHNOSCAPES

Volume 11

ON THE AESTHETICS OF ARCHITECTURE

ON THE AESTHETICS OF ARCHITECTURE

A Psychological Approach to the Structure and the Order of Perceived Architectural Space

RALF WEBER

Routledge
Taylor & Francis Group

LONDON AND NEW YORK

First published in 1995 by Avebury (Ashgate)

This edition first published in 2025
by Routledge
4 Park Square, Milton Park, Abingdon, Oxon OX14 4RN

and by Routledge
605 Third Avenue, New York, NY 10158

Routledge is an imprint of the Taylor & Francis Group, an informa business

British Library Cataloguing in Publication Data
A catalogue record for this book is available from the British Library

ISBN: 978-1-032-86590-4 (Set)
ISBN: 978-1-032-82034-7 (Volume 11) (hbk)
ISBN: 978-1-032-82091-0 (Volume 11) (pbk)
ISBN: 978-1-003-50288-3 (Volume 11) (ebk)

DOI: 10.4324/9781003502883

Publisher's Note
The publisher has gone to great lengths to ensure the quality of this reprint but
points out that some imperfections in the original copies may be apparent.

Disclaimer
The publisher has made every effort to trace copyright holders and would
welcome correspondence from those they have been unable to trace.

New Series Introduction to
RLE: Ethnoscapes

The neologism *Ethnoscapes*[1] was created by David Canter and David Stea in 1987 when they happened both to be in Yogjakarta at the same time. They wanted a term to cover the rapidly emerging multidisciplinary field of research into many aspects of how individuals, groups and cultures interact and transact with their surroundings. It was derived as follows:

Ethno (combining form) indicating race, people or culture.

Scape (suffix-forming nouns) indicating a scene or view of something.

Ethnoscapes (plural noun) Scholarly and/or scientific explorations of the relationships people and their activities, have with the places they create and/or inhabit; historical, psychological, anthropological, sociological, and related disciplines that study the experiences of places, attitudes towards them, or the processes of shaping, managing, or designing them. The term was subsequently used to provide an umbrella for a series of books. These cover topics that are so multidisciplinary that they do not sit comfortably in any of the constrained silos of academic and scholarly research. As indicated on the opening page of the first book in the series, many disciplines "have developed marauding sub-groups who move freely across each others' borders, carrying ideas almost like contraband, without declaring that they have crossed any disciplinary boundaries."

They include domains labelled as Behavioural or Perceptual Geography, Environmental/Architectural Psychology, Urban History, Social Ecology, Behavioural Archaeology, Urban Planning, Behavioural Architecture, and Landscape Architecture. There are also many other areas of research and practice that, whilst not being overtly psychological, social, or cultural, do explore and act on the built and natural environment in a way that recognises the importance of the human transactions with those settings. These professions include interior and product design, comparative linguistics, and even aspects of criminology and mental health providers.

Like all such implicit and explicit transactions between different domains, a community of interest and support has emerged in which those who cross the boundaries often find they have more in common with other transgressors than with their mother disciplines. This has given rise to common means and forms of communication, with a shared understanding of the issues and approaches that are of value. Although, of course, these are not always understood in the same way by all those involved,

The *Ethnoscapes* series of books provides a forum for these multifarious, cross-disciplinary, determinedly international, studies and practices. Each of the books takes on board one or more of the environmental challenges that that individuals, societies and cultures are facing. Emphasising a social perspective, rather than the dominant 'hard' science viewpoints embedded in physical, geological and climate changes.

It may now be regarded as rather prescient that it was over three decades ago that the need and importance was recognised of bringing together the many strands of environmental social research and practice. But there is no doubt that there were academics and professionals exploring Ethnoscape topics, going back to the 1960s, often in isolation and with little recognition, that are today front-page, and podcast, news. The challenges in the environmental social sciences that Ethnoscapes explores are just as pertinent now as they were when initially identified.

The series, in essence, deals with four challenges the environmental social sciences embrace.

1. Addressing "the awareness of governments and public alike of the problems of environmental degradation and pollution."

This includes the challenge of providing acceptable housing and related environmental conditions that also encompassed the support for environmental and related cultural heritage. It also requires detailed consideration of the assessment and evaluation of designs and design proposals as well as background research on policy related issues.

2. Developing ways of conceptualising human interactions with the physical surroundings.

This may seem somewhat abstract but has practical implications. The dominant view that people are passively controlled by their sur-roundings supports a paternalistic, management of what it is assumed people need. That ignores the active way in which people make sense of their environment, drawing on cultural and historical influences. This recognises the importance of user participation in decisions about built and natural settings. That, in turn, requires a much richer understanding of how people interact with where they are or want to be.

3. A much wider range of ways of exploring people's transactions with the environment is needed to contribute to policy and practice as well as developing richer insights into human experiences.

The stock in trade of surveys, or the inevitably artificial laboratory-based experiments, whilst of value for some explorations, need to be augmented by methodologies that enrich an understanding of what the experiences are of being in, acting on, and developing places. They need to connect not just with the endeavours of individuals but also with how cultures and societies express these transactions.

4. Finding ways to enable practitioners and researchers to express their own encounters with the contexts they are influencing or studying.

Much of the research that is carried out in what are curiously called 'Ivory Towers', even when it is studying the big wide world, allows the pretence of distancing from the direct experiences of the issues being studied. Yet the challenges of moving across disciplinary boundaries are as much personal challenges of finding new ways of thinking, communicating, and acting, as an academic demand to develop more effective intellectual systems. The Ethnoscapes series recognises the value of exploring these challenges by hosting a variety of formats. Many of these go beyond the staid and limited formulations that academic discourse assumes to be the norms.

The Ethnoscapes series brings together a vibrant mix of cutting-edge explorations, from all over the world, of human transactions with the built and natural environments. This includes, for example, consideration of vernacular architecture that contrasts with the architecture and urbanism of the colonial enterprise, the meaning of home, aesthetics, well-being and health, and consideration of how environmental psychology has become 'green'. All of these topics, and more, provide an exciting basis for dealing with current challenges in the environmental social sciences.

Note

[1] Not to be confused by the term *Ethnoscape* later concocted by Arun Appadurai in 1990, to refer to **human migration**, the flow of people across boundaries. This includes migrants, refugees, exiles, and tourists, among other moving individuals and groups, all of whom appear to affect the politics of (and between) nations to a considerable degree. Ignorant of the lexicographical origins of the term 'scape' he rather confusingly added it to many ideas of flow, such as the flow of technology – technoscapes and the flow of ideas ideoscapes. Appadurai, A. (1990). "Disjuncture and difference in the global cultural economy." *Theory, Culture and Society* 7(2–3): 295–310.

Routledge Library Editions: Ethnoscapes

1. *Environmental Perspectives* David Canter, Martin Krampen & David Stea (Eds) (1988) ISBN 978-1-032-81616-6

2. *Environmental Policy, Assessment, and Communication* David Canter, Martin Krampen & David Stea (Eds) (1988) ISBN 978-1-032-81635-7

3. *New Directions in Environmental Participation* David Canter, Martin Krampen & David Stea (Eds) (1988) ISBN 978-1-032-81646-3

4. *Vernacular Architecture: Paradigms of Environmental Response* Mete Turan (Ed.) (1990) ISBN 978-1-032-82023-1

5. *Forms of Dominance: On the Architecture and Urbanism of the Colonial Enterprise* Nezar AlSayyad (Ed.) (1992) ISBN 978-1-032-84164-9

6. *The Meaning and Use of Housing: International Perspectives, Approaches and Their Applications* Ernesto G. Arias (Ed.) (1993) ISBN 978-1-032-84781-8

7. *Placemaking: Production of Built Environment in Two Cultures* David Stea & Mete Turan (1993) ISBN 978-1-032-86434-1

8. *Environmental Psychology in Europe: From Architectural Psychology to Green Psychology* Enric Pol (1993) ISBN 978-1-032-83324-8

9. *Housing: Design, Research, Education* Marjorie Bulos & Necdet Teymur (Eds) (1993) ISBN 978-1-032-86388-7

10. *Architecture, Ritual Practice and Co-determination in the Swedish Office* Dennis Doxtater (1994) ISBN 978-1-032-81774-3

11. *On the Aesthetics of Architecture: A Psychological Approach to the Structure and the Order of Perceived Architectural Space* Ralf Weber (1995) ISBN 978-1-032-82034-7

12. *The Home: Words, Interpretations, Meanings and Environments* by David N. Benjamin (Ed.) (1995) ISBN 978-1-032-86411-2

13. *Tradition, Location and Community: Place-making and Development* Adenrele Awotona & Necdet Teymur (Eds) (1997) ISBN 978-1-032-84608-8

14. *Aesthetics, Well-being and Health: Essays within Architecture and Environmental Aesthetics* Birgit Cold (Ed.) (2001) ISBN 978-1-032-86577-5

Other Ethnoscapes series titles also available:

Integrating Programming, Evaluation and Participation in Design: A Theory Z Approach Henry Sanoff (1992) HBK 978-1-138-20338-9; EBK 978-1-315-47173-0; PBK 978-1-138-20339-6

Directions in Person-Environment Research and Practice Jack Nasar & Wolfgang F. E. Preiser (Eds) (1999) HBK 978-1-138-68674-8; EBK 978-1-315-54255-3; PBK 978-1-138-68677-9

Psychological Theories for Environmental Issues Mirilia Bonnes, Terence Lee & Marino Bonaiuto (Eds) (2003) HBK 978-0-75461-888-1; EBK 978-1-315-24572-0; PBK 978-1-138-27742-7

Housing Space and Quality of Life David L. Uzzell, Ricardo Garcia Mira, J. Eulogio Real & Joe Romay (Eds) (2005) HBK 978-0-81538-952-1; EBK 978-1-351-15636-3; PBK 978-1-138-35596-5

Doing Things with Things: The Design and Use of Everyday Objects Alan Costall & Ole Dreier (Eds) (2006) HBK 978-0-75464-656-3; EBK 978-1-315-57792-0; PBK 978-1-138-25314-8

Rethinking the Meaning of Place: Conceiving Place in Architecture-Urbanism Lineu Castello (2010) HBK 978-0-75467-814-4; EBK 978-1-315-60616-3; PBK 978-1-138-25745-0

On the Aesthetics of Architecture

*A Psychological Approach to the Structure and
the Order of Perceived Architectural Space*

Ralf Weber

University of California, Berkeley

Technical University of Dresden

A v e b u r y

Aldershot ▪ Brookfield USA ▪ Hong Kong ▪ Singapore ▪ Sydney

For Rudolf Weber

Published by
Avebury
Ashgate Publishing Limited
Gower House
Croft Road
Aldershot
Hants GU11 3HR
England

Ashgate Publishing Company
Old Post Road
Brookfield
Vermont 05036
USA

British Library Cataloguing in Publication Data

Weber, Ralf
    On the Aesthetics of Architecture:
    A Psychological Approach to the Structure
    and the Order of Perceived Architectural
    Space. - (Ethnoscapes: Current Challenges
    in the Environmental Social Sciences Series)
    I. Title   II. Series
    720.1

    ISBN 1 85628 977 X

Library of Congress Catalog Card Number: 95-75555
Typeset by
Annabelle Ison
San Francisco CA
USA

Printed and Bound in Great Britain by Athenaeum Press Ltd., Gateshead, Tyne & Wear.

Production of this book was funded in part by a grant from the Graham Foundation for Advanced Studies in the Fine Arts and by a COR Grant from UC Berkeley

Contents

Preface

This book is about form: specifically, the role form plays in the experience and judgement of architecture. Its title expresses a tautology that is intentional given my main hypothesis, which is to equate aesthetic experience with the perception of form.

Ever since architecture's emergence as a profession, architects have pondered the concept of form. In their treatises, architects like Vitruvius, Alberti, Palladio, and Corbusier all gave considerable attention to compositional principles of beautiful and harmonious form. Yet, despite the prominence given to form in architectural theory, the *ultimate* meaning of the term remains ambiguous. Is the form of a building the same as its shape? Does it include color or texture? Can form be considered separate from meaning? Can form have meaning in itself?

Through the course of history two major definitions can be identified from the varying uses of the term. In the first sense, 'form' has been used to describe how a particular object is constructed by virtue of principles — in other words, how its constituent parts relate to a whole configuration. In this sense (which one might call 'objective') form means order or arrangement.

However, form has also been used to denote that which is 'directly given to the senses', that is, the perceptually accessible qualities of one's environment. Form here refers to the appearance of things, but not to their significance or meaning. A specialized case within this second, 'subjective' use of the term is provided by the Kantian concept of form. In this view, form is a construction of the human mind based on *a-priori* concepts that are imposed onto a perceived thing.

Although these two uses of 'form' are based on different premises, there is no logical reason they cannot be linked: precisely this is the intent of my book. In the pages that follow I attempt to show how the objective and subjective views can be joined if form is considered the structure or internal organization of an object *as perceived*.

When I originally set out to write this book, I did not aim to develop a theory of aesthetics *per se*, that is, to wrestle with issues traditionally raised by philosophy. If I had, the book would have been quite a different project. Instead, my initial questions arose from the perspective of a practicing architect. What is 'good' form? What makes one building more appealing, or more beautiful, than another? Why do some cities provide a strong 'sense of place'? And, ultimately, are there principles of beautiful form which are valid in different cultural and temporal contexts?

I now realize I could hardly have hoped to answer these queries in the objective fashion I sought to pursue. Nevertheless, my original concerns still permeate my quest, albeit in a different manner. I also still refuse to adopt a position of relativism in aesthetics. Anyone who would use an argument of 'viewpoint' to elevate the suburbs of Milan, Halle or Irkutsk — epitomes of the ugly — to the level of Bergamo's Citta Veccia or to Venice is not a reader I wish to persuade. I am content with my bias: my approach remains subjective, although I hope I have succeeded in objectifying my position from my starting point.

In terms of organization, the book consists of two parts that can be read independently of one another. I first propose a general theory of aesthetics, then proceed to the specific case of architecture. Another way of thinking of this distinction is that in Part One I treat the general issue of experiencing and judging form, and then move to the question of aesthetic value in architecture and urban design in Part Two.

The text reflects a necessary interdisciplinary approach. In architecture, aesthetic concepts are often only vaguely articulated. Consideration of other disciplines is needed to bring out specific understanding of terms such as 'order', 'balance', 'harmony' and 'scale'. It is only if we establish specific meanings for these concepts that we can look for the causes of particular architectural effects. Traditionally, it has been philosophical aesthetics that has aimed at clarifying such issues. But explanations of aesthetic experience must also necessarily involve the investigations of perceptual psychology. Because I make use of such specialized areas of knowledge, the level of discourse I offer is different from that normally found in architectural writing. But it is my hope that the reader will carefully examine the discussion in the earlier, more deliberate sections, which I consider fundamental to the development of later arguments.

In terms of my position in relation to several main areas of knowledge, my philosophical perspective arises from rationalism rather than from an empirical viewpoint. In particular, I advocate a presentational theory of aesthetics rooted in Kantian thought. I do, however, disagree with those theorists within the presentational school who argue that aesthetic experience cannot, by virtue of its nonconceptual nature, be formalized through descriptive criteria. Rather, I will argue that principles of perceptual organization can be used as a basis for analyzing aesthetic value.

In terms of psychology, my thinking can be identified as organismic-organizational. In particular, my viewpoint on perceptual organization owes much to that tradition started under the name 'Gestalt psychology' by Wolfgang Köhler, Kurt Koffka and Max Wertheimer, and which has led to various schools of psychological structuralism. Even though some of the original neurological explanations this school gave for perceptual phenomena

ix

may have been superseded, its success in formulating principles of perceptual organization can hardly be questioned. It is common ground today in perceptual theory to argue that things appear as they do because of relational properties of the perceived object. Likewise, it is common to argue that percepts are organized as wholes at the outset, rather than as aggregates of discrete stimuli connected through the action of memory and 'higher' interpretive processes (as claimed by associationists and empirists). I further believe that stimuli themselves must be considered structured information, and that a strict body-mind distinction (with a passive receptor system on one side, and an active brain on the other) cannot be maintained. In this I have been persuaded by J.J. Gibson's ecological approach to visual perception, which is partly in line with, and partly opposed to, the Gestalt view.

In developing an epistemological model of information processing, I have used Jean Piaget's theory of cognitive development as a springboard, especially in relation to his position that quantitative development, that is, learning, cannot occur without qualitative, that is, structural-organic, development. Furthermore, my position displays many similarities to that of Rudolf Arnheim, whose works have brought much clarity to understanding the processes that govern the making of art. Inasmuch as psychological foundations are concerned, there is a kinship between Arnheim's theories and mine; however, there are considerable differences between us in regard to how we view the nature of expression and meaning.

The choice of a particular psychological position has been critical to this book. I agree with Paul Feyerabend, who brilliantly demonstrates in his essay *Wissenschaft und Kunst*[1] that many of the choices involved in developing scientific models are similar to decisions made in the arts. Certainly, I am not neglecting the 'aesthetic' appeal of the organismic-organizational perspective; its intellectual stature displays considerable elegance and simplicity. However, I have chosen to defend this position on logical grounds, using the philosophical models which fathered the various psychological epistemologies. Of course, should the position I adopt be refuted, my theory of form and aesthetic value would collapse. However, I still hold that architecture can be examined discursively as I have presented it in the second part of this book.

The book begins by asking several questions crucial to architects. What is successful form? And are there principles of composition that are universal despite the varying constraints of culture, time, and building technology? From here, in Chapter Two, I move to a historical analysis of three kinds of theories that have enjoyed considerable appeal in architectural circles: functionalism, proportion systems, and theories of meaning. The third chapter proposes a way around the inability of any one of these three theories to explain successfully how aesthetic judgements are made: the presentational or so-called formalist approach which attempts to relate the experience of a work of art specifically to its formal properties. The final three chapters of the first part of the book attempt to link theories of perceptual psychology to the making of judgements about architectural forms. They present an investigation of the notion of presentational properties, information processing, and aesthetic value. Arguing that perception and cognition are processes functionally independent of one another — the former being an organismically determined sensory-motor process of organizing a stimulus array into a percept, the latter standing for the organization of cognitive schemes — I arrive at a justification for the separation of form and meaning for the purpose of analysis. Then, by investigating the degree of intersubjectivity in the formation of judgements, I propose an epistemological model which describes various layers of information-processing in which formal properties are incorporated into a judgement by a decreasing extent while conceptualization increases. When defined as the experience of form, aesthetic experience must thus be embedded in all experiences. At the same time I reject the notion of purely aesthetic judgements based entirely on immediately perceivable properties, because the cognitive internalization of a perceived object must incorporate the meaning and significance which the beholder also assigns to the object. At the end of Part One I arrive at two necessary conditions for the creation of aesthetic value: perceptual appropriateness, that is, the appropriateness of a stimulus pattern to the human capacity for perceptual organization; and sustained perceptual interest, which is guaranteed through hierarchical order.

The second part of the book begins by analyzing how the dynamic qualities of perceptual space differ from the unisotropic nature of ideal, geometric space. Chapter Seven concentrates on the conditions for figural definition of space, that is, the conditions under which a void between space forming elements can assume the character of a self-contained figure. The chapter, moreover, discusses architectural spaces within larger spatial arrangements. Chapter Eight then turns from discussion of architectural space to discussion of the properties of space-bounding and accentuating architectural elements. Specifically, it elaborates on the issue of visual harmony and the concept of visual mass and stability in facades.

Overall, I did not intend in this work to develop a safe method for objectively determining what constitutes aesthetic appeal. Rather, I have aimed at demonstrating that problems of form in architecture can be dealt with systematically. Given the complexity of this topic, I admit that my approach is not fully developed. It should rather be understood as a stimulus for further discussion; and toward these ends I have intentionally included mere fragmentary thoughts on the application to design, because I was convinced that in-depth consideration of the principles in architecture only, without the backing of theoretical analysis, would make little sense. At several points I have thus had to speculate—which, given the meaning of the word, I consider a worthwhile endeavor.

In illustrating the theory with specific buildings and urban spaces, I am also aware of several other limitations. One is that architecture is always perceived three-dimensionally; two-dimensional representations cannot simulate the actual conditions under which buildings and open spaces are experienced. Space is always sequentially experienced by body, head or eye movement, and the still image does not do justice to this perceptual reality. A further shortcoming is that I have necessarily limited my discussion to the visual aspect of perception, whereas architecture is normally experienced synaesthetically.

I am also well aware that, due to its one-sided focus on architectural form, my approach does not provide a complete evaluative method. However, I do by no means intend to suggest that architecture should be treated exclusively aesthetically; this would neglect the functional and socio-cultural criteria under which a design must always also perform. Such an exclusivity of view might also detract from what architecture is ultimately about: the making of a suitable habitat.

Finally, I have tried to avoid the traditional academic format in my presentation because, above all, I aim to address architects and students of architecture. Consequently, I have tried to limit the number of academic references in the text. I am not sure whether I have entirely succeeded in avoiding psychological or philosophical jargon. But I have tried to write in a way that will help stimulate a dialogue between architects and aestheticians, and, perhaps, give some impetus to the teaching of the subject.

In the course of developing and refining the ideas for this book several people have been influential: Rudolf Weber, in who's labyrinthean place of books, paintings and memories I spent long enchanted winter afternoons of my childhood in the Erzgebirge mountains, awakened a sense of beauty and intellectual curiosity within me. Kurt Milde and Peter Gerlach from the University of Dresden introduced me to the notion of Gestalt analysis in urban form and architecture. Most importantly, however, the late Horst Rittel was a mentor for my intellectual maturation and spent countless efforts to turn a thoroughbred architect into a skeptic: my present way of thinking would differ considerably, if it were not for his insisting doubts and interjections which helped me to cast originally naive ideas into more organized thoughts; in turn, I hope to have convinced him of the worthwhileness of this topic. Kenneth Craik has been the principal critic of my manuscript: he has been an extremely thorough and sympathetic reader of virtually every sentence of the various draughts. The influence of his constructive criticism reaches beyond the limits of this approach. Richard Wollheim guided my first explorations into the field of aesthetics; through his lectures and our conversations in coffee-houses on various continents he has been an encouraging and critical teacher of a fascinating subject. Michael Trieb and Donald Olson have looked at my draughts from the viewpoint of architects and encouraged me to stress the application to design. Yael Ifrah, my student who didn't hesitate to reverse this role, has thoroughly read the first part of this approach. She asked the intimidating questions which my other readers had spared me. My deep respect and gratitude is also due to Anthony Dubovsky, my friend and teacher, and to Nezar AlSayyad for his support at various turning points in my career. In the final stages of preparing the manuscript I received invaluable support from several people: David Moffat sensibly transformed my sometimes teutonically influenced grammatical structure into readable English without altering the structure of my thoughts, Malini Krisnankutti heroically worked on locating lost bibliographic sources and organized the visual material, Anabelle Ison designed the layout for the book. David Dowell rendered the line diagrams, Jens Zander helped me with assembling the final copy, and Sharon Larner tied all the loose ends. I would like to thank the Graham Foundation for Advanced Studies in the Fine Arts and the Committe on Research at UC Berkeley for funding part of the production of the manuscript. I also would like to express my thanks for numerous free cappucini at Cafe Roma in Berkeley where many of these thoughts were conceived and discussed.

Ralf Weber
Berkeley, California, 1994

I

The Issue of Form:
Some Questions Posed

What is it that provokes the sense of profound experience, that leaves deep imprints in the memory, that moves one's spirit when one enters the cathedral at Vezelay, wanders through the winding streets of Bergamo, views the skyline of Prague, or comes upon the open space of Rome's Campidoglio? What is it that constitutes the outstanding beauty of these spaces, that gives them their unique sense of place, that has inspired writers, poets and philosophers to call architecture 'frozen music', elevated to a superior place among the arts?

What is it that distinguishes the temples of Paestum, Burgundian cathedrals, Tuscan hill towns, and certain vernacular settlements from their more mediocre counterparts? What makes certain places so remarkable that they have earned the praise of scholars as well as travelers? Do beautiful buildings and spaces have something in common despite differences in function, appearance, style, manner of construction, environmental and cultural conditions? Do they share common qualities that trigger similar experiences and judgements? And, if so, can these be applied in the making of contemporary architecture?

1

The above questions get to the root of the inquiry in this book. Over the centuries few disciplines, aside from the fine arts, have concerned themselves as extensively with form as has architecture. And, although issues of form might not always seem a primary concern for many architects and planners, they do, in fact, permeate most stages of the design process. In environmental design nearly all decisions result in form and involve aesthetic deliberation. And it is particularly in the early phases of a design, when choices among otherwise equally valued alternatives must be justified, that aesthetic judgments come into play. Form, likewise, plays a critical role in the public experience of architecture. The impact of architecture is unavoidable, since most human activities occur within the context of buildings and cities that create not only physical, but psychological environments.

Because architecture and town planning exert such a strong influence on everyone's living conditions, one might assume that architects would be aware of the impact of the visible and tangible shapes they create. But actual practice often shows this assumption to be incorrect. With regard to the 'material-functional' aspects of buildings — such as structure and construction, functional layout, lighting, etc. — the designer can rely on a large stock of factual and instrumental knowledge. And since the concepts involved are fairly clear, constructive professional dialogue normally occurs. Yet there is considerable confusion when the 'immaterial' aspects of design are discussed, because there is a scarcity of clear concepts to legitimize decisions about form or evaluate a building's aesthetic impact. One result is that the process of conceiving the shapes of buildings is often interpreted as something mysterious — the privilege of the gifted, 'creative' designer, kissed by the muse (though there hasn't been one appointed for architecture as yet). It is in this way that the aesthetic component of design is thought to be inexpressible in rational terms. Indeed, the epistemological apparatus architects use to justify their preferences for particular forms often exhibits extreme ambiguity. The result is a lack of clear discourse among architects, let alone between architects and the public.

2

Clearly, the design of the shelter, with a spatial layout adequate to the desired function and a physically sound structure, should be an architect's primary concern. But can other needs, such as those for 'beauty' in buildings, streets and squares, be neglected simply because they are so hard to formalize? If the design process is, as Rittel[1] has suggested, principally concerned with generating knowledge necessary to achieve predesired results, then the aesthetic aspect of architecture is as much in need of systematic explication as is architecture's material-functional side.

It is my view that the lack of systematic study of the aesthetic experience of form is less a matter of neglect than a symptom of a deep-rooted skepticism that has arisen within the theory and practice of architecture over the last two centuries. This tradition has been characterized by a shift from objective to subjective theories of aesthetics and marked by a resistance even to contemplating clear grounds for aesthetic judgment. If any commonly accepted standard now exists, it is *de gustibus non est disputandum* — there is no accounting for taste.

One reason is that architects traditionally have given scant credibility to scholars of aesthetics. In fact, because aesthetics has commonly been identified with 'artistic' affairs (which, supposedly, cannot be plausibly defended), aesthetics has not been considered a serious topic for architectural research. In some cases it has even been considered a hindrance to the design process. However, such skepticism toward attempts to uncover underlying principles of decision-making can also be seen to serve the architect's professional self-image. If it were possible to explain, and thus objectify, the rationale behind the formal aspect of design, then the protective myths of 'creativity' and 'fantasy' would vanish. The mystical aura shrouding design is one of the main strategies by which the architect can construct an 'asymmetry of ignorance' and so underscore the uniqueness of the profession and the need for his expertise in shaping the environment. The resulting lack of accepted criteria for evaluating aesthetic performance, however, has led to uncertainty and relativism. As a result, architecture is in danger of becoming

3

little more than a 'wrapping industry', where the teaching of form is reduced to the teaching of styles.

There are many reasons why architects, philosophers and psychologists have stayed in relative ignorance of each other and why architectural aesthetics has led such a marginal existence. For one, architects have often viewed philosophy and psychology as esoteric. For another, scholars in these other fields have found little enticement for rigorous discourse with architects. And when philosophy has treated aesthetics, it has stayed abstract and has been of little practical consequence for theories of design. The same might be said for contributions from psychology. Only in the past two decades has the emerging field of environmental psychology taken an interest in architecture and in the perceived qualities of the environment. Furthermore, even though there has been a long tradition of aesthetic treatises and polemical doctrines about 'right' architectural form, few have managed to weather the storms of changing fashion, and few have been soundly grounded in logical arguments.

And so it is that the questions with which I began this chapter are some of the most prevalent, but also the most puzzling, in the history of architecture. They carry several implications. First, they presuppose there are buildings which, to a certain extent, are more beautiful than others. Yet, while individuals may agree in principle that certain buildings and spaces are more appealing than others, there is often disagreement as to which deserve such mention. Second, the questions imply that the architectural object itself elicits the aesthetic experience, rather than the disposition of the viewer. In fact, this question — whether aesthetic judgements are determined by characteristics of the object or by the viewer's own cognitive makeup — has for centuries been one of the central battlegrounds of philosophical aesthetics.

In this centuries-old dilemma, I take this view: if an object's qualities alone are what evoke particular feelings and determine aesthetic judgements, then an investigation of the nature of these qualities and the way they are interpreted should be the principal task of aesthetic theory. On the other hand, even if feelings and judgements about the object are exclusively

4

determined by the viewer's own disposition — by a stock of accumulated experience, personality traits, and so on — then the object itself must still in some way serve as a stimulus for these experiences. In other words, there must be something about the object that triggers particular kinds of judgements in reference to a person's cognitive stock. Thus, no matter which position one adopts, aesthetic judgements must somehow be made in reference to properties of the object. (The intermediate position — that aesthetic judgement rests both on the beholder's disposition and on properties of the object — does not alter this conclusion.) Therefore, two crucial questions arise: To what degree do properties of the object, as opposed to other factors, determine judgements? And to what extent are there similarities among different individuals' cognitive makeups?

Once it has been established that the object serves to some extent as a provocateur of judgement (without implying that different people would respond in the same way), the next question to surface regards which characteristics of the object account for specific responses. It seems logical to suggest that such characteristics can be found in the object's form (defined as those of its properties which are immediately accessible to perception). In the case of architecture, this would seem to include the appearance of enclosed spaces, their bounding elements, and the elements' articulation, color and texture.

Obviously, the experience of a building entails much more than the perception of a shell. Didn't Vitruvius suggest that it was by means of *utilitas*, *firmitas* and *venustas* that buildings are judged? And isn't it true that one's actions in an architectural setting, rather than the static presentation of a building, account for the way architectural forms are brought to one's attention? One might further question whether a building can ever be experienced simply as a physical object, rather than as a source of personal and cultural associations. But claiming that characteristics of form carry a prominence in the experience of architecture does not mean that other attributes might not also contribute to architectural judgements. Memories of similar places may be triggered, and, above all, everyday knowledge of buildings cannot be discarded.

But the primary role that form plays becomes evident when one looks at the kinds of judgements that can be made and the ways in which they can be formed. To begin, all judgements about objects require concepts; this is to say objects must be placed within some frame of reference in order to define their place and value within the environment. Judgements may, for example, be made in regard to an object's suitability for certain ends and aims. In this case the concepts would be *external*; that is, they cannot be derived from the object's inherent properties. Alternatively, objects can be judged as examples within classes of objects; in this sense, *internal* concepts, based solely on inherent properties, would determine the judgement. It can further be argued that judgements of the former type will always encapsulate concepts of the latter.

Furthermore, it is possible to distinguish two separate modes of judgement: deliberated and spontaneous.[2] Of these, the former are made in regard to a set of values by which individual aspects are aggregated according to their assumed relative importance. These judgements require conscious reasoning, and their results may be quite different than those arrived at through spontaneous judgement. In the latter type, one does not deliberate on sets of evaluative criteria, and the result is apprehended immediately. It is clear, considering this distinction, that aesthetic judgements, by definition, must be spontaneous. Nevertheless, judgements of the former type will inevitably include judgements of the latter. Moreover, both types of judgement must, in part, rely on internal concepts established on grounds of morphic properties.

This line of thought leads to the question of how concepts of form are established. Even if the appearance of a building is considered the dominant factor, other factors may also be involved in the formation of spontaneous judgements — namely, factors which are *inferred,* and are perceived phenomenally in unison with the appearance of the building. For example, once it is known that certain morphic characteristics reoccur in certain types of buildings, one can predict the function of buildings based on everyday interaction with them. Similarly, so-called symbolic meanings may be perceived together with a building's forms if one is familiar with the stylistic devices of the era during which it was built. 'Meanings' of this kind clearly depend on concepts external to the physical forms of the building.

Nevertheless, if form is considered the principal factor in the immediate aesthetic experience of architecture, the question of 'good form' will become preeminent. And, in this regard, different formal configurations will obviously have more powerful effects than others. How does this occur? What mechanisms are involved? If one could answer this question, one could settle one of the most persistent and elusive issues in architectural design. It is one that has produced many dialogues — and monologues — among architects, and one that has led to many theories and manifestos with manifold consequences for the practice of architecture.

I I

Appraising Form:
Theories Compared

A central component of many theories of architectural aesthetics, the notion of good form has often been used synonymously with good architecture. Indeed, most classical treatises have given primary attention to form when discussing what good architecture ought to be. In fact, when defined as a negative condition — that bad form equals bad architecture — good architecture may necessitate good form.

But what is form? Through history, the term has been employed both descriptively and appraisingly in ways that have often been confused or commingled. Most commonly, 'form' has stood for arrangement or organization. As such, it has been used as an abstraction to characterize an object through the organization of its constituent shapes, colors and textures. This application is often synonymous with the concept of 'structure'. Used as a term of aesthetic approbation in this sense, form has normally stood for good form — as compared to amorphous things, which lack form. For example, the Latin adjective *formosus* was used to describe shapely, well-proportioned and beautiful things, whereas *deformis* was equated with ugliness.

But the term has also been used to describe a second, very different concept. In contrast to attempts to describe the structure of an object itself, 'form' has been used to denote *that which is directly given to the senses.* Such a distinction between 'form' and 'content' has played an important role in many theories of art. It leads to a further special case, that constituted by Kantian tradition. In Kantian terms, form does not exist per se; it is rather the individual who imposes form onto matter. Form is thus a construction of human thought, governed by a priori categories which are properties of the mind.

Although these two definitions of form — as structure or arrangement, and as perceptual image — stem from seemingly irreconcilable vantage points, the two can be linked if form is thought to be *the structure of the object as presented to the senses.*

Numerous architectural theories have focused on the role of form in the experience of architecture. In the following sections I will discuss three of the most prominent: the instrumental approach; theories of proportion; and various theories of expression and communication, the strongest of which equate architecture with language.

1. Architecture as Instrument: Functionalism

Instrumental viewpoints, linking the beauty of an object to its suitability for an end, have pervaded many theories of art since classical antiquity. Yet, as a pronounced doctrine in architecture, in which function is the core criterion of aesthetic approbation, functionalism has enjoyed prominence mainly in this century.

In architecture, the most conspicuous variant of the instrumental view is that in which the aesthetic value of a building is identified with the fit of its form to its function. In other words, the design of a building ought to be governed by the functions it is to assume. Louis Sullivan's phrase, "form follows function,"[1] is often said to sum up this view. Yet proponents of the functionalist position go even further, maintaining that to be aesthetically successful architecture must also *express* its ends, because the experience of form cannot be divorced from the experience of function.

This doctrine, commonly identified with architects and theorists of the Modern Movement, carries the implication that buildings are primarily experienced as means to ends. Because practical understanding pervades most aspects of our lives, the position appears, at first glance, to make sense. But when function is declared to be the primary basis of aesthetic approbation, the experience of function becomes the primary experience of architecture. But can the experience of function really suffice to explain the experience of architecture? Logically, this would require that one understand a building's function before one could experience it in aesthetic terms. Yet buildings can clearly be experienced and judged even when their functions are not, or cannot, be known. Would such uninformed judgment, according to the functionalist view, constitute 'incorrect' aesthetic experience? And, by extension, does the functionalist credo lead to the position that aesthetic pleasure cannot be derived from architecture by the layman?

Strictly speaking, the doctrine of functionalism also demands that the experience of buildings (and of useful artifacts in general) be different from that of works of art or nature. It seems to suggest that the mind is provided with two modes of experience, of useful and useless things, and that objects must be placed in one or the other category before they can be experienced. But how can an object be categorized before it is experienced? And what is to be considered useful, and what not?

Furthermore, if aesthetic impact depends on the presentation of ends, the level of aesthetic satisfaction a building provides must depend on how well it achieves this goal. Following this logic, there must be optimal solutions that relate to particular forms of judgement. In fact, the concept of architectural typology (as, for instance, propagated by Durand and his followers) does rest on the contention that there are types of buildings that best relate to particular ends. It also proposes that all buildings can be classified into functional types like plants or beasts. For example, the eighteenth-century architectural theorist

Fig.1. Typology: Elements of Architecture. From: Durand, Precis de leçons
d'architecture.

Blondel wrote that architecture "should carry the imprint of the particular intention of each building, each should possess a character which determines the general form and declares the building for what it is."[2]

Considering the above discussion, it is apparent that difficulties with the functionalist position which undermine its ability to explain the experience of architecture can be sorted into two general areas: one concerns the experience of function; the other the 'expression' of function through architecture. A series of questions may serve to bring these issues into focus. To begin: how can a building present its function if its function is deliberately vague, or if it is intentionally multifunctional? Can a building that has been converted from one function to another still provide aesthetic satisfaction;? Or is it only a building's intended, original purpose which, when successfully presented, can

12

sustain such experience? What happens when functions become obsolete? Is the experience of historic architecture, then, diluted? Above all, what is meant by function, and which of the different functions of a building ought to be expressed? The functioning of human activities? A building's function as shelter against the elements? Its structural or mechanical functions?

Apparently, most important is the function the building is to contain — that particular behavioral setting or technical process presented in the building's spatial arrangement. Accordingly, an oil refinery would seem to display its function rather well; but the difference between an atomic reactor and a planetarium might not be so clear. Ledoux's forced functional expressionism in, for example, his house for the inspector of waterworks (Fig.2), which took the form of a section through a duct, becomes almost a caricature of the instrumental view. The same might be said for the window of his salt factory in Chaux (Fig.3), which was supposed to allude to the technical processes inside.

Fig.2. Ledoux. Maison des directeurs de la loue.

Fig.3. Window, salt factory.

The issue of style is also a problem with the functional approach. Thus, one might observe that although the functions of farmhouses in the Black Forest and Norway hardly differ, their appearances certainly do. If style were thought only to express function, then different styles ought to occur only when different functions require them — for example, in different climates. However, much of Western architectural history suggests that style is not causally determined in this way. Schinkel's church in Werder (Fig. 4/5) is an example frequently cited to demonstrate this point. Schinkel originally submitted two alternatives — one Gothic, the other Neoclassical. Both versions display the traditional forms of churches. Does one express the function of a church better than the other? Or does this example suggest that the functional position needs to be diluted so that only particular formal characteristics of a building play a role in the overall expression of function?

Fig. 4/5. K.F. Schinkel: Werder Church, Berlin. Gothic and Neoclassical alternative designs.

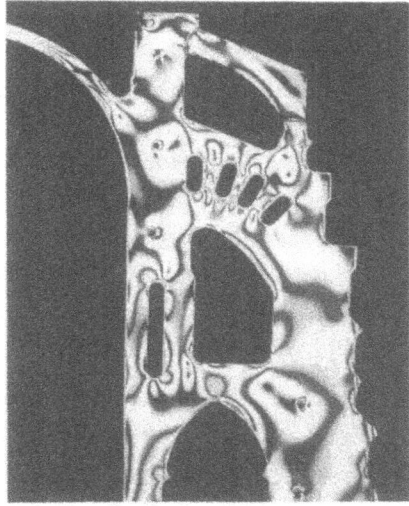

Fig.6. Centre Pompidou, Paris. Is appreciation of the building limited to engineers and plumbers?
Fig.7. Chartres Cathedral: section. Photoelastic pattern of wind loads.

There remains also the question of internal organization and articulation of a building's shapes — that is, decoration, ornament and texture. Can a church stripped of its ornament still be recognized as a church? If so, ornamentation in a church must be considered superfluous. Or is it that 'churchness' is a quality that is highly dependent on the form of certain symbolic, decorative elements? If this is so, one must admit that the design of a building's form cannot sufficiently be determined by its function; factors independent of functional constraints must play a role.

Another area in question involves a building's structural function. Some functionalists have argued that a building must display its structural function in 'honest' fashion. Frei Otto's tension structures or the Centre Pompidou in Paris obviously do this — provided the viewer has some understanding of the structural forces acting in a building. Are true aesthetic experiences of

15

buildings, therefore, the exclusive privilege of the engineer? For example, modern critics and historians generally considered the flying buttresses of Gothic cathedrals to be merely decorative until computer simulations showed that they played an important role in reinforcing the structures against lateral wind loads. Does such a change in knowledge lead to a change in aesthetic experience? Or is accurate knowledge of a building's structural system irrelevant to aesthetic experience? A further illustration of these difficulties is provided by the typical curtain-wall facade design by Mies van der Rohe. While the I-beams displayed in fig.8/9 were intended to 'express' the support system, in reality fire codes required that load-bearing structures be enclosed in concrete.

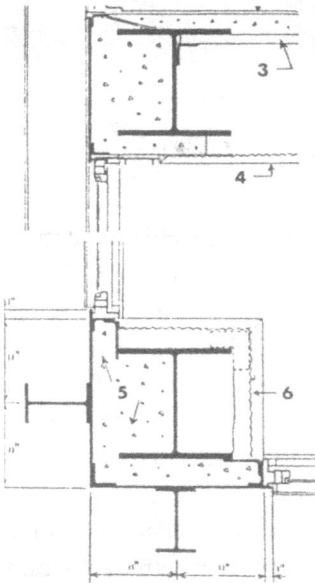

Fig.8/9. L. Mies v.d. Rohe. Apartment houses, Lake Shore Drive, Chicago, 1951: facade and detail.

Finally, functionalism as a determinant of aesthetic appreciation would seem to require considerable intellectual deliberation: to appreciate a building, one just has to determine if it displays its various functions 'correctly'. Furthermore, that it is in many cases even possible to 'recognize' a building's function is often a matter of acquaintance with similar buildings: in this way morphic similarities between certain types of buildings allow certain functions to be 'seen-in' a building. Thus, function is 'assigned' to a building after it has been perceived; it cannot be a necessary condition for a building's experience. Moreover, this process is clearly incompatible with any notion of aesthetic experience as an immediate response or experience.

Certainly, the doctrine of functionalism has value. Despite the above objections, it has played an important role in the history of architecture as a reaction to nineteenth-century eclecticism, and to the distinction between art and craft as made by Collingwood, or between architecture and mere building as propagated by Ruskin. A determination of function is also very important in the *production* of architecture. Among other things, it leads in terms of production to fundamental planning decisions. Functional concern for climate or particular methods of building has also had considerable influence on shaping styles of architecture in different regions and cultures. But, even in the production of buildings, function cannot be said to be a singular determinant; it may only limit the range of design variables at hand. In regard to function, therefore, it is probably necessary to distinguish between modes of *production* and *perception* of architecture. And, whereas function may be a constraint in relation to the former, it has very little relation to the latter.

2. Metaphysical Formalism: Theories of Proportion

To summarize theories of proportion under the label of metaphysical formalism is neither arbitrary nor incidental. A great number of the doctrines on proportion which have pervaded theories of aesthetics through the centuries have been based on metaphysical systems that have aimed to describe the underlying order of the universe through mathematical relationships.

Proportion theories present mathematical approaches to nature in terms of ordered magnitudes. These, in turn, are used to construct systems of rules to govern relationships between constituents in a configuration, and between constituents and the whole. The use of such systems throughout most of architectural history supplies strong evidence for human nature's quest for order, realized in symmetry and proportion of manmade objects.

In relation to architecture, the term 'proportion' generally refers to a relation between various parts of a building due to analogous ratios. But a 'proportion system' may also imply far-reaching geometric constructions that supply a precise underlying order for an entire plan or facade. Many of the theories of proportion in Western art and architecture may be traced to the Pythagoreans. Their discovery that the harmonious vibrations of the musical chord could be expressed in simple geometric relationships (2:1 octave, 3:2 fifth, 4:3 fourth, etc.) was seen by the Greeks as evidence that sound, space and number were all linked by a harmony that pervaded all creation. The Pythagorean-Platonic school of thought further propagated the belief that good and beautiful forms appeared so because they revealed universal proportional relationships. To emphasize the important relation between mathematical order and creation, Plato wrote ". . . the body of the world was created, and it was harmonized by proportion."[3]

Views related to the Platonic-Pythagorean tradition prevailed in the West until at least the eighteenth century.[4] The use of mathematical analogies to organize conceptions of the universe was common in Judeo-Christian mythology, medieval symbolism, and the rationalistic character of art theory during the Age of Humanism. The Bible spelled out such a view in *The Book of Solomon*: "Thou hast ordered all things in measure, number and weight."[5] And God as architect, as "the finest, greatest geometer,"[6] was a popular image during the Middle Ages. (In fact, for the most sacred structures, such as Noah's Ark or the Temple of Solomon, the scriptures did give clear instructions about the assumed dimensions.)

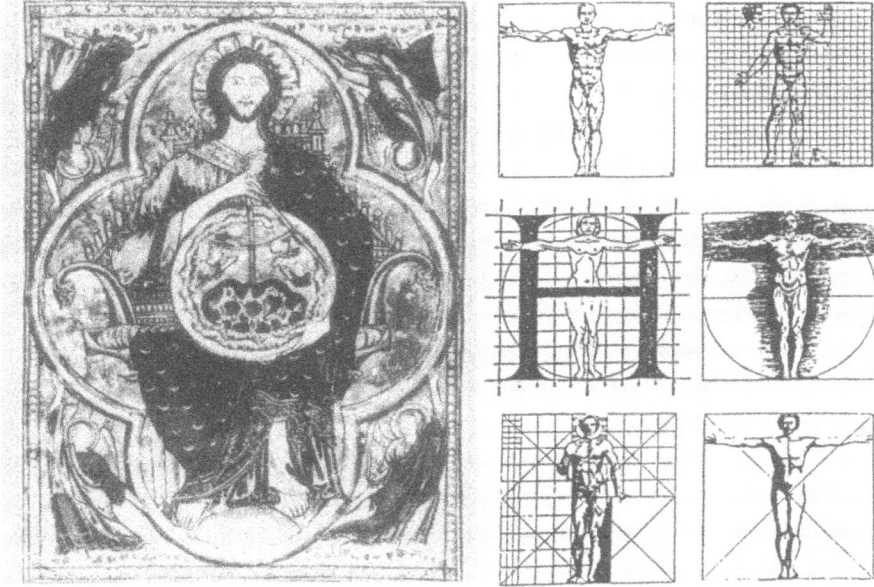

*Fig. 10. Christ as architect. Medieval illustration. **Fig.11.** Man as the measure of all things.*

In relation to architecture, the Greeks used such words as proportion, symmetry and taxis (order) to describe form. For the Romans, an object was considered beautiful when its parts were properly proportioned. Thus, according to Sextus Empiricus: "No art comes without proportions. All art therefore arises through number. Every art is a system of perceptions, and a system implies number; one can therefore justly say: things look beautiful by virtue of number."[7] To describe the qualities of beautiful form, Vitruvius used the words disposition, order, symmetry and eurythmy.[8] And later, during the Renaissance, Alberti wrote that beauty consisted "in the harmony of all the mutually adapted parts"[9] — in *concinnitas*: that is, perfect form. Even today object-oriented aesthetics is still trying to assess form in mathematical terms. Examples are George Birkhoff's theory of 'aesthetic measure', which defines beauty as a function of order and complexity, and Bense's and Moles's attempts to use information theory to define form in terms of the order and redundancy of elements.[10]

Proportion theories attempt to describe nature in terms of mathematically ordered magnitudes. These, in turn, are used to construct systems of rules governing relationships between constituents in a configuration, and between constituents and a whole. In mathematics, magnitudes related by means of the same ratio are called proportional. Since a ratio is the direct comparison of any two quantities, a proportion therefore must be composed of at least two ratios. These quantities may be related to each other in ordered sequences, or progressions. There are three types of progressions: *geometric, arithmetic,* and *harmonic.*[11]

Except during the Renaissance, there have been few attempts to use commensurable ratios, which can be expressed through real numbers, in architecture. More predominant has been the use of incommensurable ratios derived from the use of square roots ($\sqrt{2}$, $\sqrt{3}$ and $\sqrt{5}$ being the 'sacred' roots[12]), or from the so-called golden or divine ratio. (In this last, the simplest possible geometric progression, the minor dimension has the same numeric relation to the major dimension that the major dimension has to the sum of the two in other words a:b = b:a+b.[13]) Another common way to generate proportional relationships has been through the decomposition of geometric figures such as triangles, squares, hexagons and pentagons. To Plato, the five most perfect geometric configurations — those with equal faces, sides and angles: the cube, tetrahedron, octahedron, dodecahedron, and icosahedron — most closely approached the idea of beauty. Geometrical figures derived from these so-called Platonic solids, and from other polygons, later served as the basis for medieval ordering systems. Many cathedrals were thus built *ad quadratum* or *ad triangulum.*

Central to the Western tradition of metaphysical formalism over the centuries has also been a process of analogy between the universe as a macrocosm of divine creation and the microcosm of man. Such a concept has

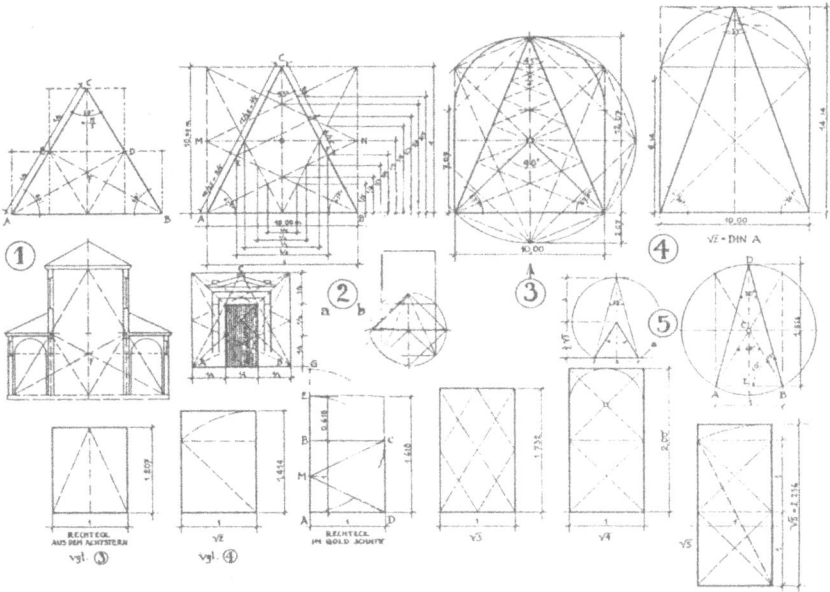

Fig. 12. Proportion systems derived from geometric decompositions (Freckmann).

demanded that artifacts, and buildings in particular, incorporate all manner of divine numbering systems. And the analogy has also worked in the other direction. Because the human body was considered the masterpiece of nature, it was supposed it could supply the perfect measures from which canons of architectural proportion could be derived. Vitruvius, for example, stated that ɔwithout symmetry or proportion no temple can have measured composition; that is, it must have the exact measure of the members of a well shaped human body. [14] During the Renaissance, artists like Dürer further supposed that the basic proportions of the human body were derived from the proportions of the golden ratio.

Art theories of the eighteenth century departed from such systems of proportion. Their rejection was based on the principal claim that the notion of

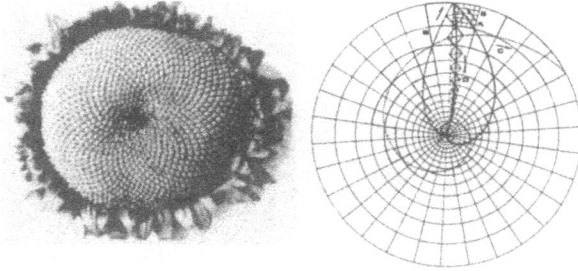

Fig.13. *Sunflower and seed pattern.*

beauty is purely subjective, a matter of the mind, or of feelings that have nothing to do with calculation or geometry, as Burke[15] stated. Nevertheless, our own century has seen several revivals of theories of proportion. Notable among these have been Hambidge's theory of 'dynamic symmetry',[16] which is based on incommensurable root rectangles; and D'Arcy Thompson's *On Growth and Form*,[17] a book which stresses the logarithmic spiral as a key to morphology in nature. Influential also has been Hans Keyser's *Harmonica*,[18] which, in true Pythagorean-Platonic fashion, proposes a whole metaphysical and mystical theory of art. In architecture, the revival found its culmination with Le Corbusier's *Modulor*, a system combining the dimensions of a standardized human figure with the Fibonacci series, a series whose numbers approach the golden ratio.

It is easy to understand why neo-Platonist mathematical cosmology continues to appeal to architectural theorists. When nature is seen as being organized according to certain constant principles — an order which we can find in ourselves — it seems plausible that buildings ought also to reflect that order. Indeed, the diversity of styles that can be achieved with similar proportion systems seems to confirm there is such a thing as universal harmony, and that it is possible to arrive at common principles of good form that transcend culture, technical concerns, or fashion.

But if this were true, such a proportional system ought to permit a clear analysis of the experience we derive from buildings. In other words, mathematical harmonies ought to be able to predict visual harmony. Yet, aside from the obvious problem that perceptual harmony and mathematical harmony may not be isomorphic, this claim has to be questioned at its very foundation: the selection of particular mathematical relationships. Nature certainly may be conceived as a system whose behavior is governed by forces interacting in some ordered fashion. But this order always turns out to be the creation of the theorist seeking explanations for particular phenomena. As the history of science shows, mathematical models are always altered or replaced by new models. Thus, if its original claim to reflect the order of the universe is no longer valid, how can the Pythagorean-Platonic model still be used as an explanation for visual harmony in buildings? Moreover, which system of proportion arising from the Pythagorean-Platonic model ought to be accepted? There exists a considerable difference in result depending on whether musical ratios are used as a yardstick, or modular systems, the golden ratio, triangulations, or root-rectangles.

Such doubts need particularly to be articulated with regard to anthropomorphic doctrines, which insist that architectural proportions should be derived from the proportions of the human body. Though order can be ascribed to nature, the forces which determine it are different in different instances. As D'Arcy Thompson has convincingly argued, the shapes of a crystal and of a flower result from entirely different processes of ordering. Should the human body, whose dimensions result from its peculiar process of adaptation within the environment, thus be taken as a model for the dimensions of a building? From an ergonomic viewpoint, this might provide useful insights. But in order to determine perceptual order, the approach appears inadequate.

A second objection to metaphysical formalism has to be made on psychological grounds. How do abstractly calculated proportions of a building relate to real experience? In music, for example, a deviation from the permeating principle is easily recognized as a violation of a structural theme, and, hence, dissonance. Visual disorder is certainly less apparent; yet, at a general level it can still be argued that the sense of order is inherent in all forms of human perception — in other words, that the need for order governs organic functioning at both physical and psychological levels. But perceptual order is not simply a matter of numerical ratios. The percept is not a photostat of the external world; it results from mental processes of organization which are selective and which take into account the structure of the whole. Thus, the proportion of the parts becomes subordinate to the principles that govern the whole, and simple geometrical order cannot suffice to explain how form is experienced. (This is especially true if, as I shall argue later, the percept is determined according to dynamic, not geometric, properties of shapes.)

The process of perception inevitably leads to an emphasis on particular structural features, to a dominance of certain parts and a subordinance of others, and to a sharpening and leveling of contours. As can be observed in many so-called visual illusions, perception is also governed by the tendency to assume the presence of the most simple configuration, even when this collides with true geometrical construction. (If, indeed, the principle of simplicity is considered pervasive, then proportional ratios that order the parts within a whole would meet the need for regularity in spatial organization and the need for clear distinction; and, because of their redundancy, similarities in dimension and shape allow the mind to establish perceptual groups, and thus permit perception with lesser effort.)

A final difficulty with proportion systems concerns the issue of scale. If mathematical regularity is assumed to be a source of aesthetic pleasure, then good proportions ought to occur equally in the macrostructure and micro-structure of beautiful objects. But scale has everything to do with the perception of order and beauty. Thus, a landscape or a settlement may show little order when viewed from the ground, but it may show much regularity when seen from an airplane. Likewise, the harmoniously ordered facade of a Gothic cathedral choir may seem a puzzling chaos when viewed up close.

Actual experience of buildings in three-dimensional settings brings attention to many of the difficulties with such strictly mathematical views of

Fig.14/15. Le Mans Cathedral: choir buttressing. Visual order is lost at close proximity. Hilltown, Santorini, Greece. A common principle unifies individual shapes into a whole.

aesthetics. For example, in the elevation drawings of Palladio's Basilica in Vicenza (Fig.16/17), the building's roof appears to dwarf its colonnades, so that it seems 'out of proportion'. In fact, this macrocephalic structure is a deliberate adjustment to the conditions of nearby urban space. Palladio knew that because of the roof's curvature, its full height would not be visible from anywhere at ground level nearby. But since only the roof ridge is visible, the proportions seem appropriate.

Similarly, the height of St. Peter's cupola in Rome (Fig.18) shows how considerations of absolute proportion and perceptual experience may actually conflict with each other. As Schubert[19] has demonstrated, the height of the cupola was primarily determined by the various view angles at which it would be seen from St. Peter's Square. In this case, strict proportional considerations were accorded only secondary importance because the cupola

25

Fig.16/17. Andrea Palladio. Basilica, Vicenza. Design drawing: elevation and actual view.

was located so far behind the plane of the facade that its lower parts were invisible. This shows that purely proportional considerations are insufficient to describe the experience of order in architecture. This is especially true of large buildings where the angle of vision does not permit perpendicular views, and in cases where buildings have several levels of depth.

Despite these criticisms, the use of proportion in architecture has value. Designing a building remains a matter of organizing diverse elements within an overall configuration, and a proportion system might prove to be a valuable tool in this complex task. But when it comes to experiencing a building, while the

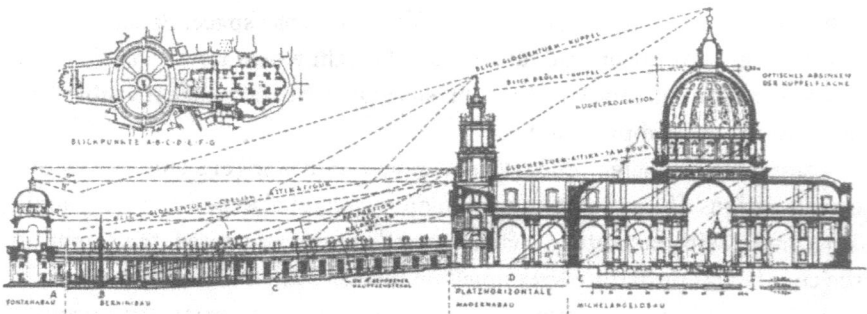

Fig.18. St. Peter's, Rome. Bernini design: study of lines of vision (after Schubert).

intellect may find pleasure in discovering ratios and mathematical coherence, this may not have much to do with real aesthetic judgement. In short, geometrical order is not the same as phenomenal order, and none of the systems of proportion that have competed through history can claim to be an absolute determinant of aesthetic value. However, proportions do become important when discussing the role of compositional structure in a building. Then, however, proportion must be viewed as a matter of perceptual order and coherence, which is beyond the realm of mathematical analogies.

3. Meaningful Form: Expression, Communication, and Architecture as Language

Though different in their aim and method of thought and stemming from diverse roots in the history of aesthetics, there are a number of theories which state that the perception of form (and, accordingly, the resulting judgement) is always laden with meaning. These range from theories of innate expression and empathy, focusing on ways by which buildings may trigger particular emotional states, to theories that regard architecture as a system of signs — or in its strongest form, even a language, or system of languages.

Before examining the critical value of these theories in regard to the direct experience of architecture, it is necessary to take a close look at their common contention. This claim is, roughly, that the experience of any object rests on a mental image of it, a 'mental object' whose properties are not identical with those of the actual object. Form, according to this view, cannot be neutrally experienced; it always expresses or signifies something. In short, perceived form is always meaningful form.

This claim is central to two, quite different ideologies. One maintains that meaning, or at least expression, is innately given in an object; in other words, objects, by their very nature, trigger certain states of awareness on the part of the beholder. The other states that meaning rests entirely on individual processes of association. In this sense meaning becomes a phenomenal property of an object only after the object has been perceived and categorized.

The notion that architecture can 'represent', 'express', or even, like a language, 'communicate' is not new. It has enjoyed diehard popularity, and been recurrently resurrected from the burial places of scholarly refutation by theorists and architects alike. 'Houses as metaphors', 'poetic discourse between buildings and landscape', 'architecture's narrative qualities', 'communication between buildings and their contexts', 'vocabulary of architectural forms' — such phrases do not just result from architects' proverbial love of metaphor. They are indicative of a conviction that there are meanings to architectural forms that transcend immediate concerns of style. The popularity of the view that architecture is a kind of language, a system of signs which allows 'communication', can be noted in the titles of such works as N.L. Prak's *Language of Architecture*, C. Alexander's *A Pattern Language*, or C. Jencks's *The Language of Post-Modern Architecture*.[20]

Among the various kinds of meaning that this third group of theories attempt to ascribe to architecture, three are especially popular: *expressive*, *symbolic* and *semantic* meaning. The most popular assumption is that buildings possess expressive properties.[21] This concept originates in the visual and performing arts, where it commonly refers to manifestations of emotional states: to *character*. Certainly, it does seem plausible to speak of expression in a painting. For example, one could imagine one depicting the temptation of St. Anthony, and in which one could clearly see the physique of an angry man. The assumption, however, that expression is a physical property of shapes and colors is incorrect on both psychological and logical grounds.

According to the psychologist J.J. Gibson,[22] the perception of pictures rests on textural properties resembling environmental patterns. Thus, expression is a matter of a represented subject which expresses a certain character, and the traditional distinction between representational and expressive properties need not be made. Expression is a mimetic property: only when something that itself is expressive is represented can we speak of expression conveyed through an

28

Fig.19. *Doric order: caryatid, or the column as a representation of man.*
Fig.20. *Are animals proud? Or does the viewer project human properties onto the animal?*

object. In the case of the painting of St. Anthony, an observer could say the image expresses anger because of the patterns depicted in the physiognomy of the saint, because the observer could draw inferences from his own behavioral patterns to the depicted physiognomy of the saint. But it is simply incorrect to speak of expression for inanimate things such as buildings.

However, there are two theories that make just such a claim: the *theory of empathy* and the *Gestalt theory of expression*. The first, which has had a considerable following among architects since it was popularized by Louis Kahn, states that viewers project their own feelings into persons and objects, and thus endow them with expression.[23] For example, one person can perceive another

29

person as being 'sad' because he or she can associate past personal experiences with sadness with the expression that appears in the face of the other. A logical extension of this theory to architecture would be that a person looking at a Greek column, for example, would be able to feel the forces acting on the column, and so empathize with its particular constellation of shapes.

There are three problems with this theory. First, there is the crucial logical flaw that the associative processes by which the perceived world is supposed to be endowed with expression cannot be rooted entirely in past experiences with similar situations. If this were possible, how could experience be acquired initially? And how is it possible to learn by association when associations are the prerequisite for learning? The second problem concerns situations in which there are no previous experiences from which to draw. The best a person could do in such a case is *sympathize* with another — for example, in trying to understand thei other's deep personal grief. But this is clearly inadequate. In such a case, what would prevent some innocent person from fatally misinterpreting the mood of a charging bull as, say, some kind of affectionate pursuit? The final problem with the associative theory concerns whether we can project ourselves into the place of inanimate things at all. The problem here is especially evident when physiognomic interpretation is impossible, as in the case of the column that may be exchanged for the caryatid.

The Gestalt theory of expression gives a better explanation of such cases. It claims that expression is an innate property of the perceived stimulus — in the same way, for example, that hue is a property of a color, or size is a property of a shape. The core of this theory is the assumption that a parallelism exists between physiomotor behavior and psychological experience, allowing physiognomic qualities and states of mind to be structurally isomorphic. Hence, as Rudolph Arnheim writes: "an observer will adequately gauge another person's state of mind by inspection of that person's bodily appearance, if the psychical situation of the observed person and the perceptual experience of the observer establish structural similarity by means of a number of intermediate isomorphic levels."[24]

A.	Observed Person	
I.	State of mind	psychological
II.	Neural correlate of I	electrochemical
III.	Muscular forces	mechanical
IV.	Kinesthetic correlate of III	psychological
V.	Shape and movement of body	geometrical
B.	Observer	
VI.	Retinal projection of V	geometrical
VII.	Cortical projektionof VI	electrochemical
VIII.	Perceptual correlate of VII	psychological

Fig. 21. Intermediate isomorphic levels in perceiving expression (after Arnheim).

In both theories objects are thought to be expressive because they refer to physiognomic correlates of emotional states. This makes expressions anthropomorphic by nature. Yet while a *person* who is perceived to be sad in this way may, in fact, be sad, can the term 'expression' be justly used to describe *inanimate* things like a building or the famous weeping willow? Arnheim argues that this tree does not look sad because it looks like a sad person, but "because its formal properties convey the expression of passive hanging, . . . a structurally similar psychological pattern of sadness in humans."[25] But the term 'passive' here can be no more than an analogy. 'Passivity' cannot be regarded as a property inherent in form. Furthermore, a psychological isomorphism necessitates structural equivalents on *both* sides. And while this can be the case with two humans, it cannot be the case with a human and an animal, or a human and a thing.

Equally popular is the tendency to define architecture in semantic terms. Like a language, it is often asserted that buildings can denote, represent, or even communicate earthly matters or metaphysical affairs.[26] Though there is no doubt that buildings can evoke an indefinite and varying number of personal associations, these are not the dependably specific semantic denotations that are required to make up a language. Thus, we cannot speak of architectural communication using these terms.

In literal languages, terms denote matters fairly unequivocally: words are 'representations', signifiers of things or events. Terms, thus, have a specific kind of meaning. But what is it that things themselves, can denote? While words have meanings that are *intrinsic* or *self-evident* by virtue of conventions, things can only have meanings that are *extrinsic*, that is, that are mere connotations, and are in no way unequivocal.

But why should a building have to represent anything at all apart from being a building? Advocates of architecture as language argue that buildings 'represent' or 'symbolize' their functions. For example, a certain arrangement of architectural parts 'represents' a church. Here, obviously, a concept used in the mimetic arts is being misapplied to architecture. In languages or representational images, a particular constellation of words or shapes can, indeed, represent something. And, to the extent a person is familiar with the conventions used, he or she can 'understand the message'. But this isn't the case with buildings because of the lack of conventions by which to assign specific meanings to architectural parts. It thus appears that the concept of representation is confused with such concepts as typology and style. A building's function can often be recognized because of previous experiences with similar buildings which allow us to formulate hypotheses about it, but this process is quite unlike that of discerning of representation and denotation in language. In architecture, there is also a Babylonian muddle when it comes to morphic types: thus, a Wall Street bank may be confused with a Jupiter temple, an apartment complex with a factory, or a telephone company headquarters with a Chippendale bureau.

Similar arguments can be made against the notion that architecture can symbolize particular socio-cultural circumstances. Buildings have been called 'talking witnesses of the Zeitgeist', and one hears of, say, 'the language of Islamic architecture'. But the morphic similarities of buildings in specific cultural and temporal periods must be subsumed under the concept of style, the art historian's tool for classification. It isn't the building which 'represents' specific socio-cultural circumstances through its form, but, rather, the knowledgeable beholder who brings socio-cultural concepts to the building and associates them with its style. Of course, deliberate symbolisms have often been designed into buildings. Medieval builders used the pentagram as a proportional device to ban evil from cathedrals. But even familiarity with the use of proportion systems cannot reveal this symbolism directly to the eye; it must be extracted by inscribing geometric patterns into a plan or an elevation drawing.

The central fallacy involved in the notion of representational meaning is thus apparent: a concept developed for a mimetic medium cannot be applied to a nonmimetic one. Form can acquire denotative function only through direct representation (that is, when a building takes on the form of the thing

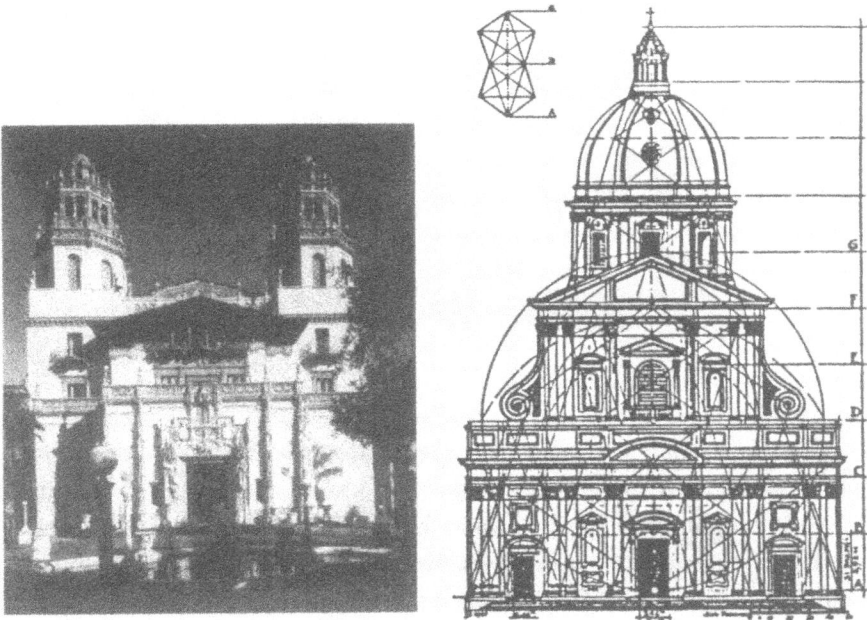

Fig.22. *Can architecture speak? Julia Morgan's Hearst Castle, San Simeon, California. Casa Grande: the facade promises a church but houses profane entertainment.*
Fig.23. *Proportion systems as grammar? Diagram of S. Ignazio, Rome .*

it represents, e.g., a hot dog), or through clear semantic conventions which determine the meaning of individual shapes. In short, architecture is not a language. If architecture were a language, one could 'understand' buildings and control their meanings through design. For this to be the case, two conditions would have to be met: there would have to be clear semantic meanings for the constituents of architecture; and there would have to be a system of rules — a syntax — by which the meaning of a whole could be derived from the meaning of the parts.

Fig.24. Examples of denotative architecture: Bob's Java Jive Cafe.

Clearly, architecture meets neither condition. Not the least of the reasons why is that the two conditions are interdependent. Thus, Frege[27] has argued that one cannot justly speak of an architectural syntax, because syntactical meanings are derived from semantic meanings. The real situation is that the majority of shapes used in buildings are without any specific meaning; and where such meanings do exist, they are usually highly individual.

But, beyond this, the crucial factor remains that there exists no commonly accepted syntax by which individual shapes can be combined into a meaningful whole. One could speculate that systems of proportion or particular formal styles could fill this role. But how then could different architectural styles rely on similar proportion systems? Could the syntax of one language really be used to order the semantics of another? In literal languages this would result in incomprehensibility. But in architecture such interchange does happen precisely because architecture doesn't communicate any specific thing. Architectural 'meanings' are different from the meanings in languages. The latter are concepts derived from combinations of terms within an accepted syntax; the former require concepts extrinsic to their discrete formal elements and overall composition.

The overall concept here is that meaning is not an intrinsic property of form; it is *inferred* by the beholder on the basis of concepts derived from cultural conventions, individual experience, and learning. On the basis of this determination, it is possible to see that meaning can be both intersubjective and individual. And in general, two conditions must be met before there can be a high degree of intersubjectivity of meaning: there must be a high denotative potential to the form of representation being used; and there must exist strong similarities between the cognitive makeup of different individual subjects. When comparing such forms of representation as words, painting, sculpture, music and architecture, the latter, together with nonvocal music or nonrepresentational visual art, would seem to have the lowest denotative potential. Only truly mimetic media possess a high degree of this; and architecture is certainly not mimetic—with the obvious exception of instances in which it consists of actual representations of things.

There is no doubt, however, that people with similar cultural backgrounds associate similar meanings with buildings. But such intersubjectivity requires similar cognitive schemes or concepts. In a few cases, as in the learning of a language, these schemes may be formed through some kind of cultural ordinance. But generally they must be acquired through learning and through one's interaction with one's milieu.

More important, however, is the connection between the evolution of architectural styles and the conventions by which meaning is associated with specific forms. It is apparent that gradual and steady evolutionary change provides the best situation for cognitive schemes to accommodate changing conditions in the environment. The evolution of meanings accessible to larger groups may, of course, lag somewhat behind the evolution of a style, because it takes time for conventions of meanings to adjust to changes in style. But when the gradual adjustment of meanings to forms is discontinued — when it is interrupted by revolutionary stylistic change, or when styles divert abruptly at any particular point — the cognitive schemes of different individuals will most likely adjust differently and cause a decrease in the overall degree of intersubjectivity. This often results in a situation where specific stylistic tendencies become meaningful only to particular subcultures, who then develop their own exclusive conventions. Once meaning deviates from common convention this way, an evolutionary process is set in motion which results in ever more diverse meanings. Because new styles are based in part on old styles, styles whose meanings are no longer largely intersubjective will form the basis for further stylistic divergences, which, in turn, will produce ever less intersubjective meaning.

The overall conclusion of this argument is that form is not neutrally experienced, but laden with meanings. Yet these meanings are by no means intrinsic. Rather, the observer 'creates' them alongside the perceived object, and thus experiences them like properties of the object. Meaning is a matter of individual concepts established through past experience. Regardless of whether one knows the intended meaning of a particular form, one always infers meaning. But the 'expression' of an object — a building, for example — is not constrained by its form. Meaning and form can, and should, be analyzed independently.

III

Adopting the
Aesthetic Attitude

The role of form in experiencing and judging architecture cannot be sufficiently explained by the three types of theories discussed in the previous
chapter. Instrumental and communicative approaches are entirely based on
extramorphic properties, and thus deny purely formal characteristics a role in
shaping the experience of objects. Proportion theories, on the other hand,
base principles of good form on systems of morphic characteristics. While
these may create abstract, and also often arbitrary, systems of order, they
neglect the role of the human subject in the experience of architecture.

A theory that adequately investigates the role of form in the experience
of the world, must take into account both the experiencing subject and the
experienced object: it must account for the process by which the visual
environment is experienced, and it must concentrate on properties of the
perceived environment which are not extramorphic — that is, properties
which the beholder can perceive directly in the object rather than assigning to
it through associative cognitive operations. By concentrating on the above
two concerns, the focus of such a theory will fall on the process of perception,
that by which the *form* of the environment is internalized. Interpretation,

then, will become a concern only inasmuch as it is able to alter primary perceptual experience.

In philosophical aesthetics the above two demands are most closely met by so-called *presentational* or *formalist* theories. These maintain that the experience of art does not rest on dispositional properties inferred by the beholder, but on properties which are directly given in an object, and are thus accessible to immediate perception. Modern aesthetic theories of this kind are rooted in the tradition of Immanuel Kant's *Critique of Judgement*,[1] but formalist doctrines were also present in theories of art from Classical antiquity through the eighteenth century, when a radical shift from objective to subjective concepts of art took place. While, previously, the qualities of objects that were thought to elicit the sensation of beauty were considered objective and real, at that time form began no longer to be considered as self-subsistent, but rather as empirically constructed by the mind. According to Hume: "beauty is not a quality in things themselves, it exists merely in the mind which contemplates them." He termed the process by which this took place an attitude of "disinterestedness."[2]

However, it was Kant who revolutionized the subject-object relation entirely. He argued that we cannot know the actual form of an object, only how it appears to us. Form, thus, is a construction of the mind based on a priori principles of sensibility by which the manifold of sensations is organized into specific patterns. His position presages contemporary organismic-organizational positions in psychology, which state that stimuli organize themselves into forms on the basis of innate predilections of the human perceptual apparatus. In laying the foundations for modern aesthetics, Kant defines as aesthetic all judgements that are of a nonteleological character, that is, all judgements executed in a mode of direct awareness. Aesthetic judgements could thus be considered spontaneous, devoid of intellectual thought or concepts, the result of a free interplay of the senses.

In the field of aesthetics, Kant's propositions have led to presentational theories of aesthetics, the pivotal concept of which is the so-called 'aesthetic attitude', which can be summarized through the following three propositions:

- The object is perceived in *direct awareness*; that is, no reasoning or application of concepts is involved. The object is perceived in an attitude of disinterestedness or psychical distance.
- The object is looked upon as a *means without an end*, or as *an end in itself*, allowing any purpose it might have to be disregarded.
- The object is contemplated by concentrating only on those properties which are *immediately perceivable*. Thus, the object may be separated from any meaning attached to it or content expressed by it.

1. Direct Awareness

The concept of the aesthetic attitude describes a mode of attention which focuses on the direct experience of an object through properties which are immediately given in it, namely, its *form*. As such, it would appear to provide a powerful tool for determining the role of form in aesthetic experiences. But this concept, so central to modern formalist aesthetics, immediately invites criticism on logical as well as psychological grounds.

The proposition that there can exist a mode of direct awareness that a person can assume at will raises the strongest objections. The understanding of 'direct perceptual awareness' has changed much in contemporary aesthetics, and now bears little resemblance to the original Kantian notion. Kant defined as aesthetic those forms of judgement and experience in which concepts not only are not applied, but categorically cannot be applied. Following this logic, whenever a concept can be adopted in judging an object, such judgements cannot be considered purely aesthetical. The idea of an aesthetic attitude, however, suggests a mode which can be deliberately adopted — as, indeed, most protagonists of this position maintain. The logical contradiction here is obvious: since the very act of adopting an attitude is deliberate and must be made in regard to a concept, it cannot involve purely perceptual awareness.

39

Modern theorists have attempted in various ways to craft a definition of the aesthetic attitude that can address this difficulty. For example, Harold Osborne defines the mode of direct perceptual awareness as "a state of mind in which we are fully absorbed in the object presented, in becoming fully aware of the object itself without being deflected by concerns for its practical or utilitarian implications."[3] The crucial questions to ask here, however, are what are the conditions for such a state of mind, and can such a state of mind be adopted at all? A more rigorous definition, by Edward Bullough, is that the aesthetic attitude requires "psychical distance."[4] This can be thought of as a state of consciousness by which the perceived phenomenon holds the attention to such an extent that any practical reference to daily life becomes neglected. This distance can be initiated by deliberate action: in other words, one's attention can be directed.

Another theorist, Jerome Stolnitz, defines the aesthetic attitude as a more ordinary mode of "disinterested and sympathetic attention to and contemplation of any object of awareness whatsoever, for its own sake alone."[5] This notion, in fact, is very close to Hume's original formulation, that of a "disinterested attitude." "Sympathetic" to Stolnitz means to "accept the object on its own terms to appreciate it"[6] — that is, to judge it as an example of a class of objects. "Contemplation" means "perception directed toward the object in its own right ...[when] the spectator is not concerned to analyze it or ask questions about it."[7] But in both Bullough's and Stolnitz's interpretations there remains the question as to whether the described mode is indeed a form of direct perceptual awareness, or simply a special attitude of interpretation.

To understand this question, one has to return to the two modes of judgement discussed in Chapter One: deliberated and spontaneous. In a deliberated judgement concepts need to be applied, according to which the values of different variables may be aggregated into an overall judgement. Concepts are categorically of a teleological nature, and therefore require (in psychological terms) that a person adopt specific cognitive sets for interpretation. This demands, however, a mode of cognition which is quite different from that of mere perceptual awareness. This would seem to imply that only spontaneous judgements can rest on perceptual, — that is, nonconceptual — awareness.

But even in the instance when no concepts are deliberately employed, there remains the question as to whether concepts may not become involved in this mode as well ; for it is questionable whether one's cognitive stock can simply be bypassed when making a judgement. It would be plausible to assume that this stock — one's present state of internal knowledge, acquired through learning and previous experience — cannot simply be ignored, for there can be no acting in the world without prior knowledge. Even if some innate determination were assumed to play a role, one's present behavioral structure would be at least partly based on prior experience. Experience — that is, knowledge — inevitably produces a cognitive model of ordered relationships of the components of one's world that unavoidably creates expectations when approaching the world. In other words, knowledge is ultimately a matter of concepts.

Is, then, the aesthetic attitude a mode of ignorance? For example, when confronted with an object or situation whose significance and purpose cannot be discerned — say, a fetish from another culture — a person cannot possibly be expected to judge it according to 'correct' concepts of utility, history or culture. Will his judgement in this case rely exclusively on properties open to perception? Or will he apply extramorphic concepts regardless of their 'correctness' — namely, concepts derived from objects in his own culture which may share properties with the unfamiliar object. For instance, the observer may consider the fetish an 'ornament', and apply a familiar concept about ornamentation. Similarly, when a person encounters a building of a particular type or style he has never seen before, he may simply apply concepts derived from previously experienced buildings.

Because previous experience cannot be suspended, interpretation is unavoidable, even when this interpretation is 'incorrect'. Unless the phenomenon in question cannot be evaluated by virtue of any concept — that is, when it has no discernible external value — perceptual awareness can never stand as the sole ground for judgement. The problem here is that cases in which phenomena have no external value are rare. Kant's famous example of the sunset may be one of a very few. Even though we know that the setting sun results from the earth's revolution, we still perceive it as plunging into the ocean.

Thus, if the aesthetic attitude is to be defined as pure perceptual awareness, it can only be negatively defined: direct awareness is only possible when no cognitive sets can be applied. In other words, the more one knows about a given object or situation, the less one can approach it aesthetically. Hence, it is only when a perceived object has no purpose, or when no specific cognitive set can be adopted (when one is ignorant of any purpose the object might serve), that one's judgement of it rests exclusively on purely aesthetic qualities.

Despite the above analysis, it must be pointed out that it certainly *is* possible to judge most objects without concern for their practical implications. But this may occur only when the judgement is deliberated and the non-utilitarian aspects of the object are intentionally discounted. However, this clearly involves an attitude adopted as a matter of conscious choice (and thus not intuitive in nature), or alternatively, a routinely applied attitude such as that adopted when entering a museum of the fine arts or attending a concert. And this is where a key flaw in modern presentational theories arises: in order to discount the practical nature of one's concerns, one must do so *deliberately*.

Though it is possible deliberately to set aside concerns for utility, in the case of art, as Wollheim[8] has shown, it is senseless to demand we free ourselves entirely from any concept, as proclaimed by the attitude theorist. People will always have expectations about objects, especially in relation to those they consider art: the more we know about art — for instance, about a particular style — the more we will expect of objects that claim to represent it. The artistic object, therefore, is not only judged against common categories of knowledge, but within a specific class of objects, namely, works of art. Thus the aesthetic attitude, adopted deliberately, requires prior cultivation of the concept of art. Hume's 'distant' or 'disinterested' attitude is instructive in this regard. Art, as he puts it, appeals to "men of delicate and refined taste."[9]

(Thus appreciation of art requires the connoisseur!) And judgements on art are, as Arthur Danto[10] has shown, logically dependent on theories which presuppose knowledge about the history of art.

As the above discussion indicates, the notion of the aesthetic attitude rests on a false theoretical conception. Developed under the concept of art, the aesthetic attitude, deliberately adopted, can only be understood as a form of focused attention by which a person judges an object against selected concepts, rather than through direct perceptual awareness. This misconception, however, does not automatically lead to the implication that perceptual properties cannot play a role in judgements. One might instead ask why it is necessary at all to draw boundaries between moral, scientific and aesthetic judgements, or between teleological and nonteleological ones, as is the case of the Kantian tradition. Most judgements cannot be confined to such exclusive domains. Instead, as I hope to show, judgements about physical objects always contain, to varying degrees, embedded aesthetic judgements which are based on immediately perceivable properties.

2. Buildings as Means Without Ends:
Is Architecture a Fine Art?

While things may exist that can be treated purely aesthetically (such as those for which no concept is adequate or for which no end is evident), the crucial question remains whether such purely aesthetic judgement is possible in the case of architecture. Not only is this issue of interest in terms of the role of aesthetic judgements, but it is also important in regard to the claim that architecture is autonomous of the idea of 'mere building'. The primary condition that would allow architecture to be considered purely aesthetic would be if it could be considered a means without an end or an end in itself. In order to examine this idea, I shall consider two modes by which architecture may be approached: *production* by the designer, and *reception* by the user.

First, in relation to the receptive mode, is it possible to treat a building as autonomous — that is, to disregard its purpose and divorce its experience from that which is known about other buildings? In cases of deliberated, conscious judgement this is certainly possible: this kind of focused attention enables a person to judge a building against any number of selected concepts, such as those involving style, ideology or fashion. Yet such deliberated evaluation is clearly different from everyday unconscious experience, which relies less on selected concepts than on one's cognitive stock at large. In everyday experience judgements about buildings will be informed by what is generally known about them. Since this involves concepts, extramorphic information will always come into play. In fact, the less one knows about a particular building, the more one has to rely on concepts acquired through previous experience. And, when no particular concept about function can be applied, a building will be judged as an example of a kind, namely, as one of many buildings. Because buildings are an integral, indispensable part of one's interaction with a world of aims and functions, it seems implausible one could have no concept about them. Buildings cannot, therefore, be experienced spontaneously as purposeless, since previous experiences cannot be discarded.

There is even less aesthetic freedom in regard to the mode of production, which is, by definition, instrumental. Buildings are erected due to demands; in particular, the production of a building is bound to the patronage that initiates the design process. This relationship implies desired results, which, in order to be achieved without unforeseen side- or aftereffects, require deliberation and planning at all stages.[11] In this regard, architecture is different from other artistic activities, where, ideally, there are no constraints other than those dictated by the medium itself. Buildings are always created within a given context — although not always planned for it — and cannot be conceived in isolation from this larger context. Where the artist has a great deal of control over design variables, the architectural designer must always respond to a host of context variables (building codes, climatic conditions, and so on) and performance variables (desired qualities of the building). A work of art may be produced exclusively for contemplation, but a building is always meant as a shelter for human activities. Though function does not constrain specific form, formal considerations cannot be fully independent of the building's ends.

3. Three Considerations for Further Development
of a Presentational Theory

A brief recapitulation of my line of reasoning to this point is now appropriate. I have so far argued that three of the most prominent theories of architectural aesthetics prove inadequate to determine sufficiently the extent to which the experience of form enters into judgements about buildings. From general theories of aesthetics the presentational approach was found to come closest to the demands of this question. But the core concept of this approach — the notion of the aesthetic attitude — was found to be inconsistent with the need of a presentational theory to be concerned only with properties that are directly given in the object. I have shown that the aesthetic attitude can be better understood as a mode of focused attention, leading to judgements which are deliberated on grounds of isolated concepts. It now remains to show how the presentational approach, further developed and liberated from several cumbersome concepts, can provide a workable basis on which to develop a theory of architectural aesthetics.

At this point a definition is necessary: by aesthetic judgement I will henceforth refer to those modes of awareness that rest on perceptual rather than extrasensory factors. With this in mind, I propose three conditions for further development of a presentational approach. First, aesthetics needs to be separated from the concept of 'taste'. Not only has this term been used in confusing variations at different times and in different languages, but it is a concept which simply does not contribute to explaining aesthetic judgement. Though Kant defined taste as that faculty to which aesthetic judgements pertained, colloquial usage of the word now more or less refers to individual preference based on instinctive feelings. Yet even if the simple determination "I like it" is not an aesthetic judgement as previously defined, might it still not be a judgement based on concepts of truth, goodness, or utility? Is taste not a matter of education, as in 'good taste'? Taste must be recognized as an elliptic term: it refers both to individual gustation and to a standard acquired through a process of discrimination and selection that reflects socio-cultural status. Taste thus results from learning and socialization and involves the application of concepts in spontaneous judgements.

The second for the further development of the presentational approach is that if aesthetic value is to pertain only to judgements of a nonconceptual nature, it must be separated from notions of art. The linkage of these two concepts has formed a major hindrance to previous investigations of aesthetic experience, because concepts developed in relation to the notion of art — a concept which has never been unequivocally defined — have unfortunately been generalized to all aesthetic experiences. Though aesthetic experience may contribute a great deal to the experience of art, the artistic is, as Binkley[12] has demonstrated, not logically dependent on the aesthetic: a work of art cannot be sufficiently explicated in aesthetic terms.

The third requirement for the further development of the presentational approach is that aesthetic experience and judgement should not be separated from other modes of experience and judgement. Although I aim to show that the aesthetic mode is, in psychological terms, functionally independent of other modes of experience, phenomenally it cannot occur in isolation. Rather, it must be seen as embedded in, and in most instances, a prerequisite for, experiences at large. Another approach to this idea is to consider that aesthetic and other forms of judgement do not exclude one another: deliberated judgement may contain intuitive judgement; likewise, intellectual thought does not prohibit simultaneous nonconceptual thinking. In fact, as I will show, all judgements about physical objects must contain aesthetic judgements based on perceivable properties. The key issue becomes the degree to which aesthetic judgements contribute to other judgements.

In conclusion, it must be noted that philosophical aesthetics has provided considerable insight to the issue of aesthetic value. It has raised the issue of good form, and provided a basic epistemological framework for its reso lution. But it has not answered the question of how properties of form constrain the experience of an object. This issue can only be pursued further by turning to psychology, to the investigation of the actual cognitive processes by which judgements are made. A number of issues can be more adequately addressed by investigations in psychology: How are concepts formed? Are value concepts connected with morphic representations when judging an object? Is it possible to distinguish between perception — upon which aesthetic judgements are supposed to rest — and cognition? Or is cognition a function of perception or part of a single process? Finally, are there commonalities between people in regard to those cognitive processes that lead to aesthetic judgements?

Form and Its Interpretation:
The Role of Perception and Cognition and the Formation of Concepts

In order to further develop a presentational theory by which the role of form in the experience and judgement of architecture can be explained, I now turn to the psychological processes through which things become known and valued. The pivotal issue in this chapter is the question of commonality between individuals in the acquisition of knowledge and the formation of judgements, because further investigations of the role that form plays in the experience and judgement of architecture will only be fruitful if such universals can be established in relation to the *perception* of form.

Several questions need to be addressed in connection with such an agenda. First, is it, in psychological terms, justified to distinguish aesthetic experience from other types of experience so as to allow the isolation of an object's presentational properties from any 'meaning' properties that may be associated with it? Next, what is the role of form in constituting knowledge of an object? How are the images of the perceptual world formed, and how do they acquire value and function within a person's universe of knowledge? Is it justified to distinguish between different kinds of knowledge — particularly between perceptual knowledge, which refers to the form of things, and other kinds of knowledge, which pertain to value? And what then would be the relationship between perceptual and overall knowledge? For example, does perceptual knowledge precede the acquisition of overall knowledge, or is it a function of it?

Similarly, before turning to the problem of judgement, it is necessary to ask how the concepts that allow judgement are formed. Indeed, what are concepts? Are there different types? What are the cognitive processes that lead to judgements? To what extent do aesthetic and other kinds of concepts enter into the judgement as a whole? And do presentational properties play a greater role in spontaneous judgement than they do in the deliberated mode, where different cognitive sets are purposefully adopted? Or must all judgements about objects contain some embedded aesthetic judgement of form? If so, how does the aesthetic component condition the overall result?

The starting point of this investigation must be the question of how we know the world. This is an epistemological issue that has long stirred controversy among philosophers and psychologists. What is reality? Is it matter — that is, the world and its things? Or do we live in Plato's cave, where the perceived world is only the approximation of our imagination? Are the phenomena of the world and their neurological substrates different aspects of one complex reality, or do they belong to fundamentally different realities? Is one's individual world imposed by the objective world, or does it result from a construction of thought? Are the objective and the subjective worlds independent of one another, or are they synchronized? Is the manner in which we cognitively organize space exclusively a matter of learning and past experience, or is it innate? This question is crucial, for if innate determination exists, then there must also exist commonalities in the perceptual structuring of the world. And if there is innate structure, there must be causalities between actual and perceived reality — that is, between the order of the world and the order of the percept. It is only if such a relationship can be assumed that one can justly speak of presentational properties. For if perceived form is the result of internalized processes only, with no causal relationship between percept and object, then all properties would have to be inferred by the subject.

When psychology began exploring perception, cognitive development, and learning, it took on the long-standing philosophical controversy between *empirism* and *rationalism*. These two schools of thought have long defined the ends of a wide philosophical spectrum: the former states that the acquisition of knowledge is entirely determined by *prior experience*; the latter that *innate structure* governs the organization of knowledge. The empirical position presumes that the mind originates as a blank slate to be filled with information, and that the way this occurs determines further acquisition of information. In psychology, the empirical view dominates, for example, B.F. Skinner's 'behaviorist' theories. To a lesser degree it also imbues the 'transactionalist' theory of Ames, which stresses a dependence on learning and past experience in both perception and the resulting transformation of information into knowledge. In contrast, the 'organizational' or 'organismic' position in psychology promotes a rationalist notion based on innate physiological processes that govern perception and cognitive development. This notion is basic to Gestalt psychology and its successors. It can, for example, be found in Piaget's 'structuralist-developmental' approach.

1. Perception: A Functionally Independent Process

What is perception? Is it a process of conceptualization, or of physiological organization? Is it an active process of interpreting the world? Or is it the organization of the stimuli of the outer world into a structured image, which must be formed before it can acquire meaning in one's universe of knowledge? Is perception a form, or even a function, of knowledge? Or is knowing a function of perceiving and acting in the world? Does what one perceives depend on what one knows? In other words, is perception a subsystem of cognition, or a functionally independent activity?

Before addressing the issue of whether a distinction exists between perception and cognition, I shall first offer the following tentative definitions.

Perception is that process by which a mental image, or percept, of an object or phenomenon is acquired. This is a process of segregation and unification by which environmental stimuli are organized into specific forms. *Cognition*, on the other hand, is how the percept acquires value — that is, place and function in the individual's universe of knowledge. This is the process by which the percept becomes a meaningful image, and so it necessarily involves recognition, memory and thought. In short, cognition is conceptualization.

Historically, there are two crucial questions on which different positions in psychology have been adopted regarding the processes of perception. The first is the controversy between *nativists* and *empirists*.[1] Nativists assume that *innate structuring processes* govern perception; empirists state that perception is a form of knowledge based on *past experience and learning*. The second dispute concerns the existence of causalities between the structure of the environment and the structure of the percept. One side in this dispute conceives of the environment as a source of stimuli that impose themselves onto the sensory system; the other denies that such a causal relationship can exist. The intermediate position is held by *organizational* theories, which are *both ecological and organismic* in outlook.

In John Locke's conception of the mind as *tabula rasa*, there was no place for innate ideas or structuring processes. People were thought to be born with empty minds. Experience then imprinted itself on the blank slate to produce simple knowledge of basic physical properties such as extension, solidity, motion, and rest. Locke believed these were primary characteristics of the world that existed independently of the mind. By contrast, he argued, qualities such as color and sound did not correspond to actual environmental properties, and he proposed that they were purely sensory. Whereas Locke assumed some correspondence between environmental properties and the perceived image, Bishop Berkeley[2] challenged the belief that sense impressions were in any way caused by properties external to the mind. Because we know only sensations, he argued, there is no reason to assume these are caused by an external world.

Contemporary empirical theories in psychology, as most clearly articulated in the behaviorism of B.F. Skinner, also consider the mind (whatever it might be) a *tabula rasa* that is structured through learning and resulting memory. Perception in this system is not a self-contained psychological process, but rather a form of human 'behavior'. Ittelson characterizes this position as follows: "The environment is considered real, existing in its own right, and can therefore be described in terms of stimuli which provoke a certain behavior. The individual's behavior can be described in terms of an aggregate of habitual responses to recurring similar situations."[3] These habitual responses, called 'stimulus-response units', are formed as a consequence of one's interaction with the environment. When there is no S-R unit adequate to a given situation, new responses are provoked, which result in either satisfaction or dissatisfaction, and lead to new S-R units being formed through 'positive' or 'negative reinforcement'. Learning is thus the result of 'reward and punishment'.

For the empirist, perception is an integral part and function of cognitive behavior. In other words, what we see depends on what we know, for, as it is argued, an infinite number of external objects can give rise to the same stimulus pattern. The one we 'choose' is only the one we are able to 'recognize'. For example, on the retina a large object at a distance may appear the same as a small object close up, and a tilted ellipse may appear identical to a circle. How else except through experience can we tell the difference? Transactionalists like Ames[4] use examples like these to argue that perception must be a selective process, a 'purposive action' upon which assumptions about the nature of the perceived object are built. In light of knowledge from the past, such 'actions' determine the nature of present perceptual experience. Perception is thus considered a 'creative' act.

A weakness with this view becomes evident when one considers simple visual illusions. These show that knowledge alone cannot suffice to explain why given patterns are seen as particular forms. For example, even when the Fraser illusion (Fig.25) is understood and has been experienced many times, it still appears as a spiral instead of a series of parallel circles. Köhler[5] has further pointed out that the underlying assumption of the empirical view, that there

Fig.25. Fraser illusion.

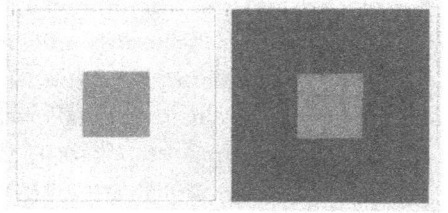

Fig.26. Simultaneous contrast.

is a one-to-one correspondence between retinal stimulation and resulting perceptual experience, cannot be maintained. He points out that, according to this view, changes in local stimuli ought to result in changes in the percept. But this is not always the case, as can be seen by so-called perceptual constancies. For example, a tilted disk can still be perceived as a disk. Color perception provides further evidence of flaws in the empirical position. Perceived color depends not only on the hue, chroma and value of isolated colors, but on the characteristics of surrounding colors. As Wallach[6] has shown, the stimulus for achromatic surface color is not constituted by the absolute intensity of the light in its region, but by the ratio of intensity of light there and light in surrounding regions (Fig.26). One can conclude from such examples that perceptual stimuli must be considered in relational terms. Empirists have long tried to counter this suggestion by arguing that the stimuli in these cases are ambiguous, and that past experience must be invoked. But the circularity of this reasoning is clear.

There are other problems with the empirical view. Perhaps most importantly, the implicit assumption that perceptual organization is only possible as a consequence of past experience and learning is also flawed, as Zuckerman and Rock[7] have argued. They ask what people can see before they learn to interpret a retinal pattern, and how they can subsequently learn to see only that which is 'appropriate'. The empirist's notion of the clean slate suggests that in the early period of life, the human visual world consists of a blurry mosaic of sense impressions rather than a field of segregated and unified shapes. Only through learning and experience, it is argued, can the person then convert these sense data into shaped areas. But how can memory traces be established in the first place if there are no previous memories? How can an initially amorphous, unorganized mass of sensory data of previous perceptions organize subsequent sensory data? Thus Zuckerman and Rock rightly ask, "how can we learn to see, if we need to see in order to learn?"[8] Perceptual organization must occur prior to any association with existing memory; otherwise it would be impossible for unorganized sense data to trigger appropriate memories. Past experience can only enter the process after some primary level of sensory organization of stimulus material has been achieved.

The logical problem inherent in the empirical view thus originates in an overemphasis on the role of memory. On the one hand, this emphasis embodies the assumption that people are born with fully equipped sense organs; on the other, it argues that perception has to be learned. The empirist thus separates sense organs from the brain: the former deliver data, while the latter analyzes it into percepts. Among those who have advocated this view are Helmholz, Wundt and Titchener, who have claimed that sensations must be converted into perceptual data by 'association' with memory traces. For these 'associationists' sensation belongs to 'lower processes', and perception to 'higher' ones.

The organizational theorist J.J. Gibson[9] has dubbed this view the "homunculus theory of perception," for it assumes the eye is little more than an optical instrument through which a small picture is produced for the brain to 'look at'. According to Gibson, such a conceptual separation of sensory nerves and brain is not justified.[10] Nerves are not just stimulus receivers obtaining data that must be computed in the brain: rather, the senses and the brain constitute one perceptual system. In this way, the eye can be considered an extension of the brain, and sense impressions do not have to be converted into a 'picture'. Instead, the very process of perception involves the selection and organization of environmental stimuli.

Gibson further argues that perception need not be learned. He writes that "as the infant learns to use his perceptual system more skillfully, his attention becomes educated."[11] In other words, he learns to see in the sense of learning to identify meaningful things in a meaningful world. However, "he doesn't learn to convert sense data into perceptions."[12] In Gibson's view, learning is not simply learning to see or discriminate, but rather learning to see what things look like. This occurs "not by association, but [by] learning of associations."[13]

Gibson argues that the common fallacy of theories which suppose that mental operations process sensory inputs is that "knowledge of the world cannot be explained by supposing that knowledge of the world already exists."[14] This is precisely the case with associationist theories — whether they assume that the outer world is deduced by unconscious inferences (which implies an ability to correlate the two); whether they claim people form hypotheses about 'distant' stimuli based on 'proximal' stimuli (which implies that proximal stimuli can somehow be 'understood'); or whether it is maintained that the decoding of sensory input takes place through the application of memories (which implies accumulated memories at the outset).

A similar fallacy can be observed in nativist theories. The nativist maintains that the world is a place of sense impressions arranged and controlled by the mind in accordance with innate categories. Kant referred to such knowledge that exists independently of experience or thought as 'intuition' or 'a priori' knowledge. In relation to it, he defined categories of space, time, cause and effect, and substance, which he argued are imposed by the mind on sense impressions. In Kant's words: "our intellect does not draw its laws from nature but imposes its laws on nature."[15] However, one must ask how such categories can be classified

before the idea of categories has been established. And, if basic categories are innate, where does this form of knowledge originate? Again, knowledge is explained by assuming knowledge to exist.

Both the empirist and nativist views assume that environmental stimuli do not contain information; hence, the claim must be made that sensory images need to be 'processed' to yield knowledge. However, if one adopts the *organizational position*, it is not necessary to localize and describe such a procedure. Organizational theories state that perception is governed by fundamental biological processes that are initiated by relations contained in the stimulus pattern itself. Thus, perception requires, in Gibson's words, "a sentient organism with certain perceptual abilities, but also . . . an environment with certain perceivable characteristics."[16] The viewpoint is thus both *organismic* and *ecological*. Perception is seen as a mode of interaction between the organism and its environment. It cannot be described by either physiological principles or the composition of the stimulus pattern alone.

A central notion governing organizational theories was formulated by the founders of Gestalt psychology: Wolfgang Köhler, Kurt Koffka and Max Wertheimer. This is that visually perceivable properties of form are not simply 'assimilated' from the outside world, but are always 'newly formed' in every instance of perception. The formation does not occur through mental processes but because of an innate human physiological inclination.[17] It is thus the organization of the stimulus pattern itself (in interaction with innate human perceptual biases) that creates segregation and unification in the visual field. In this way, organization of perceptual stimuli precedes learning. According to Köhler: "The excitation of the sensory surface and the corresponding somatic field will, with sufficiently protracted stimulation, reach a stationary, or at least quasi-stationary state, in which the acting electrochemical forces tend to reach an equilibrium with a minimum of potential energy and maximum entropy. The stimulus pattern itself thus gives rise to perceptual organization."[18]

According to Gestalt psychology, the character of the perceptual field is primarily *macroscopic*, that is, *topological* and *nodological*; percepts possess a whole character which transcends the character of their parts. Perceptual organization is thus not a matter of aggregating discrete stimuli, but compromises a reaction of the cortial field to configurational properties of the stimulus pattern. For proof, psychologists have turned to experiments showing the topological similarity between retinal stimulation and the activation patterns of the striate cortex (Fig. 27).

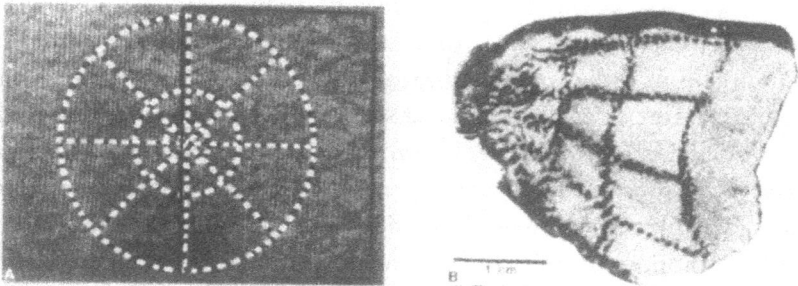

Fig 27. Target and excitement pattern of a striate cortex.

When the stimulus is explained in relational terms, in cases of perceptual ambiguity (such as optical illusions) there is no need to invoke past experience, as must the empirist. Neither is it necessary to posit ready-made categories, as does the nativist. For example, the pattern shown in Fig. 28 simply offers at least two possible organizations: either it can be seen as two sets of squares or one set of stars. That it is first seen as a pattern of squares is due to the fact this is the simpler solution.

The reasons why things look as they do has been explained by the Gestalt school by means of a number of principles of perceptual organization, verified by empirical and neurophysiological studies.[19] Such principles were first described by Wertheimer[20] as laws of grouping: 'proximity', 'similarity of size and color', 'good continuation of contour', and so on. Rubin[21] then described

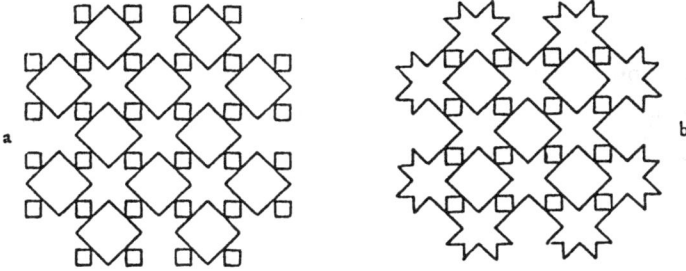

Fig 28. Competition between shapes: squares and stars. Simpler shape prevails.

the so-called 'one-sided function' of perceptual contours, and thus explained how a distinction appears between 'figure' and 'ground'. These principles have been formulated as descriptive generalizations which can be employed without the need to invoke any theory of information processing by the brain. Underlying all of them, however, is the so-called 'law of good gestalt', or 'principle of tension reduction'. This states that unification and segregation of the perceptual field is governed by an innate human need to find the simplest solution under given conditions.

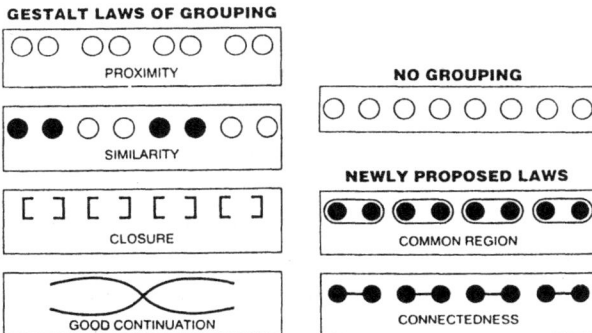

Fig. 29. Graphic representation of Gestalt laws (after Palmer).

The main tenets of the organizational position can be summarized as follows: the percept is based on stimulus relationships rather than discrete stimuli; sensory data are organized according to selective principles; and perceptual organization is innately determined. The nervous system, as Lashley[22] has argued, "is not a neutral medium, on which learning imposes any form of organization whatsoever. On the contrary, it has definite predilections for certain forms of organization and imposes these upon the sensory impulses which reach it."

The strength of these views becomes evident when one considers the example of a congenitally blind person. If this person gains sight later in life, according to the empirical view, he would have to learn to perceive segregated shapes and colors. Yet experiments with such people[23] — as with newborns — have shown that certain principles of perceptual organization need not be learned.[24] Among them are 'apparent movement', 'figure-ground organization', 'laws of surroundedness', 'separation of systems in movement', 'sound localization by head movement', 'depth based on retinal disparity', 'kinetic depth effect', and 'phenomenal identity'.

A further strength of the organizational view is that perception can be shown to be autonomous of behavioral or personality influences. A good example is given by 'afterimages' or the so-called 'Phi-phenomenon', the creation of apparent perceptual movement for which no physical equivalent exists. Here the effect has been found to be quantitatively the same for all people: when two points are consecutively projected on the retina and are seen in less than 0.6 of a second, they appear as the movement of a single point.[25]

Opposition to the organizational position has often been based on the argument that perception cannot be considered merely the passive reception of environmental stimuli, but it must rather be seen as the active behavior of a productive organism. But this argument misinterprets the organizational view. Organizational theorists also consider perception to be a form of behavior. By nature, they argue, people must always be involved in a process of adjusting themselves to the stimulus pattern. Thus, for example, visual perception requires eye movement, and the sense of touch requires variations in applied pressure. Attention drawn to specific objects is always initiated by goal-directed behavior. Perception thus is *directed* by personality factors, but the actual physiological process of perceptual organization is autonomous of such influence.

In summation, the organizational position carries several implications. First, as a process governed by the excitation of sensory receptors by ecological cues (and the subsequent organization of sensory data according to physiological predilections), perception must occur prior to cognitive processing. It must also be functionally autonomous from behavioral and personality factors. Second, if perception is considered functionally autonomous, different people must arrive at largely similar perceptual organizations when presented with the same stimuli. Third, causalities of some kind must exist between ecological cues and perceptual organization. Victor von Weizsäcker has aptly described the nature of this relationship as follows: perceived order is not identical with objective order; rather, perception is the "probability but not reality" of the objective environment. While perceptions are, as he calls them, 'falsifications of objective facts', as visual illusions show so effectively, perceptual order is still determined by objective order. Space and time, Weizäcker argues, are thus properties of the environment, and not innate forms of organization, as proposed by Kant.[26]

Before moving on to a discussion of cognition, it is important to address one more argument that has been raised to challenge the functionally autonomous nature of the process of perception — namely, that perceptual differences develop along cultural lines. For example, certain art historians have maintained that different forms of art have evolved because the world is 'seen' differently by different cultures — an argument convincingly challenged by Ernst Gombrich and his theory of 'schema and correction'.[27] Comparative studies, including those of Western Europeans and Africans,[28] have in fact discovered no evidence that such differences exist in perceptual organization, even though the *interpretation* of perceptual material may differ considerably between two cultural groups. For example, African aborigines were unable to recognize anything in photographs presented to them, and became irritated when shown perspective line drawings that included figures in the distance at

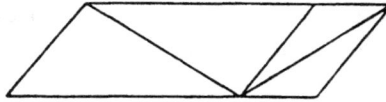

Fig. 30. Sander's Parallelogram

a smaller scale. The dimensions in typical right-angle illusions, like the Sander parallelogram (Fig. 30), were also gauged less correctly by the African group.

Yet were these tests really about perception, or were they about interpretation? Perception of photographs is, as Gibson[29] has demonstrated, quite different from perception of environmental arrays, because pictures are two-dimensional representations of a three-dimensional reality, and their interpretation relies on acquired visual conventions that may be as arbitrary as linguistic conventions. For example, regarding the gauging of dimensions, it can be argued that length is a matter of cultural concept. Moreover, certain kinds of experience are more likely to occur in some cultures than in others. For example, anyone who has grown up in a 'carpentered world' will be more able to judge dimensions of right-angle illusions correctly than someone who has not. The authors of one study[30] concluded that their original hypothesis that cultural differences lead to differences in perception of the world could not be upheld: "However plausible and widespread, the proposition cannot be considered to be unequivocally demonstrated by empirical data."

From the above considerations, it is possible to draw a crucial principle for developing a theory of form. By adopting the organizational position (which is, as I have argued, more consistent in logical terms than other views, and more plausible with regard to empirical evidence), the process of perception can be considered autonomous of cognition. However, as I will discuss in the next section, the processes of perception and cognition are actually paired phenomenally; that is, objects are perceived and identified as meaningful in the same event. Thus, meaning is given in the percept, but only as a result of cognition. Functionally, however, perception occurs prior to one's becoming aware of the object's significance and value — that is, prior to cognition. Therefore, *a distinction between form and meaning is justified*. Meaning, unlike form, does not directly result from a stimulus pattern; it is a matter of interpretation by which value is assigned on grounds of extramorphic concepts.

2. Cognition: The Formation of Operational Schemes

Now that perception has been established as a physiological process autonomous of cognitive and behavioral factors, it is justified for the sake of analysis to isolate the presentational properties of an object (those that are immediately accessible through perception and hence determined by the form of the object) from properties that are subjectively inferred (by means of information processing based on cognitive sets acquired through prior experience). The key to further elaborating the difference between these types of properties is a recognition that knowledge of the world cannot be constituted in perception alone. Only when perceptual representations are abstracted into symbolized form (so that they are free of concrete referents and can thus be easily manipulated in relation to each other), can objects be known in a meaningful sense. The philosopher Ernst Cassirer has formulated this distinction as follows: "[Concrete] acquaintance means only presentation; [abstract] knowledge includes and presupposes representation . . . [but] we must have a general concept of the object, and regard it from different angles to find its relation to other objects and determine its position within a general system."[31]

Such a distinction between concrete acquaintance and abstract knowledge raises some important issues. First, how is it possible to isolate and describe perceptual properties? Second, in the formation of judgements, what is the importance of perceptual properties in relation to those properties which are associated with the percept and subsequently determine an object's significance and value? In other words, how do modes of cognitive information processing, such as remembering, imagining or reasoning, interact with perceptual information? Can the perceptual aspect be overridden by individual cognitive sets? Or does form — that is, perceptual appearance — play a direct causal role in the formation of judgements?

Another way of considering this question is to ask whether overall judgements must contain embedded aesthetic judgements. If this can be positively answered, it will follow that all judgements about perceived objects must in some way contain universal parts. From this position, one can then proceed to question the degree to which such universalities allow the formation of similar concepts between people. But in order to address these issues, one must first ask how knowledge is attained. What is cognitive information processing? And, more specifically, how are cognitive sets, or value-concepts, formed?

In relation to information processing, the same logical inconsistencies appear with the nativist and empirist views as have already been outlined with regard to perception. According to the nativist view, people are equipped with innate, ready-made categories through which sensory stimuli are filtered and organized into meaningful entities. Cognitive development, or maturation of intelligence, is thus seen as a matter of learning, and involves the assimilation of information into ready-made slots. But this view, which explains maturation in purely quantitative terms, fails to account for the qualitatively distinct differences that develop from childhood to adolescence in the ability to structure the world. The position thus neglects transformations the organism itself may undergo in adapting itself to a milieu. It also accords too little importance to previous experience in explaining a person's increasing ability to manipulate the world abstractly.

For the empirist, on the other hand, knowledge is equivalent to the imprint of environmental stimuli on the nervous system. Since no innate determination is assumed, this view implies that knowledge must be a mere copy of the external world. The development of each person's cognitive abilities is therefore completely subject to environmental contingencies: the clean slate is passively inscribed with information by which stimulus-response units are formed; these, in turn, govern further interaction with the environment. But, as with perception, the question must be asked: if knowledge depends on learning and memory only, how can memory be formed and meaningfully organized in the first place? According to this view, there must be previous memory. How is this possible when the claim is made that a newborn's memory is completely amorphous? Succinctly put, how is it possible to establish concepts when the formation of concept requires concepts?

The organizational position attempts to address these problems with the nativist and empirist positions by advancing a view of "genetic epistemology."[32] As with perception, this entails both an 'organismic' as well as an 'ecological' outlook. The development of knowledge is thus the result of an interaction between the person and the surrounding milieu. In particular, Jean Piaget and his followers have propagated the view that, like biological growth, maturation of intelligence (defined as the ability to perform abstract manipulations of external and internal information) is "not something added to the organism and coming from outside, but corresponds to the nature of the organism."[33]

This biological-developmental approach does not begin with an empty slate, but with adaptive actions of the living organism to its environment. Hans Furth writes that "in interaction with the environment the organism builds up within itself coordinated schemes of knowing and gathers correspondingly meaningful knowledge about the outside environment."[34] Thus, every person is born with some intrinsic level of intellectual structure independent of extrinsic factors. The organizational position is thus essentially *biological*: behavior, intellectual maturation, and learning are all understood in terms of, and in relation to, underlying physiological organization. Within such a framework, intellectual development does not derive from specific innate processes which unfold over a specific time and are independent of environmental factors (the nativist view); nor is it solely the result of external factors acting as stimuli which provoke specific responses (as believed by the behaviorist). Rather, intellectual maturation is subject to natural order, or 'biological structures'.

According to Piaget, the notion of biological structure is comprised of three key ideas.[35] The first is 'wholeness': thus, the development of the intellect can be thought of as "system closed under transformations," involving laws that "never yield results external to the system nor employ elements that are external to it." The second is 'self-regulation': the intellect is viewed as a self-regulating physical system which "tends to preserve its own structure and at the same time extends the application of its own structure to include as much of the milieu as it can."[36] The third idea is 'transformation': the above principles hold the intellect in a state of "dynamic equilibrium," where it is constantly forced to undergo transformations to a higher order, or at least to change so as to adapt itself to, and interact with, the environment.

Knowledge is therefore the result of a process of cognitive structuring, in the true meaning of the term. It is neither assimilated from the outside, nor innately preexistent in categories. Rather, it emerges from interaction with the environment. According to this view, stimuli are intrinsically related to intellectual structure, since only if they can be assimilated by it, can they be said to be a true stimulus. Likewise, the intellect's response to stimuli does not simply take the form of an echo, but is rather the response of a living organism.[37]

One further important distinction is made by the organizational position — namely, between 'cognitive development' and 'learning'. The former involves a *qualitative* change in structural organization; the latter concerns a *quantitative* change in cognitive structures, caused by the incorporation of specific information. Here the process of abstracting reality is viewed biologically as a process of interactions and a series of equilibrations between the organism and its environment. Intelligence — the ability to abstract, or symbolically conceptualize the world — is therefore neither innate, nor simply the result of prior experience. The motivation for biological and psychological development can instead be found in the drive for adaptation. Thus abstract knowledge is attained through learning, but the mode of its formation is based on innate biological structures.

Piaget further describes the structuring of knowledge as being character-ized by two complementary functional invariants, 'assimilation' and 'accom-modation'. Assimilation is the "psychological relation of a stimulus to the reacting organism . . . [that] expresses an inner correspondence between an environmental phenomenon and the structure within the organism." It is an "inward directed tendency" of a person's intellectual structure allowing it to assimilate a new environmental event. Accommodation, on the other hand, is an "organism-outward tendency of the inner structure to accommodate itself to the particular environmental event."[38] Assimilation involves the modification of existing cognitive schemes to adjust to newly internalized elements. It does not consist merely of associating new stimuli with already-existing memory traces. Rather, the assimilation of an object or situation into an existing scheme alters the scheme and coordinates it with other schemes.[39]

Intellectual maturation and learning — that is, qualitative and quantita-tive development — thus stand in a dialectical, *reciprocal* relationship. Maturation is only possible through learning; yet at the same time, the way

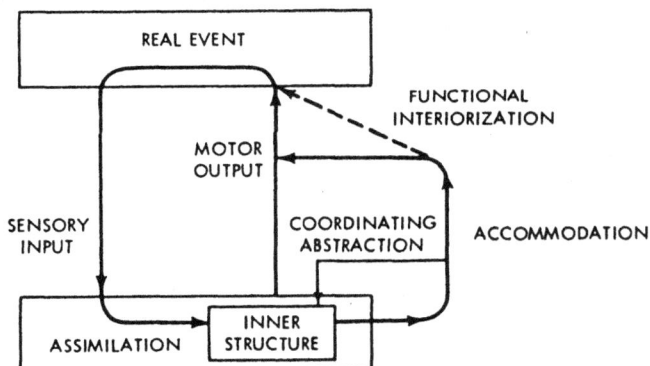

Fig.31. Diagram of Piaget's model of assimilation and accommodation.

one learns depends on one's degree of maturation. Cognitive development thus is understood as the degree of organization from lower to higher states of order: "from a state of relative globality and lack of differentiation to states of increasing differentiation, articulation and hierarchic integration."[40] This describes a progression from concrete acquaintance with the world to abstract knowledge of it.

Building on this primary idea, Piaget separated cognitive development into qualitatively different stages, each of which is characterized by a period of formation and a period of attainment. Thus a composite structure of mental operations is arrived at, where each stage forms the starting point for the evolution of the next. In Piaget's theory, the order of succession is constant, whereas the ages at which each stage may be attained may vary according to factors of the milieu. The sequence is inclusive: each new level of structure integrates its predecessors.[41]

During the first stage, the 'sensory-motor' stage, infants live in a space of action where they are the center of all reference. The infant here acts through 'habitual sensory-motor schemes' — mere reflex activities. At this time the environment is not yet stably represented in cognitive images, and exists only when perceived. The infant's world is thus 'pre-representational': it lacks meaning or symbolic function. During the second, 'preoperational' phase, the child progressively reaches a basic invariant of knowledge: that objects exist permanently, independent of his of her actions. At this point, representations are still static and are not yet coordinated into reversible structures. Only in the third, 'concrete-operational' stage does the child gradually form a system of operations which are reversible. He can now carry out various thought operations, such as those involving elementary logico-mathematical concepts. Yet even at this level thought processes are not fully separated from their concrete content: thought is still bound to the here and now. Only in the final 'formal-operational' stage is the child able to construct a theoretical world made up of concepts abstracted from concrete referents or actions. At this point a 'hypothetico-deductive' level of thought is reached, meaning that hypotheses can be formed and consequences predicted. The process of development from one stage to the next is one in which practical — that is, sensory-motor — intelligence is gradually transformed into operational intelligence, allowing knowledge to be gradually dissociated from its sensory-motor and perceptual content.

An important conclusion can now be drawn in relation to the potential for similarities between judgements by different individuals. This is that *similarities* in the cognitive (qualitative) development of different people may arise based on biological structure, while quantitative development — that is, the incorporation of specific knowledge into cognitive structures — may be dissimilar. But, as will become evident in the following section, the formation of concepts by different individuals also must show similarities in relation to the structuring of cognitive representations.

Finally, it is important to note that the organizational school of thought has suggested a parallelism between ontogenetic and phylogenetic development.[42] Thus the short-term development of specific cognitive sets must show similarities with general processes of conceptualization. Moreover, every process of conceptualization ultimately must be based on internalized sensory-motor images — that is, on the perception of form.

3. The Independence of Form and Meaning: Morphic Concepts vs. Value Concepts

Having established that perception and cognition can be considered functionally separate processes, I now turn to investigating the degree to which perceptual universals influence the formation of judgements. This analysis must begin by asking what role perceptual properties play in establishing internal representations of objects within a cognitive scheme, or within systems of interlocking schemes.

Piaget's epistemological model provides a starting point for such an investigation by distinguishing between two separate aspects of knowledge:

that which is 'figurative', and that which is 'operative'. The former is a "concrete" mode of knowing, "related to the percepts or images of successive or momentary configurations of the world by immediate contact"; the latter is an "abstract mode related to operations which intervene between the successive states and by which the subject transforms parts of the world into patterns or schemes."[43]

The *figurative aspect* of knowing represents the sensory-motor adaptation the organism needs to make in order to accommodate itself to *perceiving* a given situation. *Operational knowledge*, by contrast, is formed by the coordination and organization of adaptive action into operative schemes. This is a precondition to acting in the world, and involves the *formation of a behavioral structure*.[44] Operational knowledge is thus achieved by internalizing sensory-motor images of things and events; yet it is only by assimilating such images into a scheme in symbolized form that they become meaningful. It is clear, therefore, that concrete perceptual acquaintance does not suffice to make an object known; this only occurs when operative processes transform the internalized image into an object of knowing. This implies a reciprocal relationship; in other words, figurative knowing can only occur as a result of operative adjustment. Simply put, a person must be motivated by behavioral factors to accommodate himself to an event or object before he can make sense of the patterns of stimuli by which it appears. In this way, the meaningfulness of an object is derived from a person's action vis-à-vis perceived form.[45]

The above discussion allows an assessment of the role of the figurative aspect in the formation of operative knowledge. First, as explained above, perception results from actions of the subject stemming from the application of operational schemes, which cause existing schemes to be structured so as to permit assimilation. (According to such a formulation, figurative and operational processes can still be considered functionally independent because the sensory image is formed according to physiological predilections that are independent of a person's cognitive structure.) Second, the formation of the sensory image occurs prior to its incorporation into an internal scheme.

Third, the resulting internalized cognitive representation does not show a one-to-one relationship to the sensory image; rather, the internal representation is determined by the structure of existing cognitive schemes. This means that the internal representation must contain properties of individual schemes by which the object's significance, as well as its relationship to other schemes, is established. Fourth, single perceptual representations of specific objects or events may assume a diminished importance once representations of them have been internalized. Thus it is plausible to assume that generalized classifications may be substituted for highly individualized representations. As Hart and Moore note, "to achieve higher order of abstraction, objects of thought are replaced by hypothetical-deductive propositions."[46] Cognitive representations are thus further represented by denota in order to be freely manipulated.

It follows, then, that abstract knowledge need not be exclusively a matter of external assimilation; it can also be created by internal reclassification of cognitive schemes. What is commonly called 'imagination' or 'fantasy' can thus be understood as the result of such cognitive reorganization — the creation of a world free of concretely existing referents. In this way, hypothetical worlds can be 'imagined', and ideal, irreal or surreal settings can be composed utilizing sets of previously internalized perceptual particulars, recombined into new wholes.

Though schemes are formed by images of actions with the object, the representation of the act and the scheme cannot be identical, for no two actions are alike. Hence, the scheme must contain generalizable aspects of the coordination of external acts.[47] Operational knowledge thus must be the result of a process of *classification* and *generalization* — that is, the application of concepts.[48]

A distinction now needs to be made between two different types of concepts that can be applied in making a judgement. On the one hand, in order to attain *significance* within the world of other objects, the object of experience must be internalized through some form of cognitive representation. On the other, there must be a frame of reference in regard to which the object attains value in relation to a person's behavioral motivations. Hence,

71

a distinction needs to be made between concepts reflecting the *internal representation of an object*, and concepts against which the *value of the object* is established.[49]

Let me take up the idea of *object concepts* first. I use this term to characterize the internalized, cognitive representations of perceived objects as entities of operational knowledge. To know — that is, to identify a perceived thing through its place within the known — requires that it be cognitively represented using both *morphic* and *functional properties*. The first refers to properties of the *sensory-motor event*; the second to the *significance* of the object, established by the internalization of the properties of the action that caused the object to be experienced. Though these aspects have a different status, the object can only be known as a concept when they act together. The object's cognitive representation, therefore, must contain morphic as well as extramorphic properties, for the object cannot be known when it cannot be related to a person's present frame of knowledge.

Within such a formulation there remains, however, the question of whether cognitive representations of objects must contain the same morphic properties as their percepts, or whether these are substituted by mere denota (as in the use of symbols to create a language). Several arguments can be made to support the position that actual perceptual properties must be internalized. First, there is the case of *recognition*: when objects previously perceived can be recognized, their internal representations must contain structural invariants of actual form. Second, the *identification* of objects as belonging to particular classes or types requires a deduction from structural similarities available in memory. A third argument involves *imagining* or inventing objects by recombining properties of previously experienced objects. All three processes indicate that assimilation must be reversible. And, to permit such reversibility, perceptual data must be stored in an unadulterated manner, or through structural invariants, in an abstracted, symbolized form from which particular instances can be deduced. The symbolic representation of an object therefore *must embed characteristics of its form*.

It is now possible to state that it is only through morphic properties that general classes of objects can be established and that an object can become known within a class of objects. Such a process of identification does not necessarily have to occur based on exact similarities but may take place by virtue of family resemblances. It is plausible to assume that form is assimilated through typological properties that merely preserve structural relationships and similarities and differences between objects of a type. This would allow a condensed storage of information and permit deductive reconstruction in individual instances.

Having thus identified some key concepts regarding object concepts, let me now turn to the idea of *value concepts*. As explained earlier, these provide a framework of reference against which internal representations may be judged. Value concepts must be independent cognitive sets, for it must be possible to apply them to a variety of objects and instances. It also must be possible to form them on grounds of properties other than those derived directly from the morphic qualities of an object. Value concepts thus constitute *external* sets, and so have to be assimilated independently of object concepts.

It is clear that value concepts must be the result of learning. But such learning cannot be derived from perception of the object itself. Value concepts are based either on individual learning through manipulations with the object (through which its appropriateness for a certain behavioral end is deduced), or through education, by which already-formed concepts are acquired as a matter of individual or socio-cultural convention. Moreover, once value concepts are established, they can form the basis of new value concepts established on the basis of reorganization of already-existing internal information.

An important distinction needs to be made here between *general* and *specific* value concepts. On the one side are concepts which are acquired over a lifetime, and form a general cognitive set which is intuitively applied in impromptu judgements. But there may also be cases where concepts are selected and applied as a matter of choice in a specific deliberated judgements, such as when an attitude of interpretation is adopted. In the latter case, the process of conceptualization is specific; that is, specific cognitive sets (which, however, are a result of general conceptualization) are selected and applied to the judgement. General and specific conceptualization thus maintain a dialectic relationship. The results of specific deliberated judgements using selected concepts may be included in one's general cognitive set, thus altering general world views that govern impromptu judgements.

My main arguments about perception and cognition can now be summarized as follows:

• By adopting the organizational position, it is justifiable to make a distinction between presentational and extramorphic properties. Presentational properties result from processes of perceptual organization which are functionally independent from processes of cognitive organization, by which properties are associated with the object.

• Perception can be considered a process autonomous from the application of concepts acquired by previous experiences. It must occur prior to — and indeed it must be a prerequisite for — the formation of operative knowledge. Hence, the internalization of form cannot be constrained by meanings associated with the percept through the application of acquired concepts. Accordingly, perceptual properties are universal.

• Because presentational properties must be internalized to allow cognitive representation of an object, all judgements about perceivable things must partly be constrained by properties of form. In other words, all impromptu judgements about objects must contain embedded aesthetic judgements.

V

The Roles of Form and Meaning in the Formation of Judgements

In the previous chapter I argued that the formation of judgements is partly, and indeed necessarily, based on internalized morphic properties of things. In this way I established a basis by which to claim that there are universal components within judgements. The question now is to what extent these components lead to similarities in experience among different individuals.

In this evaluation, I will first look at the different kinds of information that are derived through experience of things, and then examine how this information is transformed through various stages into judgements. This involves the construction of a model of cognitive information processing, one which assumes layers of cognitive structure. These may in turn be linked to the kinds of information an object — or, more precisely, its internal representation — provides. The model will attempt to illustrate the role of perceptual properties in the formation of judgements by showing how varying degrees of intersubjectivity may exist at different levels of information processing. One may note here that the distinctions between different types of information and layers of information processing are not based on actual neurological structures — of which none have hitherto been identified.

Rather, they are based on the distinction between figurative and operative knowledge, as proposed by the organismic-organizational position and outlined in the previous chapter.

1. The Subject: Similarities and Differences in Information Processing and the Formation of Judgments

The model of information processing is based on three functionally distinct, yet interdependent, levels of mental operation, each resulting in distinct structures of knowledge, which together form the larger structure of a person's cognitive stock. The first level of mental operation is *perception*, which results in *morphologic-typological structures*; the second is *qualitative cognitive information processing*, which results in *referential structures of knowledge* (i.e., general concepts of value and significance); the third is *quantitative cognitive information processing*, which results in *particular structures of knowledge* (i.e., individual object and value concepts). Although there can be no qualitative cognitive development (that is, maturation) without learning (that is, quantitative information processing of specific instances), the distinction between a qualitative and a quantitative aspect of cognitive information processing is necessary. These modes represent different qualities, because the individual instance of incorporating specific information into cognitive schemes must be distinct from the development of a general capability to make abstractions and form the referential frameworks that structure individual instances of knowledge.

Before proceeding to a discussion of the three levels described above and the cognitive structures that accompany them, I must first point out that the organismic-organizational approach implies that the microgenetic development of individual instances of knowledge must be similar to the broader pattern of human ontogenetic cognitive development. For the approach developed here, it follows that in order to establish a cognitive representation of an experienced object, three separate stages in the internalization of information must be passed. In order of occurrence, they are the *sensory-motor process of organizing the percept; the provision of a mode of abstraction*; and *the actual formation of individual structures of knowledge.* However, the formation of a cognitive representation will always involve the three stages in a unified process, and none of them can occur in isolation. Furthermore, the sequence of the stages must be inclusive: each must incorporate its predecessor, which must be functionally independent from its successor. The key implication here is that perceptual information processing cannot be determined by cognitive information processing.

Perception — Morphic Structures of Knowledge

Let me turn to more in-depth exploration of the three levels of information processing. The first level, perception, is defined as a sensory-motor process by which an array of environmental stimuli is transformed into a perceptual image. Although initiated through individual motivational-operational behavior, the actual physical process of perception is independent of any influence exerted by an individual's existing set of cognitive schemes, and therefore also independent of such internal cognitive processes as imagination, memory, and recognition. The perceptual image thus rests on unmediated experience of presentational properties — that is, on the structure of the stimulus pattern organized according to organismic capabilities. Perception thus may be presumed to be *almost entirely inter-subjective.*

The proper functioning of organismic perceptual abilities permits the formation of *single sensory qualities* such as hues of color based on wavelengths of light, dimensional frames of reference allowing differentiation along continua such as light and dark or warm and cold, and *configurational qualities* which allow such effects as the unification of perceptual figures and their segregation from a ground, the perception of groups by virtue of similarities and differences between parts, and the hierarchical organization of patterns of stimuli.

77

Qualitative Information Processing — Referential Structures

The second level of the model of information processing involves the formation of referential structures: structures which exist in isolation from particular instances of perception.

It is important here to distinguish between two kinds of referential structures: those that are biologically determined, and those that are developed as a result of individual maturation and cognitive development. The first type provide the simplest form of knowledge and are based on what some psychologists have termed 'innate releasing mechanisms'. IRMs are a result of a learning process during the evolution of the species, and they form a part of every person's genetic makeup. Lorenz and Eibl-Eibesfeld[1] have identified several such instinctive behavioral patterns among animals and humans; among them are aggression, sexual attraction, and basic physiognomic behavior. To be triggered, IRMs require unique and unambiguous patterns of stimuli such as simple shapes or movements or high concentrations of brightness and color contrast. Innate referential structures thus rely on formal properties, are innately given, and can be assumed to be highly similar between individuals.

The second type of referential structure, developed over time in response to a person's experiences in the world, involves the ability to make spatial and temporal abstractions. According to Jean Piaget and his followers, an individual's increasing ability to conceptualize the environment rests on the formation of composite structures of mental operations. Such an ability of abstraction develops through a person's interaction with his milieu, and with the assimilation of specific experiences into cognitive schemes. It seems plausible to assume that once a person gains the general ability to conceptualize the world in this way and perform logical and reversible operations, that person need not redevelop these abilities every time he is presented with new information. Rather, such *abstract referential structures* seem to remain with a person to help him organize newly assimilated information. It is clear such structures must exist independently of cognitive representations of specific instances of knowledge. However, specific perceptual representations must incorporate aspects of abstract referential structures in order to become *symbolic abstract representations.*

Abstract referential structures can thus be thought of as predispositions gradually developed based on individual experience with presentational properties. They are neither biologically given, as are IRMs, nor are they derived from cognitive 'meaning properties'. This last point is crucial. Although learning in the individual instance does entail the incorporation of extrapresentational properties — which themselves are derived from specific cognitive schemes — the cognitive ability to make spatial and temporal abstractions is an ability the organism gradually develops to process presentational properties more efficiently. Since such qualitative development actually represents an attunement of biological structures, the development of referential structures too can be thought of as having a high degree of intersubjectivity.

Quantitative Information Processing — Specific Knowledge Structures

Whereas the qualitative level of information processing provides the basis for intelligent behavior (that is, the abstract manipulation of knowledge), the third level of the information-processing model involves individual structures of knowledge. Such individual conceptualization results from the fusion of two types of information structure: *object concepts,* and cognitive sets that serve as *referents of value.*

The first of these, the object concept, involves the formation of both an *individual morphic representation* of an object, as well as an aspect of *signification* in relation to other objects. This dual nature of the object concept is necessary to allow individual recognition of objects as well as a means of identifying them as members of types and classes.

To qualify this statements further, one can say that the process of forming an object concept involves *double denotation.* In particular, the twin imperatives of generalization and classification mean that in addition to an internal representation formed in accordance with actual referential structures (the morphic representation), an abstracted image must also be internalized, much as words represent things in a language. The value of the latter is that it can substitute for the internal representation and allow abstract manipulation and communication. The signifying aspect must thus be stored symbolically so that it may be freely manipulated against the significatory aspects of other objects. It must be noted, however, that denota of this second type cannot suffice as the sole source of internalization; otherwise, neither classification and recombination into 'imaginative' new morphic forms, nor recognition based on the reversibility of internalizations, would be possible. In other words, the signifying aspect cannot substitute for the morphic representation; it only accompanies it. Furthermore, although the morphic and signifying aspects of an object concept are structured individually and preserve their identity from one another, it is only as a single confederative structure that they can create a complete internal representation.

It is particularly important in relation to the question of intersubjectivity to separate these two aspects of the object concept. The *morphic aspect* will show a *high degree of intersubjectivity* because it rests on a organismically determined process of perception and on referential structures — both of which may be assumed to be highly similar among different people. This is not true of the *signifying aspect,* however. Since it is determined almost completely by individual experience with an object, it may *differ considerably* between individuals.

I now turn to the issue of *value* in relation to the object concept. The object concept must always have more than mere factual existence as quantified data, because human actions are a matter of choice and preference. Thus, while those properties of the object concept discussed above are of an intrinsic nature, concepts extrinsic to the internal representation must be applied to determine the object concept's significance in relation to behavioral ends. The value of an object concept is thus not judged on grounds of properties of the referent, but in relation to deontic, procedural or interpretive ends. This must involve application of cognitive sets that are independent of individual object concepts; otherwise, free association of one value frame with different object concepts could not occur. However, both the object concept and whatever relevant cognitive value sets are applied to it must merge in actual experience and judgement.

The above formulation carries substantial implications in relation to the distinction between impromptu and deliberated modes of judgement first introduced in Chapter One. Specifically, it is important to understand how these two interpretive modes relate to the two general types of cognitive sets that may be applied in establishing the value of an object concept: *long-term (or general) cognitive sets,* and *specific cognitive sets.*

Long-term cognitive sets may be formed in a number of ways: by manipulating objects and establishing their value in relation to specific behavioral ends; by imitating the behavioral patterns of other people; by incorporating other people's already-formed sets through persuasion or learning; and by reorganizing information into new sets internally. Thus, long-term cognitive sets are based on instrumental and factual knowledge. But, because they partly reflect collective knowledge of specific groups (for example, moral and ideological concepts, superstitions, and religious beliefs), long-term structures are largely *ethno-specific* and *culture-specific.* Even though in some instances general cognitive sets may be formed deliberately as a result of a particular need, they are generally applied intuitively, or by habit, and are thus rather stable. In other words, they will most commonly come into play in cases of impromptu judgement.

By contrast, specific cognitive sets are applied mainly in specific deliber-ated judgements, and are adopted as a matter of choice — as can be seen in a person's ability to look at something from different percpectives. Such a focused attitude of evaluation may lead to quite different results than would be attained through off-hand, spontaneous judgement. Deliberated judgements also presuppose reasoning to decide between specific sets of value, and determine the relative weight of different values in an overall judgement. However, long-term and specific cognitive sets are mutually dependent: the adoption of specific concepts depends on one's general cognitive stock, which, in turn, may incorporate the results of previous deliberations. In other words, the outcome of the adoption of a specific cognitive set may alter the general structure of value-related knowledge.

To summarize the model of information processing so far, one can see that it involves a *progressively decreasing intersubjectivity with increasing conceptualization* of internalized information. At the most innate level, perceptual organization and IRMs can be supposed to be almost totally independent of individually acquired structures of knowledge. At the next level, some individual difference can be assumed in the formation of abstract referential structures; but intersubjective differences here can still be considered marginal. Such differences only become pronounced at the third level, that which involves the acquisition of particular knowledge structures. Yet even here intersubjective similarities will exist in internal organization because of commonalities in the development of abstractive abilities. Such commonalities pertain regardless of individual organismic differences and differences in the age at which abstractive capabilities are first developed. Differences in specific structures of knowledge thus can be assumed to occur principally in regard to applied attributes of significance and value.

However, in conjunction with *increasing individuality at the higher levels of information processing*, the model also proposes a reciprocal *decrease in the influence of perceptual characteristics* in the formation of cognitive structures. Thus, at the perceptual and abstract-referential levels, the formation of knowledge is almost exclusively a matter of the internalization of perceptual properties. However, extraperceptual properties begin to play a role in the structuring of object concepts. And, finally, at the highest level, *value concepts* may be formed entirely without incorporation of perceptual referents.

The process of experiencing and judging the world involves the operation of all these levels in unison. In other words, in each instance of perception, all the above structures must fuse to form one specific structure of knowledge vis-à-vis an object. However, as I have noted, a one-directional general relationship always prevails between levels, by which the lower level is independent of higher levels, which must incorporate the structure of lower levels. The key principle here is that *perceptual organization always determines the organization of subsequent cognitive processes*: this includes the formation of object concepts, which, together with value concepts derived from extrapresentational sources, combine to create the complete internal representation of an object. Thus perceptual structures always influence larger structures of knowledge, and all experience of the world must be partly determined by perceivable *form*.

The above determination has important implications for a general theory of aesthetics. Principally, it implies that if aesthetic experiences are defined as those related only to perceptual modes of experience, then there are few such instances. Perception is always part of a larger process of experiencing and judging the world, which also involves internalization of properties related to the way objects are encountered. If entirely perceptual experience were to exist, it would contradict a person's history of intellectual maturation through which the cognitive schemes of operational knowledge are formed.

Of course, it may be argued that there are instances in which an object is merely contemplated, without reference to any utilitarian end or without being manipulated — for example, watching a sunset or a movie, listening to a piece of music, looking at a painting, or strolling through a town as a tourist. But the factor of recognition doesn't permit purely perceptual experience. When an object or event can be recognized, concepts established through processes of classification and generalization must be involved, and this will necessitate retrieval of referential and particular structures of knowledge. Thus, in cases of recognition, inferences of meaning are unavoidable. Therefore, the act of experiencing the world cannot stop at the sensory-motor level.

Rather, aesthetic experience (that is, pure experience of perceptual properties) might more properly be considered a form of preoperational knowledge embedded in the larger process of experience, and from which certain kinds of satisfaction can be derived.

On the other hand, based on the determination that perceptual structures are functionally independent of structures through which operational knowledge is attained, one may justly speak of *aesthetic experience*. Such experience will be embedded in a more general type of experience, and the degree of its impact will depend both on the kinds of phenomena perceived and on an individual's cognitive stock. The same conclusion cannot be drawn in regard to the term *aesthetic judgement*, however. Simply put, there can be no judgement without the application of a frame of reference — that is, without partaking of extrapresentational properties. Referential frames of value will thus always be involved in judgements, both because they are an inherent part of the internalization of an object, and because (as I explained in the previous chapter) concepts will be applied regardless of whether they are 'appropriate' or not.

2. The Object: Its Structures of Information

In the previous section I proposed a model that distinguished between three levels of information processing, which together are required to form cognitive representations of experienced things. I will now focus on the *object* itself, and address the issue of how its characteristics may determine experiences and judgements. This will include looking at different kinds of properties objects may possess, and relating them to the various levels of information processing discussed in the last section. The goal will be to discriminate between properties of objects which function as *invariant* determinators, and properties which are *variant* — that is, that depend on subjective inference, thus allowing the meaning of an object to be influenced by individual personality factors and previous experience.

To begin, it is important to distinguish between two kinds of psychological processes through which knowledge may be attained: information derived via perceptual processes, and via cognitive acts. The traditional distinction between *form* and *content* here finds an equivalent in the distinction between *environmental* and *conventional* information.[2] Whereas environmental information consists of information given in the percept of the object, conventional information involves information established on grounds of previous knowledge — that is, through those individual or intersubjective 'conventions' by which the percept is interpreted and its value established in a larger structure of knowledge. In other words, environmental information results from the transformation of environmental affordances into stimulus invariants by virtue of physiological processes. Conventional information arises from the transformation of the resulting perceptual referents into thoughts by means of processes of psychological association, which in turn involve symbolic abstraction according to social or individually acquired conventions.

Based on the one-directional nature of the model of information processing, one can derive an important further principle from the above distinction between environmental and conventional information. This is that *conventional information will always presuppose internal referents* and so necessitate prior perceptual information processing. And, while perceptual information is acquired directly from the environment, conventional information may only be obtained through the mediation of information extrinsic to the object. Thus, one can say that the acquisition of environmental information rests on the perception of morphic structures and is *aesthetic* in nature, while the acquisition of conventional information is based on extramorphic structures and is *semantic* in nature.

Based on the above distinction, form is environmental information: it consists of those aspects of the internalization of objects and events which rest entirely on perceptual properties. Form can be defined as the totality of the constituents of a perceived configuration and their interrelationships. As a structure, therefore, form consists both of the similarities and differences between individual constituents as well as the syntactic relationships between them. In visual media, constituents can include shapes, textures, and colors; while relationships may include proportion, figure-ground distinctions, etc.

The definition of *meaning*, on the other hand, involves a number of difficulties which show that the traditional division of *form* and *content* in many theories of aesthetics is insufficient. This is because in many such theories the form-vs.-content dichotomy is only justified as a rough approximation — namely, only insofar as form refers to presentational properties, and content to individual cognitive inferences based on extramorphic concepts.

In his writings on information theory, Abraham Moles[3] suggests several concepts that give the traditional distinction greater clarity. Moles distinguishes two types of information that can be derived from an object: 'aesthetic' and 'semantic' information. Aesthetic information is not translatable; it only initiates sensations and inner states of feeling. Semantic information, on the other hand — provided familiarity with certain conventions of presentation — is logical and decipherable by virtue of signs. This is not to say that aesthetic information cannot be formalized in logical terms; only that such formalization will be bereft of meaning. Formalizations can only attain meaning through the association of semantic conventions with the perceived form.

In Moles's definition, the conveyance of an 'intentional' meaning, therefore, requires an unambiguous system of conventional schemata as well as specific knowledge involving instrumental, cultural and historic concepts. Meanings, therefore, are not inherent to form, and the form of an object does not constrain its meaning — only concepts do. The above views imply that meaningful form must always be considered historical: thus, at different times and within different socio-cultural settings, a given form can symbolize, or 'mean', different things. Intended meaning cannot therefore be considered an invariant characteristic; when conventional schemata become altered, originally intended meanings may be 'lost'. Thus, for example, dances that were once fertility rites may change into stylized formalisms; the layouts of medieval cities in northern Italy, once symbolic of the city of Jerusalem, may be interpreted as picturesque tourist attractions; and the pentagram, which once served as a symbol against evil, may be reduced to a mere geometric abstraction. According to Moles's view, the 'correct meaning' of an object, one that it was originally intended to carry, can only be understood when a person is aware of and chooses to apply the same concepts according to which the object was created.

Of course, the above principle also implies that different types of knowledge will be required to understand different types of phenomena. For example, to understand the meaning of tools, one would need instrumental knowledge; to understand pictorial representations, one would need to be familiar with the schemata of representation used to make them (as well as any particular symbols depicted in a given image); and to understand works of art, one would need a concept of art that includes knowledge of the history of art. However, such a notion of 'correct' understanding pertains only to manmade things, those things that are intentionally produced. Natural phenomena, by contrast, would only be able to attain specific significance in relation to behavioral ends.

While justified as a principal distinction, therefore, the traditional form-content dichotomy is insufficient, because it cannot account for the complexity of the information-processing model. Whereas the experience of form can be said to derive from a clearly demarcated type of psychological structure (namely, perception), judgement of meaning involves several different and distinct types of cognitive information processing. Instead, the notion of meaning needs further qualification.

I have already pointed to a distinction between significance and value, whereby the former denotes that which an object is and enables it to be identified and recognized, while the latter refers to cognitive sets by which value is attributed independently of specific representations. It must now be pointed out that there are different kinds of significance. For example, a difference clearly exists between an object's status within the realm of other known objects and its purpose as a useful instrument. Whereas all objects can have significance as identifiable entities of the former type, not all have instrumental significance in relation to a behavioral end. (This is precisely the case with many natural objects.)

Furthermore, instrumental significance can, for example, be utilitarian, ideological or moral; it can even be symbolic. In relation to the latter, a further distinction can be made between the significance of mimetic and nonmimetic entities. Clearly, objects may exist whose primary purpose is to represent other objects. Such entities may include representational art and language. But it is also because of this distinction that such things as buildings in the form of dinosaurs or coffeepots have a dual reality status, a dual significance. They show us that meaning can be immediately, as well as mediately, inferred.

There is one other crucial problem with the traditional distinction between form and content. This is that when an intended meaning is to be produced, it cannot be directly associated with the physical medium presented to the senses without an intermediary structure. To convey intentional meaning, therefore, a form not only needs denotative signifiers, but also formal-syntactic relationships by which such signifiers can be organized into a meaningful whole. Such relationships depend on learned conventions of organization, which may represent a particular style of formal organization. Hence, identical meanings can be represented by different forms. But the key point here is that form can only be endowed with intentional meaning by virtue of a deliberately 'meaning-laden' presentational arrangement. (It can, of course, be argued that the meaning of form lies precisely in this association. But meaning and form would then be cognitively inseparable; and as I argued earlier in this chapter, operational knowledge requires abstraction beyond the reality of the actual referent, so as to allow manipulation of object concepts independently of their specific morphic referents.)

The above discussion indicates that in order to craft a convincing theory of the structure of meaning as embodied in an object, one has to move beyond the simple distinction between form and content. I now suggest a threefold distinction to take the place of this traditional dichotomy. This is that the meaning of an object exists first in the *idea* or *meaning* of an object or event as an abstract cognitive entity; second in a *meaningful form* that carries the idea through a presentational arrangement of denotative and connotative signifiers according to conventional systems and syntactic schemata; and third in a *perceivable object* composed of physical

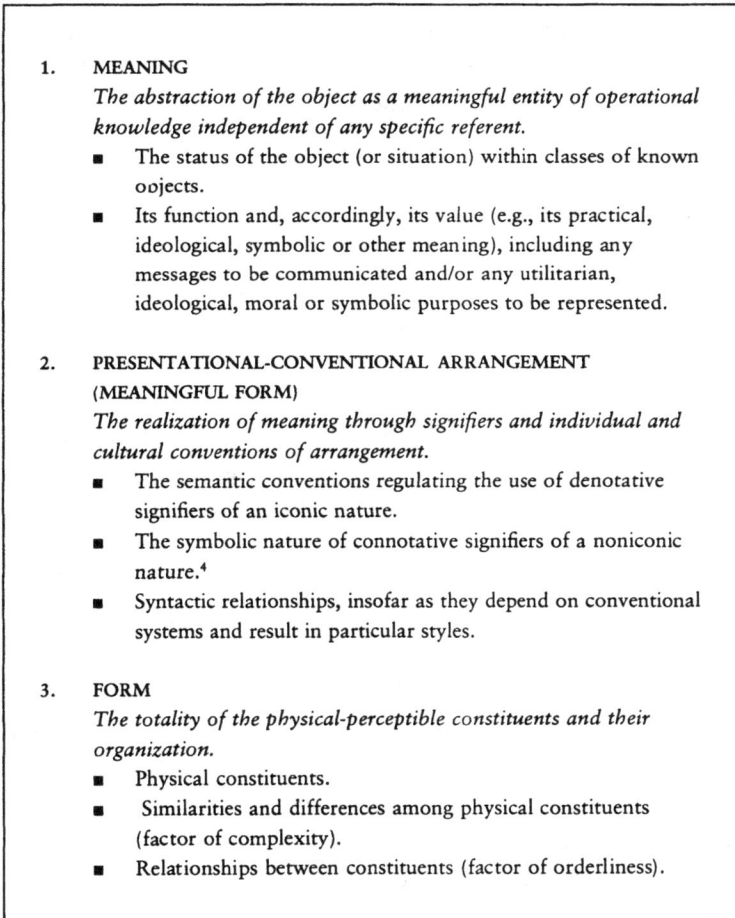

1. MEANING
   The abstraction of the object as a meaningful entity of operational knowledge independent of any specific referent.
   - The status of the object (or situation) within classes of known objects.
   - Its function and, accordingly, its value (e.g., its practical, ideological, symbolic or other meaning), including any messages to be communicated and/or any utilitarian, ideological, moral or symbolic purposes to be represented.

2. PRESENTATIONAL-CONVENTIONAL ARRANGEMENT (MEANINGFUL FORM)
   The realization of meaning through signifiers and individual and cultural conventions of arrangement.
   - The semantic conventions regulating the use of denotative signifiers of an iconic nature.
   - The symbolic nature of connotative signifiers of a noniconic nature.[4]
   - Syntactic relationships, insofar as they depend on conventional systems and result in particular styles.

3. FORM
   The totality of the physical-perceptible constituents and their organization.
   - Physical constituents.
   - Similarities and differences among physical constituents (factor of complexity).
   - Relationships between constituents (factor of orderliness).

Fig.32. Three-layered chart of meaning properties.

89

constituents and their basic relationships. Key features of these three levels of meaning are summarized in the accompanying chart (Fig.32).

In addition to the individual attributes of form and meaning listed in Fig.32, it is important to reiterate the principle that objects and events are always experienced as generally meaningful; this is to say that none of the listed sets of properties in the chart can be experienced in isolation. However, according to the framework of cognitive organization, the interdependence is one directional. Thus, meaning is always constrained by the presentational-conventional arrangement of a meaningful form, which cannot exist without physical form as such. In turn, form cannot be constrained by meaning, and meaningful form cannot be constrained by abstracted ideas — only by conventional schemata.

To this point, I have delineated the model of meaning aspects as a general abstraction. However, the model must be further qualified to reflect specific classes of phenomena as well as the kinds of media in which they may be realized. The reason is that the weight of individual meaning aspects will vary accordingly. For example, in the case of architecture the equivocal nature of applicable semantic conventions is relatively high in comparison to, for example, that for languages and pictorial representations. Strictly speaking, denotative signifiers are rare in architecture; they are by and large more characteristic of mimetic media, to which architecture, apart from some borderline cases, does not belong. Instead, architectural signifiers are mostly of a connotative kind; that is, they trigger particular individual associations as a result of previous experience. Interpretation of architecture, then, rests largely on individual, rather than on public and strictly formulated, semantic conventions. Those denotative signifiers that do exist in architecture are generally limited to decorative instances, such as a cross attached to a church or specific ornaments used to represent specific symbolic content. While one might think that architectural features such as stairs, doors and windows could denote specific functions, there are, in fact, no conventions by which a building's parts can be said explicitly to convey such meanings as 'monumental', 'enticing', and so on. Indeed, even the function of a building is normally realized as a matter of connotation rather than fixed association.

In light of such denotative ambiguity, it is mainly through the organization of parts within a whole that specific knowledge of a building's status can be obtained. Yet no precise denotative meaning is 'communicated' through these 'syntactic' relationships, because this would require specifically defined conventions of combination. Moreover, as I have pointed out already, syntactic meaning of this kind depends on being able to work with established and generally recognized denotators — a condition, that, unlike in languages, is not fulfilled by architecture. In architecture it is rather the recurrence of similar solutions for similar functions that allows a person to speculate on a building's meaning. Likewise, information about a particular style, or about the historico-cultural circumstances surrounding the evolution of a building, cannot be perceived directly in a building, but can only be inferred as a correlative of form. There is, however, one borderline case in architecture between denotation and connotation, which I will call *tectonic expression*. As I have noted, the fact that a person may perceive a building as a meaningful form — as top-heavy, fragile, stable, etc. — largely results from previous individual experiences with buildings. But such perception is also, as I will explain later, a matter of general kinaesthetic analogies derived from the stimulus pattern itself.

To pursue the case of architecture further within the context of the three-level model above, one must isolate individual aspects of meaning for further analysis. To do this it ought to be possible to describe architectural form mathematically through *magnitude, order* and *distribution*. (The same might be said to apply to the form of the segregated space that results from and depends on the arrangement of the space bounding and articulating components.) But, as I will discuss in greater depth later, such strict Euclidean analysis fails to account for the *unisotropy* of perception and perceptual space. Thus, the actual effect of a work of architecture must also be described through principles of perceptual organization — that is,

1.   MEANING
     ■   The building's *status* within classes of objects.
     ■   The building's *function* (practical, symbolic, ideological, etc.).

2.   PRESENTATIONAL-CONVENTIONAL ARRANGEMENT
     (MEANINGFUL FORM)
     ■   Semantic conventions (insofar as they relate to specific
         meanings of the constituents of the building):
         * Denotative signifiers: symbols, ornaments.
         * Connotative signifiers: buildings parts (e.g., windows
           and doors).
     ■   Syntactic conventions:
         * Functional-typological conventions: these may be
           predictable based on individually perceived
           redundancies in spatial and formal solutions in similar
           buildings. Functional 'expression' can partly rest on
           the use of symbols.
         * Stylistic conventions: syntactic routines specific to
           distinct periods or cultures may allow the identification
           of a building within specific socio-cultural and temporal
           settings, provided an individual is familiar with these
           schemata.
         * Tectonic conventions: both by conventions and
           kinaesthetic projection the building is endowed with
           tectonic 'expression' (e.g., stability, solidity, fragility,
           top-heaviness, etc.).

3.   FORM
     ■   Spatial form: the form of the space segregated by corporeal
         entities.
     ■   Corporeal form: the form of the space-bounding and space-
         articulating entities.
     ■   The internal articulation of each of these through:
         * Similarities and differences of the constituents.
         * Their syntactic relationships:
           Topological: the position of discrete entities within the whole.
           Dynamic-topological: perceptual dominances that result from
           the arrangement of perceptual masses within the stimulus
           pattern and the segregation and unification of elements of the
           pattern into groups and subgroups.
           Geometric: characteristics of shapes and their mutual
           relationships in space (e.g., proportions).
           Arithmetic: dimensional relationships (e.g., between colors,
           rhythms and scales).

Fig.33. Three-layered chart of meaning properties, as qualified for architecture.

through phenomenal properties. The table delineating aspects of meaning, as qualified for architecture, thus takes on a form as in Fig.33.

3. Constraints of Experience: Degrees of Aesthetic Freedom

The model of information processing I outlined in the first section of this chapter showed how cognitive structures constituting knowledge of particular experiences must incorporate morphic structures of information. It implied all experiences of perceptible things (and the judgements that result) must be determined in part by properties of form. Because form was shown to be an outgrowth of common perceptual processes, I suggested that experiences and judgements of phenomena must contain aspects that are highly intersubjective. It is now appropriate to examine more closely the nature of, and conditions for, this intersubjectivity.

So far I have argued that with increasing conceptualization (and an increasing participation of meaning properties), the impact of perceptual properties (and, accordingly, the degree of intersubjectivity) decreases. But the reverse is also true: the less it is possible to infer meaning in a given case, the stronger must be the role of perceptual properties and the higher the degree of intersubjectivity. And because I have equated aesthetic experience with perceptual information processing, it is further possible to call this tendency of perceptual properties to predominate in a given instance the *degree of aesthetic freedom*. The degree of aesthetic freedom will depend on two factors: the capacity of an object to permit meaning to be inferred, and the individual's status quo of knowledge.

Based on the previous discussion, it is logical to assume that the extent to which meaning properties will enter into the formation of a particular structure of knowledge will vary depending on both the type of phenomena and the media employed. For some classes of phenomena, especially those of mimetic kind, the experience of meaning may be determined predominantly by inferred meanings, and in these instances the degree of aesthetic freedom will be low. But the experience of objects which cannot be immediately connected to a particular purpose, or which do not allow other types of 'conventional' meaning to be inferred, must to a large extent be determined by the experience of form. To the former class of phenomena belong language, examples of representational art, objects designed for utilitarian ends; to the latter, natural objects and examples of nonrepresentational art. The above distinction may be further qualified if one examines the different types of meaning an object may have. For example, an object may have both a general significance in relation to other objects and a specific meaning in regard to an end. In general, it is possible to say that meanings can be broken down into two categories: those that are *denotative,* and those that are *connotative.* In relation to denotative meaning, one can make a further division between those that are *representational* and those that are *utilitarian.*

In relation to the above distinctions, 'representational denotative' meaning must rely on schemata of denotation based on arbitrary and conventional symbols. Such meanings can be highly unequivocal — provided, of course, the meaning of the denotators used in this system is familiar. Languages are such conventional systems: given familiarity with the meaning of individual terms and the use of prevailing rules of combination, statements in a language may permit clear communication of abstract ideas. Likewise, representations in two- and three-dimensional media may provide a high level of representative denotative meaning when the organization of the representation's structural invariants is identical, or nearly identical, to that of the actual instance. In other words, the more a representational medium can provide a symbol of a real object, the more unambiguous the meanings will be.

The second kind of denotative meaning is obtained when objects (by virtue of conventions acquired through manipulation of objects or public conventions acquired through learning) denote a specific end. Such 'utilitarian denotative' meaning may arise by virtue of repeated individual usage of an object, or by public convention acquired through learning. Meanings known in this way are instantly 'perceived': for instance, a hammer may be immediately identifiable as a tool for performing certain tasks. Objects of use may assume a high degree of denotative meaning, however, only among those familiar with their use.

The less an object can be connected to a denotative meaning of either type noted above, the more its meaning will be determined by connotative associations and presentational properties. The meaning of nonvocal music, for example, is entirely connotative. The same might be said for most natural phenomena when no specific behavioral end can be associated with them. Almost all phenomena will permit associations of connotative meaning, however, the key determinant of the extent to which this may occur is a person's previous experience with similar objects. Connotative meanings are thus mainly based on a process of recollection, by which information acquired through past experience is projected onto present circumstances. The less such associations are possible (either because objects are unfamiliar or because they have only minor human significance), the more the judgements of them will rely on presentational properties.

It can be stated in this regard that the less meaning a medium in which a phenomenon is realized permits to be associated on grounds of conventional schemata, and the less the phenomenon can denote in regard to an end, the higher the prevailing degree of aesthetic freedom will be. Thus different media provide characteristically different degrees of aesthetic freedom. To the class of systems with a low degree of aesthetic freedom must belong language, representational forms of art, and objects designed for utilitarian ends. To the class with a high degree of aesthetic freedom must belong natural objects and examples of nonrepresentational art. Architecture will thus present a moderately high degree of aesthetic freedom, because only a few architectural elements are directly denotative. Among these might be listed symbols that refer to the use of a building and particular prototypical formal solutions that may also have acquired symbolic character, such as typical patterns of religious and residential buildings in specific cultural circumstances.

The second factor involved in determinations of aesthetic freedom, the status quo of an individual's knowledge, can also be thought of as the degree of relative ignorance of the experiencing subject. A simple principle applies here: the less a person is able on grounds of previously acquired knowledge to conceive of an object as a meaningful entity within his world of knowledge, the more his experience of it must be determined by morphic properties. This is not to say that an object is less meaningful when no 'correct' concept (relating to the intentional meaning) can be applied, merely that concepts will be applied, regardless of their 'correctness', simply by their being available in a particular instance. This will lead to a situation where objects will be experienced as meaningful, even though meanings may differ between individuals. The availability of 'correct' concepts will also differ according to different people's past experience with similar objects.

In general, the more a person knows, the more he can deduce about present circumstances from previous experiences. However, when a person has no concept which can be applied at a given instance, the experience must be dominated by presentational properties as well as by connotative associations. When an individual has no knowledge, say, about the function of a hammer (that is, he cannot apply a correct concept of utility), the hammer will assume a status similar to that of a 'useless' piece of driftwood. In such a case, any meaning that may be derived from an object will arise largely through connotative association. In the same way, when no particular knowledge can be associated with an originally meaning-laden symbolic form, the form may be perceived as little more than an abstract geometric pattern.

To understand the implications here, one must return to the notion of distinct modes of production and reception in the interpretation of meaning. In short, the factor of ignorance does not relate to the application of concepts in the *production* of an object, only to the availability of concepts through which it is interpreted. This is because, in the receptive mode, the experience of form is initially unconstrained by associated meanings. But in the mode of production, the choice of form is constrained from the beginning by intended meaning. Thus, the same form may assume different meanings in the receptive mode, depending on an individual's stock of conventions by which to interpret it. This is not to say, however, that meaning cannot also be public; individual conventional schemata can overlap within particular cultural conditions. And in this latter case, meaning can show great invariance. But such public conventions need not be stable, and meanings of this sort may change over time, and so contain a historical component.

Another implication of the process of associating meaning with an object is that there may, in fact, be cases in which form can be experienced as 'meaningless' — that is, where no, or only very little, conceptual content can be applied. This is because in instances where no value concepts are available (either 'correct' or 'incorrect'), experience must rely on the object concept, which is dominated by perceptual structure. One must be careful how far one takes this concept of 'meaningless' form, however. Even though there can be a *high degree of aesthetic freedom in the receptive mode*, there can be *no aesthetic freedom in the productive one*. Form in this mode can never be 'meaningless', for manmade form always results from intention, and so cannot be bereft of motivation. In other words, forms will always be meaningful for the communicator, regardless of whether this meaning is communicated successfully. In other words, a building or other object can never be totally 'meaningless', for it is always designed with some purpose in mind.

The validity of this last statement becomes further apparent if one considers the way value concepts enter into the production of form. According to the model of cognitive processing, the sequence of the incorporation of perceptual structures into cognitive structures is assumed to be inclusive. Thus, there can be perceptual experiences without a high degree of conceptualization, for the formation of object concepts is independent of value concepts. But, in the case of production, this is different. The reason is that design is a process involving successions of judgements, and there can, by previous definition, be no judgements without cognitive sets through which values are determined. Therefore, the structure of the imagined object must incorporate meaning, — that is, extramorphic concepts. Design can be considered a process of 'imagination' involving the recombination of a person's existing structures of knowledge into new forms. Since the formation of cognitive structures of particular instances is assumed to be an invariant sequence of the various layers of information processing, in retrieving images for imaginative recombination, form cannot be disconnected from the other, value-laden, aspects of cognitive representations.

The above should not be interpreted as a claim that the choice of form in design is determined by particular meanings, because there many forms may be associated with a particular meaning. Of course, a producer may strive to create particular forms which, in his estimation, seem to fulfill particular functions 'optimally'. But since the formation of meaning is not constrained by form but by conventions and individual experiences, meaning will always be an individual affair. Rather than 'following' function, therefore, the choice of form is constrained by conventional schemata, a person's individual stock of knowledge, and the medium in which the form is presented.

4. An Intermediate Conclusion

In Chapter One I posed the question of what constitutes aesthetically 'good form' in relation to the design of buildings and cities — a matter of a rather elusive nature, yet one that has permeated the history of architecture. However, prior to addressing the question directly, I had to scrutinize its principal assumption: that the appearance of architecture can be experienced and judged in a purely 'aesthetic' manner without regard for utilitarian or social considerations.

I began my examination of this issue by evaluating the potential of theories by which the subject of architectural aesthetics has traditionally been approached. I found that these did not suffice to formulate necessary and sufficient conditions to evaluate form strictly on aesthetic terms. Either human perceptual abilities were not adequately considered, as in theories of metaphysical formalism, or the experience of form relied to too great an extent on extramorphic characteristics, as in the case of instrumental and meaning theories.

The potential for an adequate theory was found to lie in the presentational approach, as introduced by Kant and his followers, which distinguishes between properties open to direct awareness and properties mediately inferred by the subject on the grounds of concepts. In Chapter Three, however, I explained how the key notion of the presentational approach, the aesthetic attitude, was insufficient to explain the role of form. The aesthetic attitude was shown to better describe a specific type of focused attention in which certain concepts could be deliberately adopted. The presentational approach also did not define the nature and impact of presentational properties adequately, nor did it justify in psychological terms a separation between perceptual experience and conceptual thinking.

To address these difficulties, I turned from philosophical aesthetics to psychological analysis of processes by which human beings experience and judge the world. Particularly crucial here was my need to question whether images of known objects are constructed according to one unified, inseparable process, or whether knowledge is the result of functionally independent but interlocking processes. In other words, I asked if it is justified to make a separation between perception and cognition, and, accordingly, between presentational and other kinds of properties. If such a separation could be made, I would next need to ask to what extent psychological processes are organismically determined and, hence, common between people. And beyond this, I would need to analyze the relationship between universal and individual factors in aesthetic judgement.

Within a range of empirist, nativist, and organismic-organizational positions in psychology, I therefore opted in Chapter Four for the latter, rejecting the others on grounds of inherent logical fallacies. In line with this position, I defined perception as a process of segregation and unification of environmental stimuli, and I determined that this process must occur prior to cognitive information processing, and so be functionally autonomous from personality factors. Since perceptual organization could thus be related to physiological laws and the actual

99

structure of the stimulus array, I argued that the results of perception must be substantially similar among different individuals.

Next, I considered how and to what extent perceptual properties enter into the formation of knowledge about particular instances. Specifically, I addressed the question of whether operational knowledge is partly determined by perceptual properties, or whether perceptual properties are dominated by concepts individually acquired through learning. This led me to consider the role of learning and cognitive development; and in this regard, I adopted an organismic-structural position — as introduced by Jean Piaget and his followers. According to this view, cognitive maturation — that is, the increasing ability of abstract manipulation of knowledge — is an adaptation of the individual to his or her environment through a process which involves the assimilation of ecological events into cognitive schemes, and the subsequent accommodation of these schemes to changes in the environment. This brought me to the following two conclusions in relation to the intersubjectivity of knowledge structures: first, that there are similarities in the formation of concepts to the extent they are determined by abstract referential structures; and, second, that individual schemes of knowledge must incorporate perceptual properties in order to guarantee reversible operations — for example, recognition and imagination.

Thus, at the end of Chapter Four I concluded that when an object is to attain meaning — that is, to become an entity within a system of operational knowledge — two independent kinds of concepts must be involved: object concepts, which are internalizations of the sensory-motor acts in manipulating the object; and value concepts, which are frames of reference that allow the value of the object to be established in regard to behavioral ends. Whereas the first must incorporate morphic representations, the latter is generally of an extramorphic nature.

Based on the above consideration of perception and cognition, I was, at the beginning of this chapter, able to suggest an epistemological model delineating three functionally independent levels of information processing.

Each level corresponded to particular types of information that could be derived about an object at particular points in the process of knowing it. And, in accordance with a central premise of the organismic-organizational position, the interdependence of the layers was defined as one-directional. In other words, each level incorporates its predecessor, which, in turn, is functionally independent of its successor. Experiences must thus start with perception, which leads innately to internalization of an image. This process must be governed by abstract referential structures to permit classification and generalization. However, it is only when extramorphic value referents are attached to an object concept that its significance and value may be fully established, and it may be judged in relation to other objects.

A key point established by these investigations was that in order to allow cognitive development, the internalization of form cannot be constrained by meanings that may later be associated with it, and that the experience and judgement of perceivable things must in part be constrained by presentational properties — that is, by form. This allowed me to determine that the degree of aesthetic freedom prevailing in a specific instance of perception is based on two factors: an individual's status quo of knowledge and the capability of the object and its medium to permit meanings to be inferred on grounds of conventions. Experience based solely on presentational properties is thus virtually impossible when an object is to be known in an operational sense. But aesthetic experience can still be considered a kind of preoperational experience embedded in all experience and judgement.

At this point, further consideration of the issue of 'good form' is justified on two grounds. The first is that, because perception must occur without cognitive interference, presentational properties can be analyzed separately from other properties which may enter into the knowledge of an object. The second is that the perception of form is an outgrowth of intersubjective processes that are largely determined by organismic and ecological factors, autonomous of learning and personal association.

V I

Aesthetic Value:
Analyzing the Effects of Form

1. Has Form an Intrinsic Value?

Having argued that there is a justifiable distinction between perceived form and inferred meaning, I shall now focus more narrowly on the experience of form and the possible kinds of value form may have within an overall judgement. In the model of information processing developed in the last chapter I suggested that all judgements about perceived things must be determined in part by properties of form — that is, by presentational properties made manifest through processes of perceptual organization. Because these processes are genetically determined rather than learned, it follows that judgements involving them must contain universal aspects. However, before turning to an analysis of these common aspects, there are two crucial questions that must be addressed. Can form have value of its own aside from that value assigned it by cognitive processes? And if the answer is yes, what kind of value is it, and how can it be demarcated and described?

For an object to become known, two basic conditions must be fulfilled: it must be *identifiable* from among the other objects that make up the

103

environment, and it must be *classifiable* as a potential source of behavior in a person's milieu—i.e., it must have assigned value. Thus, the sensory-motor act of perception is only one part of the transformation of an array of perceptual stimuli into a known object, because this does not yet constitute operative knowledge. For this to happen, the object's perceptual structure must fuse with those cognitive structures that determine its value relative to behavioral actions. The value of an object, thus, is always connected to the application of cognitive sets, which may also be called *concepts*. In this most strict sense, then, form cannot have value, for value cannot be established exclusively on perceptual grounds. Such a conclusion, however, would seem to contradict one of the most prominent notions of aesthetics, namely, that form can be pleasing on its own. For this reason, philosophical aesthetics has consistently been concerned with how it is that people seem to enjoy perceptual experience for its own sake — for instance, why they appear to enjoy scenes in nature or works of art without any regard for ulterior purpose. The answer to this question may lie in the fact that even though an object's value may be determined by cognitive concepts, percepts are not entirely neutral in the process of cognitive information processing. If the overall value of an object results from the fusion of cognitive sets with perceptual structures, form must also play a role in determining value. But what kind of role?

Previously, I described value as an object's potential in regard to a behavioral end (for instance, as a source of danger or nourishment, or as an instrument for an activity). Value, therefore, is *extrinsic* to an object, and *assigned* to the percept on grounds of independent frames of reference. Yet it may also be suggested that objects can possess another kind of value — a value which serves as a determinant for the formation of the percept. Moreover, it would be logical to look for such value in two areas: in the suitability of an object for arousing perceptual interest, and in its ability to permit unambiguous perceptual organization. As I will attempt to explain, such kinds of value must lie within the structure and orderliness of the presented array. In other words, such value must be *intrinsic* to form.

But if form can have innate value in this sense, how can such value be described? In philosophical aesthetics the value of form has traditionally been thought of as a kind of pleasure derived from purely perceptual experience. But introducing such customary epistemological apparatus here is not useful, for most aesthetic doctrines simply presuppose certain ideas of beauty or particular forms of pleasure without adequately questioning their roots. Terms derived in this way are mere abstractions of preferences. Thus, Beardsley[1] notes that if beauty is to be considered simply that quality in an object that pleases us, then we can progress no further than saying, "that what pleases us is what pleases us." Alternatively, if beauty is considered to be a peculiar kind of feeling aroused in an observer, then one must ask what kind of feeling it is. Is it really of one definable type? And if so, how can we be sure it is derived from purely perceptual factors? If one attempts to isolate the presentational facet of a judgement (setting aside the question of whether this is possible at all), that judgement will become conceptualized, no longer a matter of direct awareness. Analysis along these lines invariably leads to major logical difficulties.

Of course, on the basis of the above discussion it is impossible to *deny* that form plays a causal role with regard to an individual's preference for certain objects, or satisfaction in relation to them. But since knowledge can never be purely figurative (but is, according to the position I have adopted, always to a varying degree operative), it is impossible to establish any strict cause-and-effect relationship between specific properties of form and individual responses to them. It would therefore seem futile to attempt to define a particular species of satisfactory feelings that are triggered by certain presentational properties. It must rather be admitted that (as I argued in Chapter Four) all operative knowledge must be preceded by figurative knowledge. Consequently, form will always play a role in judgements, be they impromptu or deliberate.

On the basis of the above argument it becomes evident that all considerations of value must begin at the operative level of knowledge — that which includes all three layers of information about an object. Nevertheless, it is still important to examine how particular experiences, preferences, or feelings of satisfaction occur. Generally, it can be said that such states of awareness must result from some type of a correspondence between an individual's existing cognitive stock and the information presented in a specific instance. This means that whenever newly assimilated information shows structural iso-morphisms with existing and relevant cognitive schemes, this correspondence will form the basis for judging the new information. But when no isomorphic relationships are possible, the assimilated information must be related to those schemes that most closely approximate it. And subsequently these schemes must be altered to accommodate the new information.

It is thus through an individual's existing cognitive disposition that particular values may be assigned to certain experiences. In other words, something will be considered beautiful, good, or appropriate to an end if its properties correspond to properties it is expected to possess according to a person's existing cognitive stock. By extension, it may be argued that it is possible to rank objects according to their appropriateness within a person's system of expectations (as this is developed from classifications of previously experienced objects). Thus, judgements are subjective, for the experiences of each individual — his feelings, satisfactions and dissatisfactions, preferences and aversions — will certainly differ from those of other people based on his particular history of experience and learning. One might then ask how it is possible to demarcate any aspects of form that might contribute to the inherent value of an object.

To address this issue, one must ask which of the factors that shape an individual's cognitive disposition are not individually determined. Recalling the model of information processing, one can see that the overall value of an experience is created by incorporating all sublayers of information process-ing. The fusion of object concept and value referents gives overall value to an object in relation to a behavioral instance. However, in terms of individual microgenetic development of structures of information, superior layers of structure will always incorporate functionally independent, inferior layers.

Thus, operational knowledge always includes preoperational structures of information — to an extent that depends on the degree of aesthetic freedom prevailing in the circumstances of the object's presentation.

The above formulation implies that even though the value of an individual instance of operational knowledge may vary between people due to subjective variances in those substructures of information processing that result from individually assimilated information, the particular values determined by organismically determined substructures will still be similar. This is especially the case in regard to perceptual organization and to qualitative modes of structuring this information within specific cognitive sets. It follows, then, that values established through sensory-motor information processing will combine with values determined by referential structures to govern the value of any succeeding structure in which they are incorporated. The value of form thus partly influences the value of resulting experience. By this logic it is possible — when the aspect of form is isolated for the purpose of analysis — to formulate necessary, yet not sufficient, conditions for the formation of overall value.

But the question remains: what kind of value is it that is intrinsic to form? And how is it embodied in an object? As trivial as this may sound, one approach here is simply to point out that an object must first be perceived before any overall value for its cognitive representation may be established. And two conditions must be met before an object can be perceived: its form must be assimilable by the brain — hence, there must exist some possibility of isomorphism between environmental and perceptual order (as determined by the brain's capacity for structuring the displayed array into a percept); and the stimulus array must be such that it arouses and sustains perceptual interest. On the basis of these two conditions I suggest that two types of intrinsic value can be identified as attributes of form: one concerns *the appropriateness of the stimulus pattern to the brain's capacity for perceptual organization*; and the other involves *a sensory-motor satisfaction derived from the perception of such appropriate forms.*

If one accepts the two conditions above, one must next ask about the nature of this value. Here two possible explanations may be suggested. First, it has been established that disturbances to a person's innate perceptual-motoric sense of order result in organismic dissatisfactions — as, for instance, in a loss of that sense of balance through which we maintain our orientation in the world. If disturbances of one's innate sense of order result in dissatisfaction, might it not also be possible to assume the reverse — that one derives satisfaction from objects and situations that reinforce this sense of order?

A second possible explanation for the mechanism of value formation emerges if one looks more closely at innate releasing mechanisms, the most basic form of knowledge, which I discussed in Chapter Four. Based on studies of animals and cultures in early stages of development, Arnold Gehlen and Konrad Lorenz have both argued convincingly that human beings, like other animals, react strongly to particular morphic configurations consisting of unusually bright colors, regular shapes, and/or rhythms. Such reactions, which they claimed are based on IRMs (or instincts), are derived from a type of knowledge that is neither learned nor a matter of extrinsic value association through cognitive processes. The existence of this type of reaction would seem to suggest that certain configurations possess intrinsic value for certain species. And, in this regard, Lorenz[2] has actually shown that certain preoperational knowledge does consist of genetically determined responses to otherwise highly improbable configurations in a species' milieu. Furthermore, reactions to such configurations are normally found to be connected with feelings of satisfaction through consummatory actions.

However, not all perceptions are connected to immediate ends and thus lead to consummatory actions. Gehlen[3], for example, has argued that the influence of instinctive behavioral patterns has decreased with human evolution and with the increasing ability to abstract knowledge — that is, to engage in intelligent behavior. Yet, despite the fact that action based on IRMs has atrophied to certain basic forms (such as sexual arousal or aggression-defense mechanisms), human beings remain under the influence of morphic trigger stimuli. Gehlen argues this simply no longer requires a consummatory response, only the experience of pleasure. In technical terms, this pleasure is the result of 'discharge actions' which stand for consummatory behavior. Thus, anthropologists have noted how instincts are often transformed into rituals, dances, or ornamental forms which recall the stimulus patterns of IRMs. Furthermore, it may be pointed out that the stimuli that trigger IRMs usually approximate what Gestalt psychologists have called 'good' or '*prägnant*' (clear-structured) gestalt: namely, highly ordered and regular configurations which arouse strong perceptual interest.

2. Perceptual Appropriateness: Order and Wholeness

On the basis of the preceding discussion, it becomes clear that one type of value intrinsic to form involves pleasure derived from the perception of order. The importance of this characteristic of human perception becomes apparent when one considers the value of a person's sense of order to survival in any milieu. Without being able to establish a sense of order, a person could not identify the specifics of the world and assign a place for himself in it. Orientation in a city would, for example, be impossible if one's mind could not impose order on the layout of streets and buildings. Similarly, ideas could not be communicated without some ordered medium of discourse, and technical processes could not be controlled if the nature of their function could not be comprehended. It is only through recognition of underlying order that the phenomena of the world can be generalized and categorized and a sense of their relative importance determined.

The cognitive models by which people order their environment are subjective: they are imposed individually onto the world based on those individual processes of cognitive organization by which we assign significance and value to the facts of the world. Yet, even though the cognitive models of different individuals may differ due to our various experiences, cognitive order is also partly the result of environmental order. As I have already argued, this is due to the fact that cognitive order necessarily presupposes perceptual order. And since perceptual order is a consequence of physiological processes that are based on innate biological principles, each individual's sense of cognitive order will, to some degree, be intersubjective. In terms of the model I presented in Chapter Five, this effect arises in the formation of object concepts.

A simple proposition to guide further exploration of aesthetic value may now be stated: *that which is to be perceived, needs to be intelligible to the senses; that which is to be perceived must possess in itself a kind of order that can be apprehended within the biological parameters of human perception.* Although this may sound obvious, it must be pointed out that not everything in the environment is thus suitable to perceptual processing: there is much that is either 'invisible' or 'ignored'. For one, limits exist to the capacities of human receptor organs; the eye, for example, can perceive only that spectrum of electromagnetic energy apparent as light. Furthermore, in keeping with the basic relational nature of perception, perceptual appropriateness will also depend on the *organization* of the stimulus pattern.

As explained previously, the segregation and unification of stimuli into perceptual patterns is determined by innate laws of perceptual organization. These laws explain why the environment is perceived as orderly despite the bewildering complexity of stimulation it presents. Such laws explain, among other things, why similar elements form groups, why some things appear in front of others, why figures are segregated from a ground, and why certain features appear dominant and others subordinate. According to the organismic-organizational school of psychology, this deeply ingrained human tendency to perceive regularity is but one manifestation of a universal tendency among physical systems — the principle of least action. Thus, in experiments on human perception, the founders of Gestalt psychology (of which the organismic-organizational position is an outgrowth) observed how people tend to organize their perceptions so as to give preference to the simplest, or most regular, configuration in a given circumstance.[4] The

Gestaltpsychologists thus formulated a general hypothesis that perceptual organization in the visual cortex shows the behavior of inhomogeniously stimulated fields, which tend to organize themselves into states of equilibrium. In this way the segregation and unification of parts of the cortial field could be related to the biological tendency of interacting electro-chemical forces to seek quasi-stationary states embodying a minimum of potential energy.[5]

Due to what they called the 'field character' of perception, early Gestalt psychologists explained how the organization of a percept preserves only configurational aspects of the stimulus array — that is, topological relationships such as adjacencies and spatial distributions. They further argued that the segregation of a figure from a ground depends on its degree of simplicity, or regularity, with respect to an entire field of perception. They based this claim on the simple principle that the more regular a configuration appears, the more likely it will be to resist fusion with the rest of the field. It is the effect of the entire field of forces that leads to the organization of a figure's boundaries, contours, and internal articulation. By extension, it is possible to see how a complex configuration must either organize itself into subsystems and groups, which can be perceived together as a larger, confederate whole; or else it must be perceived as a multiple of unrelated patterns. (It is important to note that the above principle of perceptual organization according to simplicity and whole character does not contradict the validity of the underlying correspondence between the order of the object and the neuro-physiological order of the percept. A large body of empirical research on visual perception has made this apparent. The tendency towards regularity is evident, for example, in the filling in of contours in the region of the blind spot on the retina or an increase in the regularity of afterimages.[6])

In general, experiments have shown that the tendency to perceive figural regularity is present in two characteristic ways. First, people 'improve' shapes perceived under difficult conditions. Tests showing this effect include short-term tachistoscopic presentation of figures,[7] presentations of very small figures, and displays of shapes at the periphery of the field of vision.[8] Second, the more regular a configuration, the more readily it will take on figural character. From the many possible perceptual combinations available in response to an array of stimuli, the simplest will usually win. Thus, while the pattern shown in Fig.34 is constructed from the repetition of a single complex shape (a star), it is perceived as being composed of two sizes of squares, because the square is a simpler shape. Similarly, although the pattern in Fig.35 could result from the connection of two curved lines, it is perceived as consisting of a straight line and an S-shaped curve. And since the cross-shaped figure is the simplest possible combination in Fig.36, it is preferred over other possible forms of figural segregation.

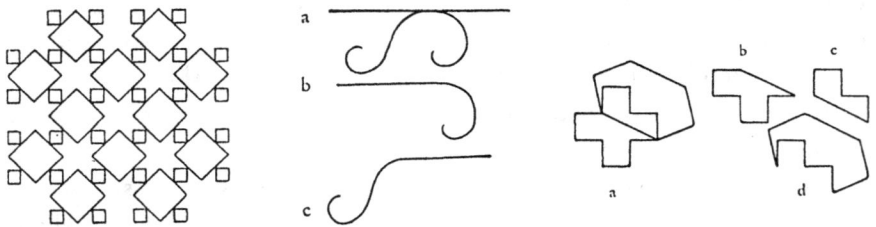

Fig.34,35,36. Effects of good shape: simplicity prevails.

Principles according to which figures are formed and the parts of configurations are combined into groups were first formulated by Max Wertheimer. He listed these as proximity, closure, similarity of shape and direction, symmetry, regular continuation of a contour, concavity, and uniformity of articulation.[9] In addition, the tendency of the percept to take on as much regularity as possible has been formally named the 'principle of good gestalt', or the 'law of *prägnanz*'. The fact that form is organized according to the law of *prägnanz* should, however, not be confused with a tendency towards entropy, or dissipation of energy. This is because it is not always the most regular parts of a field that take on figural character. Often, more homogeneous parts will form the background for figures composed of heterogeneously arranged parts.

In light of the above discussion it is now possible to clarify the first criterion determining the intrinsic value of form, that of *perceptual appropriateness*. The key principle here is that only that which is organized so as to permit figural segregation of stimuli can be perceived. In other words, perceptual appropriateness is a matter of an isomorphism between objective and perceptual order. Unfortunately, this statement is of little use in determining the value of aesthetically pleasing form. If it is possible to perceive only that which is appropriate to perceptual organization, then all that is perceived must be appropriate. But if one can reformulate the concept to include the notion that perception is a matter of degree, it proves much more useful. Thus: *the more orderly a configuration, the higher its aesthetic value.*

Obviously, concern must now be focused on the nature of order. Scientific experiments have, in fact, clarified two criteria that are used in the judgement of the orderliness of a configuration: its *degree of prägnanz*, and its *degree of wholeness*. In regard to the first, tests indicate that people show a clear preference for *prägnant*, or 'good', shapes over less *prägnant* ones.[10] Degrees of *prägnanz* (constituting the 'figural goodness' of shapes) were first investigated by Wertheimer, then later by Metzger and Rausch.[11] Their tests showed a number of things: that configurations consisting of similar elements are more *prägnant* than those composed of dissimilar ones; that closed or partly enclosed shapes are stronger than less enclosed ones; that straight or regularly curved contours form more *prägnant* shapes than erratically bent ones; and that configurations with permeating orders are stronger than those lacking this quality. Their tests also showed that, from a number of regular configurations, the simpler (that is, the one with the least number of determining relationships) will be seen as the more *prägnant*.

The second criterion of order is degree of wholeness. 'Wholes' best fulfill the conditions of perceptual appropriateness because they permit parsimonious, hierarchical and complete organization of the perceptual field. In fact, the notion of an organic whole is one of the oldest and most persistently applied concepts in aesthetics. Aristotle, in his *Metaphysics*, separated the concept of an aggregate from that of a whole.[12] He defined the former as a configuration "to which the position of the parts in relation to each other makes no difference." A whole, by contrast, was a configuration in which the relation of the parts did matter. Beautiful things, to Aristotle, were those that could be apprehended as a unity through a single act of synoptic perception. Aggregates could only be connected by reason. A similar concept of 'unity in variety' enjoyed prominence during the Middle Ages and the Renaissance. To Alberti,[13] for instance, beauty was "the harmony of all parts, in whatever subject it appears, fitted together with such proportion and connection that nothing could be added, diminished, or altered but for the worse." But the key to this concept of organic unity perhaps lay in St. Augustine's[14] postulate that the unity of a whole's diverse parts could be immediately perceived through proportion and congruity.

What is the psychological relevance of this concept of wholeness — which was, originally, first erected on metaphysical foundations? Why would configurations with a strong whole character best fulfill the criterion of perceptual appropriateness? And, for that matter, how is wholeness defined? A principal claim of organizational theories of perception is that an array of stimuli is perceived 'on the whole', namely, as a *perceptual complex* rather than as a summation of discrete stimuli. Allport has stated this view succinctly: "Though form can present itself as a pattern of parts, its essential character is not their linking together in piecemeal fashion, nor even their assembly as interconnecting elements. Form has always a whole character that transcends the character of the parts. The whole character manifests itself in the relationships of the parts as well as in the changes produced in the parts themselves."[15]

What this means is that the formation of the percept is always determined in *relational* terms, so that the individual character of any part will depend on its position and articulation with respect to the other parts of a configuration. Therefore, the parts will appear differently when observed together than when they are perceived as single perceptual units. Furthermore, relational properties such as closure and proximity must be seen as belonging to the configuration as a whole, so that any change in one of the parts will result in a change in the character of the whole. This can be observed, for example, in the phenomenon of simultaneous color contrast—the change in the appearance of individual colors when alterations are made to neighboring colors. The character of the whole may also be determined by such factors as coherence, similarity and dissimilarity of constituent parts, spatial relations such as proximity and symmetry, and the degrees of *prägnanz* of subgroups of elements by which a hierarchy of dominant and subordinate parts is established.

As I have already suggested, the formation of morphic concepts must rest on the internalization of relational (that is, topological and typological) properties. It is only in this way that processes of generalization and classification can occur which may allow the free association necessary for imagination and other mental processes. Because perceptual wholes are defined in relational terms, they easily fulfill this condition. Furthermore, the ability of abstraction, especially regarding conceptions of space, depends, as Lewin[16] maintains, on nodological and topological properties. Similarly, Lynch[17] argues that the cognitive images that provide orientation in a city rely on field properties such as nodes and boundaries.

The central factor here is that a configuration needs a minimum degree of wholeness in order to be segregated from the rest of the visual field. The stronger wholes will segregate themselves more easily than the weaker ones, and they will allow a more complex internal organization. But before discussing this matter of degree, it is important to establish a proper definition of wholeness. In this regard, one can say that a whole is first of all a set of items that can be perceived as more or less segregated from other items: it must therefore be a *self-contained* and *bounded* configuration. Second, the items constituting a whole must be dependent for their appearance on the perceptual complexes to which they belong. And so all elements of such a structure must be subordinate to certain laws by which the whole is defined, and these laws must be distinct from the properties of the configuration's individual features.

115

The first criterion, which Piaget[18] calls 'self-maintenance', implies that wholes are closed structures, in the sense that the compositional laws by which they are defined do not depend on external features. Only through closure can a structure be isolated from the rest of the perceptual field and assume figural character. However, since most perceived things are multilayered, parts of a configuration must also be able to possess their own whole character. Of course, if the whole character of the parts is weak, they will lose their boundaries and form additive groups; examples of this tendency include checkerboard-like patterns (Fig.37). Other cases where the whole character of the individual parts is lost include groups of similar elements unseparated by independently perceivable negative spaces — for example, where the contours of the parts assume a so-called 'double-sided function', as in a typical curtain-wall facade (Fig.38). A third case would concern groups of similar elements of similar scale that are equally distributed over a continuous background, so that no dominating symmetry or contrast relationship arises to allow a larger grouping of shapes by the eye (Fig.39).

In contrast to the above examples, when the whole character of the individual entities in a configuration is strong, the entities will retain their boundaries and closure, and will be treated as substructures, forming confederate wholes within the overall configuration. Such configurations will be perceived as hierarchical and multilayered, composed of parts which them-

Fig.37. Repetitious pattern. Fig.38. Curtain-wall facade. Fig.39. Aldo Rossi. Facade.

116

selves are groups of wholes. The nature of such hierarchical organizations depends on such factors as regularity, scale, and multiplicity of elements. The less a structure is enclosed and self-maintained, however, the weaker its whole character will be. Thus, within a group of wholes, the weaker will function as the ground for the stronger.

Of course it is possible to point to a special paradoxical case within the above general rule. This concerns configurations consisting of sets of parts of equally strong whole character. In these instances a so-called *multistable* formation will result, as in many of Escher's reversible patterns (Fig.40). However, most spatial layouts consisting of groups and series of parts can be effectively broken into multilayered structures, each forming a self-contained whole. A classic example is Bramante's first plan of St. Peter (Fig.41). Other facades can be seen as groups of groups; these are often formed out of a number of self-contained groups, which in turn consist of subgroups with their own distinct boundaries. One might think here of the effect of risalites and their individual parts such as windows and intervening areas of wall — as well as an internal, sometimes 'ornamental', articulation of these elements.

We can now turn to the second criterion of wholeness, which calls for the existence of permeating organizing principles by which individual parts of a configuration are concatenated. Such ordering can be achieved through

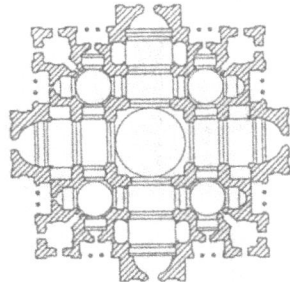

Fig.40. Multistable pattern: M.C. Escher, Day and Night.
Fig.41. Bramante. Plan for St. Peter.

congruities among the parts or through topological orders by which the parts are organized into subgroups of distinct figural character. When a configuration consists of isomorphic, syngenomorphic, homeomorphic or katamorphic items, structural similarities will tie the parts together. Such similarity can also be used to achieve rhythmical organization into simple subgroups. Structurally similar shapes (as well as heteromorphs) can also be organized into subgroups with figural character through symmetry relationships and gradients of scale, as is in many Chinese pagodas.

But a strong figural structure can also be achieved in other ways — for example, when the parts and the whole share organizing principles, or when the organization of the whole affects the organization of the parts. In simple configurations this may occur when the overall shape and the shapes of constituent parts are congruent; or in more complicated arrangements, it may occur when the parts and the whole are organized using gradients based on logarithmic curves.

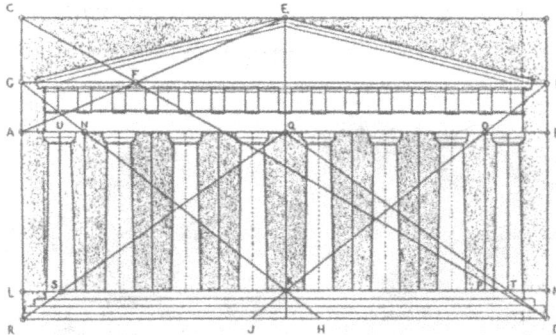

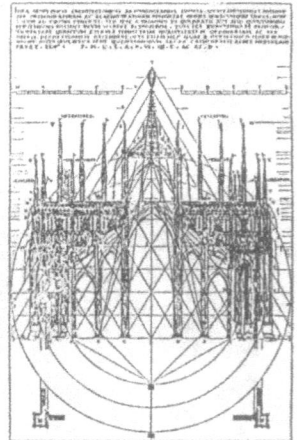

Fig.42. Parthenon. Geometric relationships.
Fig.43. Milan Cathedral. Cross-section showing proportional scheme.

118

The importance of common principles for organizing the parts and the whole is apparent when one compares 'genuine' styles with their eclectic copies. For example, Gothic and Neogothic cathedrals use the same repertoire of shapes, yet the latter often appear to lack the harmony of the former, or look 'flat'. The reason may lie in the lack of an overall proportional system to determine not only the dimensions of each part, but also the location and scale of each part within the whole (as well as the sizes and shapes of residual spaces). Thus, even though Neogothic and Gothic cathedrals use similar elements and decorations, the former lack the mathematical rigor of proportioning that characterize the connections of the parts in the latter, and are really mere collages of Gothic features. A similar observation can be made about other eclectic styles. For example, the architecture of Neoclassicism, and of the Fascist period (Fig.44),

Fig. 44, 45. Comparison between National Socialist (left) and Classicist (right) architecture.

lacks the articulation of true Classical models, particularly at the micro-structural level of ornament and texture (Fig.45). More recently, one can observe how many examples of the Postmodern style adopt features from many different styles, which are often based on the use of different orders and can be combined into a unified organization only with difficulty.

Respect for a building's compositional order becomes particularly important during restoration work or during the design of additions to existing structures. But it must be remembered that compositional order and style are not identical concerns; respecting or modifying existing orders does not call for new buildings in the old style. For example, the traditional European city underwent considerable transformation from the Renaissance on. Nevertheless, until the turn of the beginning of the twentieth century there were many examples of how different styles could be made to coexist without a clash of compositional order or a loss of overall wholeness. Such order, transcending differences in style, was generally achieved through similarities in materials, color, and the format of the main shapes of buildings and their parts.

To summarize the above discussion, it is possible now to formulate two criteria for wholeness: the first is the degree of figural regularity, or *prägnanz*; the second is an interdependence between the complexity of a structure and the number of possible relationships between its parts. Structures of low complexity, which employ only a few heterogeneous elements, require few organizational relationships to achieve orderliness. But very complex structures, which employ many different items (often showing heterogeneous internal articulation as well), either require organizing principles of a higher order or a greater number of connecting relationships. Thus, in order to have a high degree of wholeness, a less complex structure will require comparatively fewer relationships than a complex one. In fact, complex structures usually require multilayered organization involving a manifold of relationships in order to allow those processes of information-reduction which keep the brain from being overtaxed during perception.

3. Hierarchical Structure: Sustained Perceptual Interest

In the previous section I argued that unity of organization is the primary condition for the perceptual appropriateness of form. If, according to this position, unity is understood as the atunement of forces in a stimulus array, then *simplicity of organization* must be considered a key characteristic of perceptual appropriateness. However, it can hardly be maintained that aesthetically pleasing forms are, by definition, 'simple'. Therefore, the notion of simplicity needs further exploration.

When used in a way that is merely the opposite of 'complexity', simplicity would appear to imply a maximum of entropy, that is, the existence of a statistically most probable state of organization. Ultimately, this state may be thought of as the most homogeneous possible distribution of elements in a configuration. In physical terms, this would mean a state of mechanical disorder, one in which, as Max Plank has noted, "the single elements . . . behave in complete independence of one another."[19] Hence, maximum simplicity would seem to imply minimum wholeness.

However, when referring to the level of orderliness of a given configuration, simplicity may also characterize a state of equilibrium: the most ordered or balanced state attainable under given circumstances. In this sense, the notion of simplicity is not dependent on the notion of homogenous statistical distribution. Wolfgang Köhler called this tendency toward equilibrium in a system (which also operates in perceptual organization) the "principle of dynamic direction."[20] It does not imply a most probable arrangement of parts, but rather a compliance of all parts with rules of a whole. In this sense, a maximum of simplicity will prohibit parts of a system from acting independently of one another.

However, maximum simplicity in the latter sense — that is, in the concatenation of a configuration's constituent parts in regular fashion so as to permit the formation of groups and the segregation of perceptual units — still does not suffice to define aesthetic value. Such a characteristic of form

121

only concerns the brain's ability to assimilate environmental information, and, as pointed out earlier, a second condition must be met: *perceptual interest must be stimulated* in the first place.

Stimulus material must have some degree of heterogeneity to stimulate the brain; it must possess a minimum of structure. Thus, a perfectly homogeneous array, in which no stimulation of receptor systems occurs, will arouse almost no interest. But perceptual arousal is more than a simple matter of degree. A maximum heterogeneity will also prohibit perceptual organization, for structures can only be segregated from a perceptual field by virtue of topological relationships between parts that share similarities. In other words, maximum heterogeneity doesn't permit order to arise. It follows, then, that the formation of percepts is based on two interdependent requirements: *structure* and *orderliness*. Between a homogeneous stimulus field that possesses no structure, and a heterogeneous field that possesses no orderliness, there must exist a range of optimal conditions for perceptual information processing.

Before examining the interdependence between order and structure, it is important to investigate the notion of perceptual arousal. The findings of information psychology and information aesthetics can be very useful here. A famous experiment by Heron[21] showed that people's general feeling of well-being (as well as the proper functioning of human thought processes) requires a minimum level of external stimulation. Subjects in the experiment who were placed in a low-stimulus environment — lying on soft beds, ears and eyes covered — experienced strong feelings of anxiety, and even hallucinations, after only a short period of exposure to sensory deprivation. If low complexity in the stimulus array produces such a dissatisfactory state, does it follow that a high complexity will result in a satisfactory one? Indeed, a test of the correlation between people's preferences for abstract paintings and the paintings' actual complexity did show a clear preference for more complex paintings.[22] Similarly, Berlyne[23] has argued that perceptual arousal and complexity are interrelated.

However, it has also been demonstrated that too much perceptual information may overtax a person's capacity for information processing. Based on a model which distinguishes between short- and long-term memory, and which assumes that short-term information processing is a precondition for the formation of long-term memory, both Frank[24] and Miller et al.[25] arrived at calculations of roughly 160 bits maximum storage capacity for short-term memory. With a maximum storage time of ten seconds, information input thus ought not to exceed 16 bits per second to guarantee the complete processing of a stimulus pattern. Based on these considerations, H.W. Franke's[26] hypothesis — that a person reaches a state of maximum satisfaction when perceptual stimuli provide as much complexity as can be processed by short-term memory — seems plausible.

It would then appear that that aspect of aesthetic value which depends on arousal could be explained through concepts proposed by the information-processing school of aesthetics founded by Moles and Bense.[27] However, on further examination one finds that their research focuses entirely on the numerically measurable characteristics of experienced objects. While it may be reasonable to assume there is some statistically determinable plateau of optimal arousal, one may question a definition of information based solely on quantitative assessment. One might also ask how aesthetic value could be related to such a definition. In fact, a major weakness in the work of this school is that their calculations of maximum permissible stimulus arousal have normally been based on temporal formations, such as sequences of tones in auditory presentations.[28] Such tests, however, ignore the crucial fact that a display in the *visual* field is perceived all at once, as a whole, and not through the successive aggregation of parts over time. An additional difficulty concerns the fact that the information theorist's approach treats all parts of a configuration as discrete stimuli, failing to consider how perceptual organization is also a matter of configurational properties. The different parts of a pattern are thus assigned information value only in regard to the statistical probability of their occurrence. The rule of information value thus implied is simple: the more redundant an item, the less information it provides. Such a *quantitative* measure obviously ignores the possibility of *qualitative* difference that may arise as a result of the location of an item within an array, its proximity relations, the organization of the total array into figure and ground, or internal articulation into subsets.

These issues highlight the information school's overreliance on quantitative measures. In fact, the school defines order through a measure of statistical redundancy — the idea being that once a part of a configuration has been perceived, its recurrence provides no further information. Thus, the more redundant a configuration, the less information it provides. While this position might plausibly lead one to conclude that a totally homogeneous display will possess no information, once the amount of information begins to increase, the content of the configuration becomes less predictable. Thus, since an entirely heterogeneous arrangement contains no redundancy, it would seem to present the highest information value. And to take this argument to its logical extreme, chaos would appear to provide the most information. Clearly, if information means 'to give form', then a measure of statistical probability alone cannot be sufficient to determine the level of information in a pattern; for how can information be derived if there is no order in a system? Moreover, the reverse — that the more order there is in a system, the less information it will provide — would also have to be correct.

Information theory, therefore, offers little prospect for explaining aesthetic value, for it treats perceptual space as isotropic. Nevertheless, an important conclusion in terms of perceptual arousal can be drawn from such theory. This is that perceptual arousal is not determined by the *absolute complexity* of a configuration. Instead, the *relative* — that is, actually perceived — complexity of a configuration is a function of the system's organization. This means that, at any given level of information, the complexity of a system can increase with the relative orderliness of the system.

With a number of qualifications, then, the basic model of information theory does offer the potential for further defining the role of arousal in aesthetic value. But before proceeding further with this analysis, it is necessary to pursue the notion of complexity in qualitative as well as quantitative terms.

As stated above, a complete definition of complexity must consider not simply the total variety of elements in a configuration but the variety of the relations between them. Complexity is thus both *elemental* and *structural*. The former criterion concerns the *variety of elements*, the latter the *variety of relationships* by which they are connected. For example, translatory symmetry is less complex than rotational symmetry, because it relies on only one reflection. Similarly, curves of higher order (such as logarithmic gradients) are more complex than simple or circular curves. However, as noted, mathematical concepts alone are insufficient to explain the structural complexity of a configuration, because they cannot do justice to the unisotropy of perceptual space. To address this issue, Heckhausen[29] suggested that the 'phenomenal complexity' of a pattern — for example, its figure-ground relations — ought to be included in measurements of total complexity. Similarly, Raab's tests[30] have suggested that perceptually relevant complexity depends on the occurrence of detail in only certain parts of a pattern and on the number of subfigures in a configuration.

Any description of perceived complexity must also take into account the effect of perceptual factors, such as the varying significance of vertical and horizontal orientation, and the varying impact of parts in a symmetrical organization depending on their distance from an axis of symmetry. However, since different configurational properties have different levels of dominance (for example, the effect of proximity in figural segregation is often neutralized by the effect of closed contours), it becomes apparent that it is virtually impossible to formulate exact criteria for measuring the dynamic properties of perceptual space.

Relational properties must therefore be seen as representing a *qualitative* aspect of order. Moreover, the degree of orderliness they create will not be determined by their kind, but by the completeness of organization they provide. In quantitative terms, then, the complexity of a configuration will increase both with the number of relationships that connect the parts, and with the increasingly complicated nature of these relationships. In the end, *the more the parts of a configuration are subordinate to relational properties, the higher its degree of orderliness, or unity, will be.*

Thus, the orderliness of a configuration is determined by two factors: *structural congruities* among the parts, and *the degree of organizational completeness* according to permeating orders. Of these criteria, the latter is the more important, for it results in wholeness and closure of a structure. In other words, the more the parts become subordinate to configurational laws, the greater will be the degree of a structure's orderliness. Thus (in contradiction to the apparent conclusion with which I began this section), a tendency toward permeating regularities emerges as the *opposite* of entropy. Whereas the constituent parts of an entropic configuration are independent of one another and the whole, an orderly configuration requires that the parts be subordinate to rules of the whole. Total completeness of organization therefore requires that there be no local disorders; for instance, there can be no deviation from permeating figure-ground relationships, and there should be no residual spaces unless these can be perceived as part of a continuous ground. Disorder is thus not a matter of difference between parts, but of insufficient subordinance of parts — or, alternatively, of the collision of antagonistic principles of ordering.

Thus, although similarities among a configuration's parts may help the whole achieve some level of orderliness, such similarity is not necessarily a condition for order. For example, an entirely heterogeneous set of parts can still be organized into a whole if the prevailing rules of order are strong enough. However, redundancy does become a major factor in the formation of multilayered complex structures. One can point to two principal types of organization in relation to such structures: *coordination* and *subordination*. Coordinated structures have no subgroups; their parts are of equal value in relation to the whole (for example, through simple alternating repetitions), and high levels of perceived complexity here will result only from high levels of absolute complexity. However, in subordinately organized structures, absolute complexity can be comparatively higher at similar levels of perceived complexity. It's important to note that, due to organization into redundant

126

subgroups, a subordinately organized structure can create a relatively low level of perceived complexity at each organizational level, even though its total absolute complexity may be high.

If the perceived complexity of a configuration is a measure of its potential for perceptual stimulation, it becomes apparent that high levels of absolute complexity can only be processed by the human brain when a grouping of redundant elements prevails, and thus allows processes of information reduction to work. Again, a concept borrowed from information theory is helpful here. Information theory defines elements that are grouped into regular patterns — 'supersigns', or superparts — and proposes that they can be treated as single elements of an overall configuration. If similar supersigns recur in a configuration, the effort necessary to grasp the whole can be reduced even further. Tests have tried to show correlations between preferences for abstract patterns and the degree to which supersigns are formed at different levels. The results have indicated a strong preference for patterns containing supersigns — that is, patterns with hierarchical, multilayered structures. Frank[31] has gone so far as to propose a method for calculating the effect of such a process of information reduction. Ultimately, his model is somewhat questionable on technical grounds because qualitative differences also exist between supersigns (based on differing levels of perceptual dominance and varying degrees of regularity). Nevertheless, the concept of such a model helps explain how the ability of the brain to perceive groupings of parts as singular elements makes it easier to grasp a complex whole.

In comparing coordinate and subordinate organizations, therefore, it becomes apparent that coordinate structures cannot achieve high levels of absolute complexity without their perceived complexity exceeding the maximum limit of arousal (16 bits per second). In contrast, a multilayered structure, in which processes of information reduction can occur, will create relatively higher degrees of absolute complexity at comparably lower degrees of perceptual complexity. For the same amount of information, then, it is possible to say that complex, subordinately organized structures may be

127

grasped as perceptual wholes more easily than simple coordinate structures.

The above discussion provides grounds for arguing that *hierarchically organized structures yield a higher degree of aesthetic value* than nonhierarchical ones. If one accepts that the optimal plateau of relative complexity is based on the brain's capacity for short-term memory (see above), one finds that a structure whose perceived complexity equals its absolute complexity can be fully grasped within roughly ten seconds and, thereafter, will sustain no further perceptual interest. But a hierarchically organized structure may sustain perceptual interest for much longer, depending on the number of its sublayers of organization. And if each sublayer consists of groupings which form the single parts for the next sublayer, then the whole can be explored at every level of structure in succession without exceeding the brain's perceptual capacity.

If sustained arousal is considered a criterion of perceptual interest, it becomes apparent why certain patterns, such as building facades with low absolute complexity, easily create boredom. Nonhierarchical organizations tend to result in a rather monotonous appearances, such as that of certain curtain-wall facades created through the addition of equal parts. One can also see how the developed styles of Gothic, Northern Renaissance, and Baroque architecture show a stronger hierarchical organization and a greater layering into subgroups than Neoclassical architecture. Fascist-style buildings, or buildings from the period of early Italian rationalism, also show an absence of hierarchical organization, an important reason for their extremely monotonous appearance. Based on the above considerations, it becomes apparent how sustained interest in an object is only possible when hierarchical organization occurs both at macro-structural levels and at micro-structural levels such as that of textural articulation and color.

As a final note on hierarchical structure, one might observe how such organizations comply with the principle of '*prägnanz*'. Simple coordination does not permit strong visual accents; and within a larger unit, such singular heterogeneous groupings will always claim dominance. The rose window of a Gothic cathedral is a good example: the most regular shape in this structure is also the most *'prägnant'* because of its isolation and its lack of repetition elsewhere.

When the two principal demands of perceptual appropriateness are considered together, it can thus be stated that *maximum appropriateness requires maximally articulated simplicity*. Perceptually appropriate form may thus be described as a hierarchically organized structure, as complex as possible, with a maximum of orderliness.

4. Two Conditions for Aesthetically Successful Form

It is now possible to summarize my arguments to this point regarding the nature of aesthetic value. I began by arguing that all judgements of perceptible things must in part be founded on presentational properties. Because of the sensory-motor nature of perception, I pointed out how values established during the internalization of form must be embedded in the overall value assigned to any object. I then addressed the nature of the kinds of value that may be intrinsic to form, and I suggested that a major criterion for determining such value is the organismic satisfaction a person derives from the perception of order. My argument here concerned the biologically determined sense of dissatisfaction that occurs when one's innate motoric sense of order is disturbed. Furthermore, I suggested that consummatory actions resulting from perceptions of orderly configurations (or the discharge actions by which these can be replaced) can be considered a source of organismic satisfaction. Finally, I attempted to formulate the conditions a perceived object must meet if it is to arouse such a state of satisfaction. These were found to be perceptually appropriate order and structure.

The above conditions can be summarized in the two principal criteria for determining perceptual appropriateness, and thus aesthetic value. First, to be perceptually assimilable, an object has to possess a kind of order that would permit its perceptual organization. In this regard, the more ecological and perceptual order are isomorph — that is, that the actual order of an object mirrors a person's existing capacity for perceptual segregation — the more completely the perception of the object can be internalized without causing dissatisfaction. The best condition for perceptual segregation thus occurs when an object permits the formation of perceptual wholes. Whole character depends on the orderliness of an object's internal organization — where orderliness is defined as the simplest possible arrangement a given structure can assume under the prevailing conditions of perception. Perceptual appropriateness in this first sense, therefore, concerns maximum completeness of internal organization, achieved through the subordination of parts to relational properties and the avoidance of antagonistic principles. The more the overall structure of a percept thus tends toward prä*gnant* form, the stronger its impact in aesthetic terms will be.

The second determinant of aesthetic value related to an object's ability to arouse perceptual interest is that it possess a minimum of structure, yet not so much relative complexity that it causes the brain's biological capacity to process information to be overtaxed. A state of sustained perceptual interest would be the most aesthetically satisfying state. This is most likely to occur when the absolute complexity of a structure exceeds its relative complexity. The important principle here is that the more a structure is organized so that its parts assume hierarchical organization into subgroups (in order to allow processes of information reduction), the greater its absolute complexity will be in comparison to its relative complexity. Thus, aesthetically successful forms are those that permit a maximally articulated simplicity of organization.

VII

Spatial Form in Architecture

Thus far, my suggestions for a presentational theory of aesthetics have been formulated broadly enough to pertain to all types of visual forms. However, different classes of objects also require qualification through different sets of descriptive categories. In particular, the experience of buildings and cities may be quite different than that of objects of daily life such as tools and coffee cups or works of art such as paintings and sculpture. First of all, the comparatively large scale of buildings makes it difficult to perceive them as a whole. Rather, they are perceived ambulatorily, in a sequence of successive perceptions of different locations that need to be fused into a single cognitive image. Buildings cannot be experienced in a single act of perception: either they surround the viewer, as in the case of an interior space, or the viewer has to move around them, as when trying to see the whole of an exterior. Moreover, unlike most other objects that occupy space, architecture also displays space. In other words, it is experienced both as the corporeality of physical objects and the shape of the void these objects create. Furthermore, individual architectural form is usually agglomerated into larger units to form streets, plazas and cities, and such contexts have an impact on the perception of single entities.

Despite these concerns, however, the organization of a building is usually far less complicated than, for example, a painting or a natural object. And so in the organization of a facade or the formation of an interior volume, architecture provides an excellent example of the way in which principles of perceptual organization operate. For example, buildings are often organized according to the cardinal axes of kinesthetic balance, and they often display symmetrical organization within their parts, as well as fairly simple separation of shapes into figure and ground.

Any attempt to formulate descriptive categories of architectural form has to start with a confrontation of the nature of perceived architectural space. The essential existence of architecture is not simply given by the shapes of which a building is composed but through the interaction of them as they segregate, bound and articulate space. The experience of architecture can be said to encompass both the experience of tangible and visible objects, and the relationships between them that segregate, bound and articulate space. This chapter will look closely at the form space takes in architecture and describe the conditions under which the void between the physical components result in a self-contained perceptual figure of its own.

1. Perceptual vs. Geometric Space

Before beginning this analysis of spatial form, however, I will look in general at the difference between perceptual and geometric space. Many attempts to describe architectural form have assumed that space may be treated as isotropic, that is, no one direction or location can be said to have inherent dominance over any other. But such a Euclidean framework does not suffice to describe the properties of architectural space. However, architectural space is always *experienced* space in that it enhances and constrains human activities. Thus, the perception of architectural space is never a homogeneous or faithful recording of geometric characteristics and dimensions. Rather, every location and direction possesses a different value depending on use and meaning assigned by the inhabitants. One might also note that architectural space is always experienced synaesthetically — that is, as a compendium of sensations involving light, sound, touch, smell, temperature, and, of course, movement. And this quality also adds to its potentially 'distorted' character.

But even if the above qualities could be ignored, the Euclidean approach to architectural space would still be deficient. The reason is it uses topological, geometrical and arithmetical properties to represent space as a matter of dimensions, angles, axes, adjacent parts, and so on. But perceived space is, as Koffka has astutely formulated, not a geometric pattern but a 'dynamic event'.[1] The percept is organized such that the constituent parts assume varying dominance based on their relation to a field. Thus, figures are segregated from a ground, certain features are sharpened or leveled, and some parts become dominant while others recede. Visual space is thus *unisotropic*; it has different properties in different directions and features a host of dynamic characteristics depending on the location, articulation and massing of elements which generate it. The effect of such dynamic properties can easily be seen in visual 'illusions', whose perceived characteristics contradict geometric reality. For example, the circular lines of the Frasier illusion appear to be spirals (Fig.26); and in the Mueller-Lyer illusion, one and the same distance appears shorter or longer depending on the orientation of the secondary arms (Fig.144).

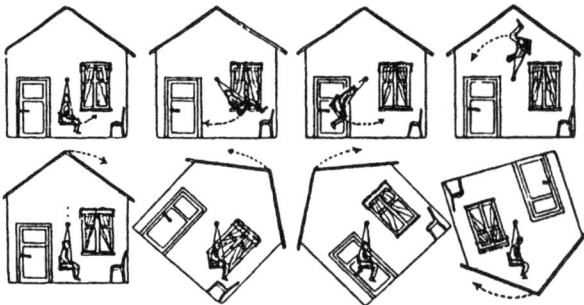

Fig.46. 'Witches swing': effects of rotating frame of reference.

133

The sense of physical balance derived is not the only biological mechanism involved in the dominance of the vertical-horizontal frame of reference,
however. Hubbel's experiments with higher mammals also show there are
particular clusters of cells in the visual cortex which react only when
stimulated by horizontal or vertical lines. Moreover, as I have mentioned in
previous chapters, there is a marked and nearly uniform tendency in human
perception to overestimate vertical dimensions. Tests have shown, for
example, that people overestimate the height of vertical objects such as towers
and masts by an average of 30 percent.[2] Such an effect is apparent in the
examples in Fig.47, which are all actually as wide as they are high. As
Gombrich[3] has pointed out, this is why mountains depicted in paintings — for
instance, Cezanne's Mount Victoire, Fig.48 — are usually superelevated
compared with their actual condition. It is also why one usually places a mark
one third higher than the actual midpoint of an upright symmetrical shape
when asked to mark its center. To compensate for this effect, architects often
make windows slightly wider than high if they want them to appear square.

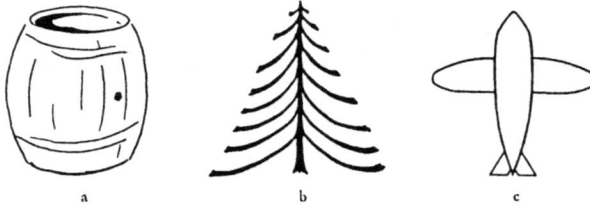

a   b   c

Fig.47. *Overestimation of height: actual height and width dimensions of the above
objects are equal.*

But the unisotropy of perceived space is not only a matter of prevalent
directions. The apparent size of a shape also depends on the size of surrounding
shapes. For example, the same circle looks smaller when surrounded by large
circles than when surrounded by small ones (Fig.50). And one and the same space

Fig.48. Mount St. Victoire. Painting by Cezanne (left); **Fig. 49.** *actual view (right).*

may look wider or narrower, shorter or longer, depending on the articulation and color of its walls, a seeming compression or decompression of space that clearly cannot be explained in Euclidean terms (Fig.51). Similarly, the perceived remoteness of a shape is not simply a matter of actual distance; it also depends on the shape's brightness and articulation. According to Koffka this effect is caused by the tendency of articulated figures to possess greater potential energy in the cortial field than less articulated ones.[4] A bright moon is a perfect example: it seems much closer and larger when perceived directly by the eye than when perceived as part of a photograph from the same viewpoint. So too can buildings which are highly articulated and regular appear closer than those that are less articulated.

All these effects which demonstrate the unisotropy of visual space can hardly be explained in mathematical terms. However, this does not mean that

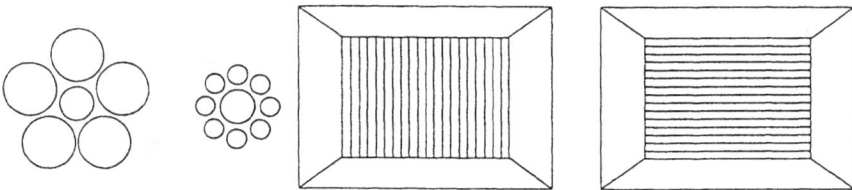

Fig.50. Ebbinghaus Illusion. **Fig.51.** *Effects of directional articulation.*

one can proceed in an examination of architectural aesthetics without analyzing them. In fact, based on the argument I have developed that percepts can be understood as fields of forces generated by the relations of elements in a configuration, it is precisely on the basis of these forces that visual space ought to be analyzed. To speak, as Arnheim does, of forces of attraction and repulsion which operate in architectural spaces, is much more than just a loose metaphor. In the end, the apparent 'remoteness' and 'connectedness' of buildings cannot be explained in purely quantitative terms — only through the influence of dynamic effects of shape, massing and articulation within the overall visual field.[5] Of particular importance may be the effect of these dynamic properties on whether the forms of architecture or the shapes of the intervening spaces lay a stronger claim to a dominant sense of figural clarity.

2. The Shape of the Void: Figural Definitions of Architectural Space

When we speak of architecture, we speak of spaces — that is urban spaces and spaces within buildings. But precisely how does one define architectural space? Does it have a presence of its own, or is it just a void created by surrounding walls or facades? In light of the above discussion, it is possible to consider the ways in which architectural space — the void between walls or buildings — can assume the

Fig.52. Mont St. Michel.

Fig.53. Palladio, Villa Rotonda.

136

quality of a perceptual figure. Such an effect of a figuredness is particularly common in architectural interiors, where the shape of a space usually dominates its boundaries. But it may also arise at the level of urban space, where either the buildings or the spaces between them can assume figural dominance. At one extreme in this relation is the architectural solitaire: the isolated structure that dominates all surrounding open space, as did a freestanding medieval monastery or an isolated Renaissance villa (Fig.52,53). At the other extreme are regularly shaped urban spaces, such as the Neoclassical boulevards of Paris, with their similarly articulated bounding facades (Fig.54,55). Most often, however, buildings and the spaces between them compete for dominance, as the spatial boundaries present visual centers which draw attention away from the primary spatial figure.

Fig.54. Rue de Castiglione, Paris.

Fig.55. Place des Vosges, Paris.

It is through the process of perception that the visual field is organized into shapes. Koffka has defined a shape as "a unit segregated from the rest of the field."[6] As such, it consists of an external *contour* containing a face, or *figure*. Perceptually, a contour has a so-called *one-sided function*: this means it belongs to the figure, and is set off from the rest of the visual field, which becomes the ground.[7] Thus, in (Fig.56) the contour belongs to the disc and not to the background, which, instead, appears to continue behind it. In (Fig.57) the contour belongs to the silhouette, and the sky becomes the subordinate ground.

137

Fig.56. The contour appears to belong to the disc, not the background.
Fig.57. Silhouette. (after Metzger) Fig.58. Multistable pattern.

As discussed in Chapter Four, perceptual figures do not exist on their own; they only arise because of forces acting in a field which cause them to be segregated from a ground. Perceptually, the ground is subordinate to the figure; it can either be shapeless, or it can consist of shapes in their own right that form (in a somewhat awkward use of the term) *negative* spaces. The stronger the figural character of the ground, the stronger its tendency to claim the common contour as its own boundary. This tendency, which Arnheim calls "contour rivalry,"[8] becomes most evident in reversible or *multistable* patterns (Fig.58). It is the distinct character of such formations that only one possible perception of it can prevail at a given moment; in other words, figure and ground can never be observed simultaneously, giving rise to the familiar experience whereby the image of a multistable pattern 'flips' back and forth.

The principles of figure-ground segregation have been well described for two-dimensional patterns by the Gestalt psychologists. Yet little attention has been given to their operation in three-dimensional space. In the following subsections I therefore propose five principles of figural segregation for three-dimensional configurations. Following their description, I will conclude this section by illustrating how they are present in several well-known urban spaces.

1. Centricity

In perceptual terms, a shape does not simply consist of a contour and a face, but is endowed with dynamic properties. Arnheim calls these 'perceptual forces' because they have direction and magnitude.[9] In particular, shapes may be said to have *centers*: foci induced by concentrations of the forces of attraction and repulsion that result from their directional properties and the organization and articulation of their contours. A shape's perceptual center does not have to coincide with its geometric center. As I have already mentioned, for example, the perceptual fulcrum of shapes which are not centrally symmetrical will be located above the geometric center due to an overestimation of the vertical. In addition, shapes may have any number of secondary perceptual centers, induced at the edges of the shape as well as at the radial points of its contours. And shapes which are both convex and concave may actually be characterized by secondary centers located outside the spatial figure, which compete against internal centers and weaken the autonomy of the shape against its ground.

However, the more regular, concave, and centrally symmetrical a shape is, the less it is characterized by multiple centers. Naturally, the fewer the

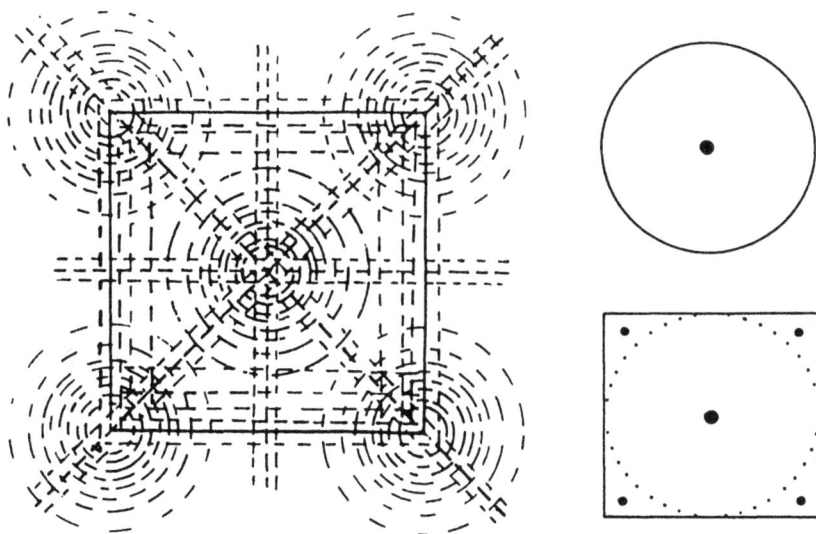

Fig.59. Distribution of perceptual forces within a square (after Arnheim).
Fig.60. Location of centers in simple shapes.

number of subcenters that compete with the main center, the stronger the figural character of the shape will be. A circular or spherical shape is the strongest possible figure; it possesses only one main center and is thus fully autonomous from its surroundings (Fig.59). By comparison, squares and cubic shapes are slightly less strong, since they are characterized by smaller centers induced at their corners. These secondary centers may either compete with the main center, or, if they are symmetrically arranged, they may enforce its presence. In many cases involving architectural space, the main center will be marked by a defining object such as a column or an obelisk, while the subsidiary centers will be emphasized by smaller architectural elements such as fountains or trees (Fig.60).

St. Peter's Square in Rome provides an excellent example of how the placement of smaller centers in an urban space can enrich the experience of individual segments of the arrangement while also strengthening the overall centricity of the composition. By all accounts, the successive arrangement of three spatial entities — the Piazza Rusticuci, the Piazza Obliqua, and the Retta — along

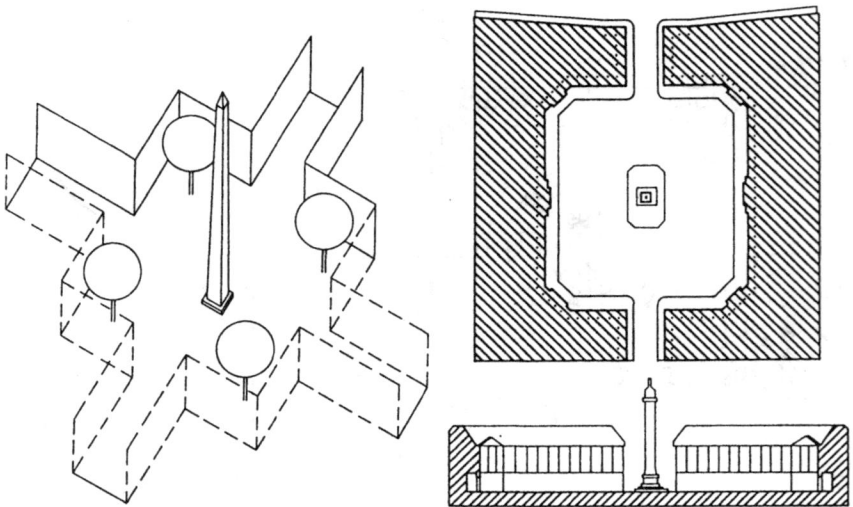

Fig.61. *Architectural elements emphasize visual centers.*
Fig.62 & 63. *Place Vendome, Paris. plan and section.*

St. Peter's principal east-west axis should result in the sense of an elongated space with a clearly pronounced orientation. However, when one faces St. Peter's, the location of the various architectural centers in the configuration, together with the application of various perspective illusions, results in the sense of a strongly centered spatial figure. One reason is that the obelisk marking the Piazza Obliqua is located so as to accentuate the center of its elliptical form, and the considerably less dominant water fountains are placed so as to create subcenters at the radius points of the peripheral colonnades. Together, these three centers induce the sense of an axis perpendicular to the main axis of St. Peter's, which qualifies the dominance of the principal axis through the space and enhances the sense that the obelisk is at the center of a single composition. The perceptual length of the east-west axis is further shortened by the nonparallel alignment of the colonnades on either side of the Retta. These create the illusion that St. Peter's is closer than it actually is: the facade of the cathedral thus appears no farther away from the obelisk than it is from the colonnades on the eastern and western sides of the Retta, while the Piazza Rusticucci appears longer because of the perspective illusion.

Another example of a strongly marked center that compensates for an elongated, non-centrally symmetrical shape is the Piazza Navona in Rome.(Fig.68,69). Because elongated formats lack a clear center, this piazza

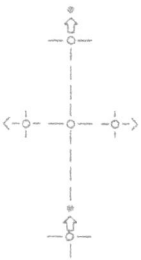

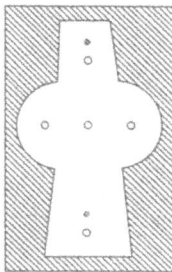

Fig.64. *St. Peter's Square: visual effects of perspective on spatial centers.*
Fig.65. *View from St. Peter's.*

141

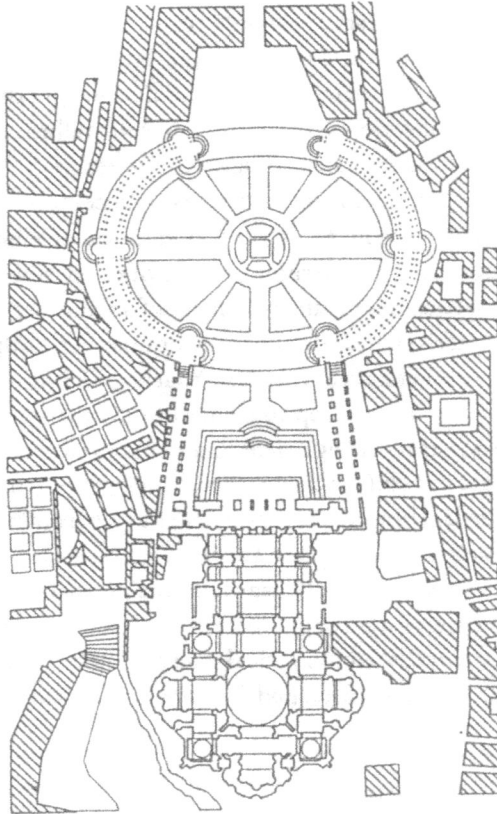

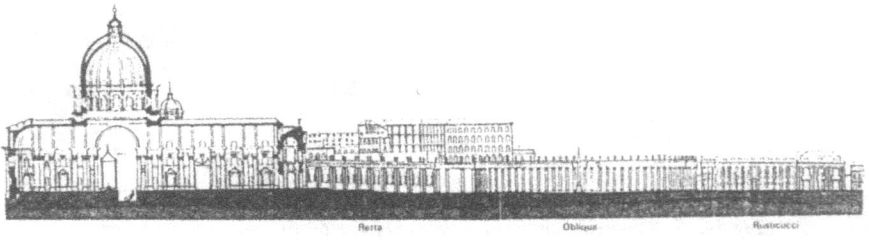

Fig.66. *St. Peter's Square: Plan.* ***Fig.67.*** *Section through cathedral and square.*

would tend to assume the stretched character of a street were it not for the three objects that mark it and enhance its centricity. In particular, the piazza's two smaller fountains are placed in equal proximity to its corners and at equal distances from the tall obelisk in its center. Such an arrangement provides a counterpull to the piazza's long format and divides the space into two smaller entities, each with a format that is less than 1:2. This allows two self-contained subfigures to form within the larger figure of the overall piazza.

2. Concavity

The law of concavity, first formulated in a two-dimensional context by Edgar Rubin[10], states that surfaces which are partly or fully surrounded by concave contours are more likely to be perceived as figures than are the areas that surround them. Since contours have a one-sided function, enclosed areas tend to monopolize the common contour and acquire figural quality. The same

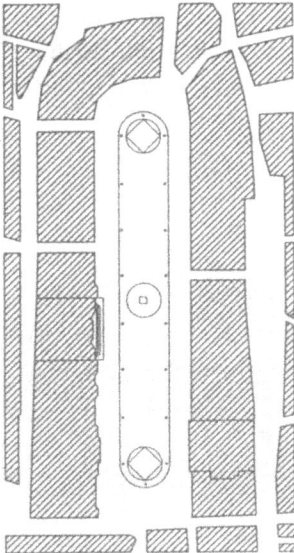

Fig.68. Piazza Navona, Rome: plan.

Fig.69. Piazza Navona, Rome: view.

143

principle can be applied to three-dimensional shapes — with the necessary
qualification that a person's location has to be taken into account because it
creates different possible proximity relations.

Fig. 70. Effects of concavity (after Rubin).

In relation to three-dimensional space, one can say that the more concave
a space, the stronger will be its perceived centricity, and thus its figural
character. Spaces with totally concave contours — that is, contours which
surround a person located inside them — form spatial figures most readily.
Ideally, in a circular plaza, or in a semi-spherical space like that of the
Pantheon (Fig. 71,72), a person in the center will perceive the boundaries as
being equidistant, and the perceptual concavity of space will be fully realized.
However, perceptual effects of concavity may be evident regardless of where
one is located in a space.

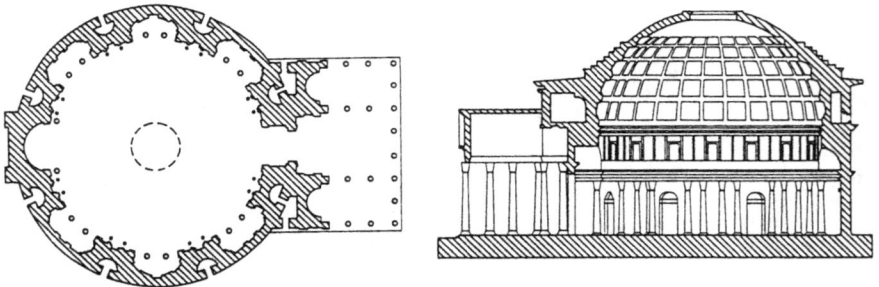

Fig. 71 & 72. Pantheon, Rome: plan & section.

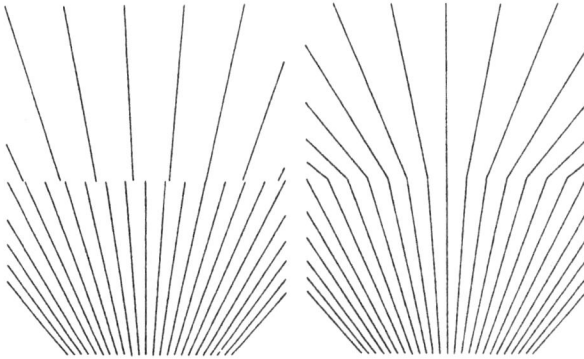

Fig. 73. Textural Gradients (after Gibson).

According to J.J. Gibson, the distances between surfaces are in part gauged by perceived differences in their *textural gradients*.[11] Thus, the left diagram in (Fig.73) indicates an inclination, while the right indicates a step. One can better understand the effect of textural gradients on the degree of perceived spatial concavity if one imagines a semispherical picture plane in front of one's eyes. Walls which curve to follow this imaginary plane show a consistent textural gradient, as in (Fig.73). However, surfaces that extend behind this plane show a increasingly dense gradient; and those that are closer to one's viewpoint show a gradient that is less dense. In the case of a concave circular shape perceived from its center, the textural gradient is absolutely even over its entire surface. However, when perceived from a point farther away from the center, textural density will increase towards the center of the field of vision — that is, toward that part of the wall that is farthest away. The effect of visual concavity here is preserved, because the contour of the space and that of the picture plane are roughly the same.

According to the above line of reasoning, an angular space will be perceived as being less concave than a circular one. Because the corners of such a space will be perceived as located behind the median of the curving picture plane, they will assume a higher textural density. The center area of the

145

opposite wall, however, whose textural gradient will be less dense compared to that of the corners, will appear closer to the eye, and will be pulled into the visual space (Fig.74). Since such a textural pattern is similar to that of a convex surface, one can speak here of an effect of 'pseudo-convexity'.

It is obvious that a maximum sense of concavity will thus be achieved in circular or elliptical spaces, because in such cases there will be little change in textural gradient around the perimeter of the space, giving rise to an enhanced

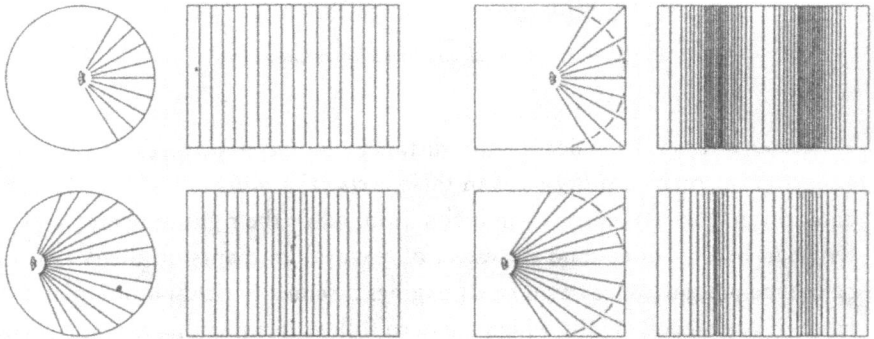

Fig.74. Effects of concavity in angular spaces.

sense of centricity and figural character. Copenhagen's Amalienburgsquare provides a good example of this effect (Fig.75). In this case the faceted corners of the space enhance the overall concavity of its contour. The overall effect is further reinforced by the location of the entering streets. Generally, when streets enter close to the center of a square's lateral boundaries, they strengthen its perceptual concavity. However, when streets enter at the corners, perceptual concavity is weakened, because the distances between the picture plane and the perceived corners of the space increase considerably (Fig.76).

Effects of concavity and centricity can be enhanced in angular spaces through the use of spatial appendixes such as alcoves or niches, or by filling the corners of the space with columns (Fig.77). In these cases distances

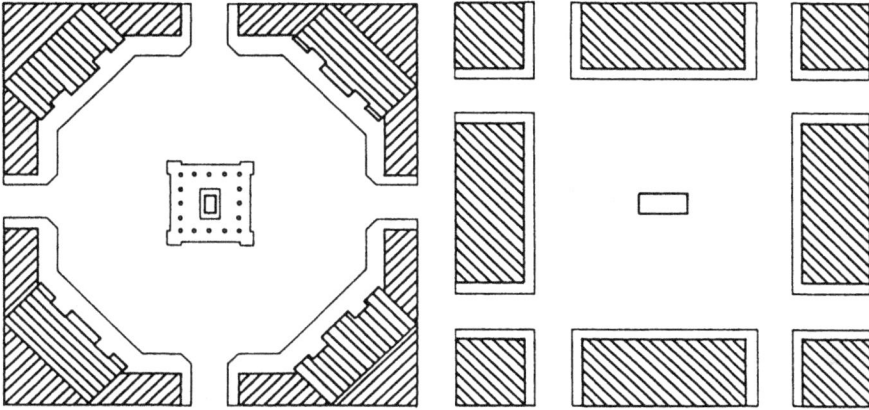

Fig. 75. *Amalienburgsquare, Copenhagen (left).*
Fig. 76. *Square with streets entering at corners (right).*

between walls and the imaginary picture plane are similar over most of the field of vision, and so the textural gradient will approach that of an ideal concave situation. Illusionist paintings on the walls of angular spaces can provide a similar effect (Fig. 78).

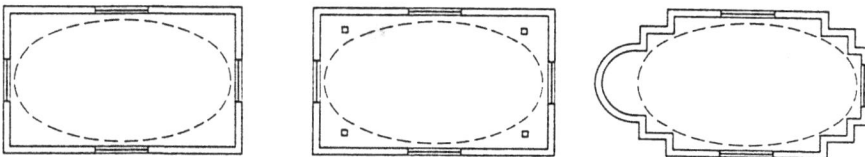

Fig. 77. *Columns, niches and appendixes enhance perceptual concavity.*

Of course, an effect opposite that created by niches or spatial appendixes can be created by using elements that protrude into a space. Such features enhance convexity and weaken the figural dominance of an enclosed space by creating boundaries that rival it. When boundaries are both concave and convex, figure and ground become visually interlocked, presenting a contour

Fig.78. *Illusionist painting.*

Fig.79. *Piazza S. Ignazio, Rome.*

rivalry that is similar to that in a multistable pattern. Bay windows, stairs that expand into a square, or convex risalites can produce such an effect. Such deliberate ambiguity was often a feature of Mannerist and Baroque architecture; an excellent example is the Piazza S. Ignazio in Rome (Fig.79). Though the buildings surrounding this space are concave relative to it, their placement results in a convex appearance at their corners. A similar effect in an interior space can be observed in S. Ivo in Rome, where the walls alternately protrude into and recede from the central space (Fig.80,81).

3. Closure and Peripheral Density

The less enclosed a figure, the stronger will be the competition between figure and ground. In urban spaces the factor of closure is especially crucial because there is no top boundary. Whether or not a space between buildings may be

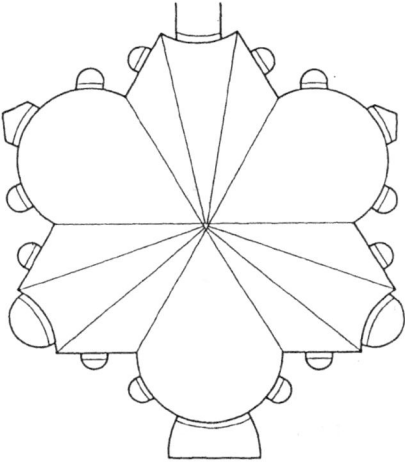

Fig.80. S. Ivo, Rome: diagrammatic plan.

Fig.81. S. Ivo: interior.

may be perceived as a figure in its own right, thus often depends on how the visual field generated by the size and mass of the architectural boundaries creates *cognitive contours*,[12] invisible boundaries which perceptually enclose the space. The diagrammatic comparison of two street profiles in (Fig.82) shows how architectural elements which protrude over a space, such as architraves or overhangs, may hint at more complete boundaries, and help establish a sense of closure.

The perception of spatial figures further depends to a large degree on the height-to-width ratio of the enclosed volume. An optimal ratio for centricity in abstract, fully enclosed space is, of course, 1:1. as in (Fig.83). However, in an urban context, lateral boundaries must be slightly higher to compensate for the lack of a full top boundary. The cross-section of the Via degli Angeli in Ferrara (Fig.84) shows about the right proportions to produce a maximum figural quality. A section with a vertical format of more than 2:1 begins to lose

149

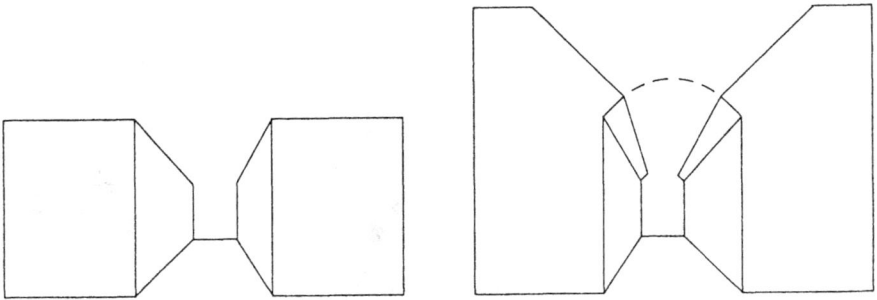

*Fig. 82a. & b. Effect of 'cognitive contours': Protruding Elements produce
perceptual closure*

the sense of a clearly defined center, resulting in a weaker figural character. In
an urban situation, one might liken this to the effect of a medieval street, such
as in Siena (Fig. 85), where centricity is weakened and where the lateral facades
become so dominant they command primary attention. Moving in the other
direction, formats with a vertical-horizontal proportion of more than 1:2 also
tend to have a weak figural character (Fig. 86). The Friedrichstrasse in Berlin
is an example of a street with a borderline figural identity; however, when a
street format exceeds the 1:2 proportion, rows of trees may be used to
subdivide it in the center, thus returning it to a format with a perceptible
figural quality. According to Trieb,[13] a space will no longer be perceived as
enclosed when its proportions reach roughly 1:7, see (Fig. 87). At this point
the field of vision is mostly filled with sky, and the lateral boundaries will
always assume a subordinate existence.[14]

  It should be noted that the establishment of cognitive contours depends
on other factors, one of which is articulation of the spatial boundaries. For
example, the more strongly a top contour is articulated by architraves and sills
protruding into the space, the more easily a cognitive contour may be
perceived. An articulated top contour also produces a strong upper boundary
for the walls of the space, emphasizing the dominance of the lower part of the
figure as opposed to the unbounded sky above. But the height of the buildings

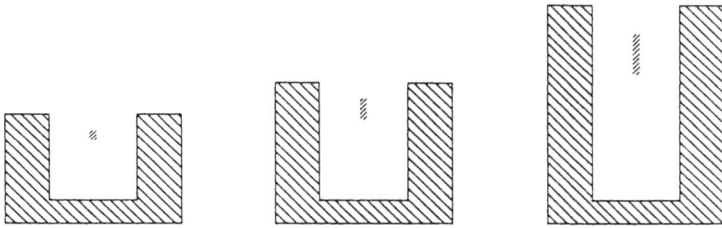

Fig.83 Square in Wangen, Germany. Fig.84. Via degli Angeli, Ferrara.
Fig.85. Street in Siena.

surrounding such an urban ensemble can vary only slightly or else the figural
dominance of the enclosed space will be lost. This is because irregular
contours result in a weak figure because they violate the law of good
continuation[15] (Fig.90,91).

Thus, a sense of closure not only results from the format and position of
the spatial boundaries, but from the *internal articulation of the periphery* —
specifically its *perceived density*. The less dense the perceived periphery of a
shape, the less the shape will seem to be autonomous from its surroundings.
This effect is more apparent in three-dimensional space than in two-dimensional images. Whereas four dots can mark a square on a flat surface, four

Fig.86. Friedrichstrasse, Berlin. during Baroque period.
Fig.87. Dvortsovia Square, St. Petersburg.

columns in the landscape do not necessarily create a space with figural character. When a person finds him inside such a space, he can never see more than three columns at a time, and therefore cannot perceive the columns as a complete contour. In such situations, the columns will tend to assume figural character because of the law of proximity,[16] which specifies that smaller enclosed shapes will always perceptually dominate larger ones. In cases of low peripheral density, elements such as columns accentuate rather than segregate space. However, when repetitively arranged — for example, in rows or colonnades — such elements can more easily form a spatial boundary; rows of trees may have a similar effect.

In both interior and exterior spaces, then, there may exist instances where the autonomy of the spatial figure is preserved despite the low peripheral density of the boundaries. For example, toward the Canale Grande the Piazetta of St. Mark's Square in Venice is bounded only by two columns, which carry the Lion and St. Theodor. Since the form of the square supports an extremely clear figural dominance of its volume over its contours, these columns are prevented from assuming separate figural dominance. However, the rivalry between the space and the columns is strong, especially because the vista to the island of S. Giorgio Maggiore — which functions as a backdrop to the Piazetta — exerts a strong perceptual dominance of its own. When seen from the opposite side of the Piazetta, the spatial boundary is actually *diaphanous*, consisting of layers.

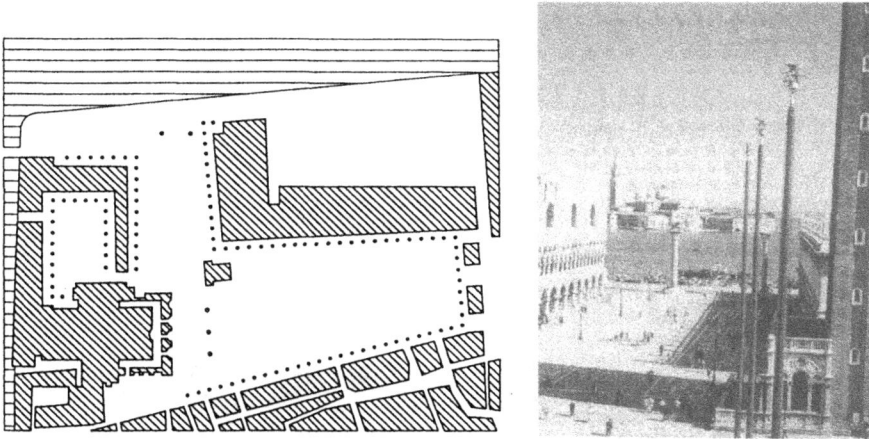

Fig.88 & 89. Venice. Piazza S. Marco: plan and view toward S. Giorgio Maggiore.

4. Uniformity and Coherence of Boundaries

The three previous principles of figural segregation have all presumed neutral, uniformly articulated boundaries. Whenever spatial contours are not uniformly articulated, some of their parts will assume dominance, causing a weakening of the overall figural strength of the enclosed space. But a call for a unified character of a spatial boundary does not require that all of its parts be literally equal in articulation, as in Weinbrenner's design for the Kaiserstraße in Karlsruhe (Fig.90). A unified appearance among spatial boundaries can be realized through morphic similarities: for example, through similar formats of facades or architectural elements; similarities in scale, internal division and decoration; or similarities in materials. Dissimilar formats of buildings can also be arranged in ordered repetition to achieve an overall unified effect.

The importance of uniformity, however, becomes evident when one compares a typical street in Castelfranco (Fig.91) to Weinbrenner's street design. The former shows an erratic agglomeration of elements, where the format and height of buildings vary, and where the overall figural character of the street is weak. Weinbrenner's design, however, shows a variation of individual elements which share principal orders: the horizontal format of the buildings,

Fig.90. Karlsruhe, Weinbrenner's design. Fig.91. Street in Castelfranco, Italy.

the common vertical format of windows, a similar degree of openness of facades, an overall similarity of architectural elements, etc. Furthermore, in terms of uniformity of boundaries, upper contours of a space can be especially important. As I pointed out in discussing cognitive contours, when upper contours vary erratically, a key principle of figural segregation, the 'law of good continuation', is violated.

Nonuniform articulation of boundaries can result either in *disorder*, or in *dominance* of the boundaries over the space between. Where disorder results from a heterogeneous arrangement of parts in the boundary, dominance may still be achieved if single elements contrast with an otherwise uniform articulation — for example, in the Baroque church of S. Agnese at the Piazza Navona (Fig.68,69). The different size, shape, and internal division of this church in relation to the other buildings that make up the boundaries of the piazza, as well as the change the church introduces into the upper contour of the piazza, result in a strong condition of contrast. A similar effect can be observed at the Campo in Siena (Fig.113). Here, the contrasting size and format of the Palazzo Publico becomes the dominant element in an otherwise uniformly articulated boundary. The Palazzo actually establishes a focus of its own, rivaling the self-contained figure of the open space.

Another important aspect determining the dominance of the spatial figure is the coherence of the internal divisions of its boundaries in relation to the overall spatial division. Especially in strongly symmetrical spaces — as in most interiors — figural character may be weakened when the internal division of the boundaries contradicts the symmetry and format of the overall spatial figure. A good example of such a contradiction is evident in the design of Balthasar Neumann's Vierzehnheiligen pilgrimage church (Fig.92,93). Here, a clearly defined space at the vertex of the two naves is contradicted by the design of the elliptic ceiling vaults, which invade the center from behind the crossing of the naves, causing the lateral and top boundaries of the space to indicate competing figures. In contrast to this Baroque structure, most Romanesque and Gothic churches show a clear and unified system for partitioning boundaries, in which vaults, pillars, columns, and floor patterns are all organized according to the same underlying module. The lack of such coherence is, however, evident in the ceiling of the Duomo in Pisa, where the original ceiling was replaced after a fire, and where the new ceiling no longer conforms with the internal division of the lateral boundaries.

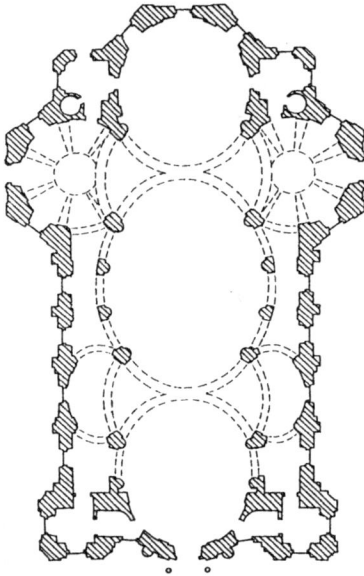

Fig.92 & 93. Vierzehnheiligen: plan and interior.

5. Internal Division of Space and Spatial Density

The last principal of figural segregation I will discuss here concerns the placement of corporeal elements within architectural space to subdivide it into smaller entities or articulate its appearance. In certain cases elements placed in a space can be so visually strong that they rival the perceptual dominance of the spatial figure. A common motif in urban design is the marker in the square: the water fountain, the monument, the freestanding campanile; common as well is the repetition of similar elements such as columns, arcades, trees or lanterns to subdivide a space. In interiors, the rivalry between spatial and corporeal figures is often provided by pillars or columns that carry the vaults or ceilings of large rooms, and so subdivide them into smaller, ancillary spaces.

Fig.94,95,96. *Amiens Cathedral and the Duomo, Pisa: interiors.*

By virtue of their position and size, space-articulating elements can either enhance the figural character of a space, or be so dominant that they are stronger than the main spatial figure. As in the example of St. Peter's Square, a space-enhancing effect can be achieved by placing isolated objects in the center of a space. Marking an otherwise latent perceptual center may draw perceptual attention to the center of the figure, and diminish the importance of its contours. Other examples of this effect include the equestrian statue of Mark Aurel at the Campidoglio in Rome (Fig.104,105,110), and the two fountains and the obelisk in the Piazza Navona (Fig.68). In the Piazza Navona, the three markers clearly create a single effect; rather than competing with the dominant central obelisk,

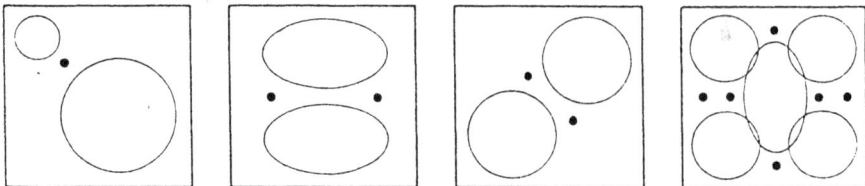

Fig.97. *Columns as a means of defining zones within spaces.*

157

the symmetrical placement of the fountains enhances its centrality in the space. When, however, a marker is positioned outside the center of a shape, it forms two competing spatial fulcrums and results in ambiguity.

Repetitively arranged objects are another way of enhancing a space. If such objects are large enough and are placed close enough together, they can create internal boundaries within a single space. For instance, columns in a

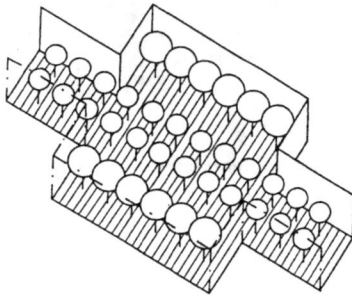

Fig.98.   Trees as spatial boundaries. Fig.99.   Duomo, Pisa: interior.

cathedral or rows of trees from an avenue that continue through a square may divide a unified figure into sections (Fig.97,98). Such an appearance, however, depends on one's position within the space: if one's line of sight is approximately parallel to the line along which the elements are arranged, the effect of a nearly solid boundary will be created; but if one's line of vision is diagonal or perpendicular, placement of the objects may create a contour rivalry, as in the Duomo in Pisa (Fig.96,99).

Whether the corporeal elements in a space can produce this sense of separate spatial units, or rather of a subdivided whole, depends on the density of their spacing. For example, the interior space of the refectory in the Marienburg Castle is perceived as one spatial unit despite the row of columns along its central axis (Fig.100). The temple for Ramses III in Medinet Habu presents an example of

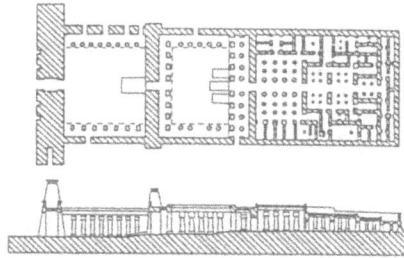

Fig.100. *Marienburg Castle, West Prussia: interior.*
Fig.101. Temple of Ramses III, Medinet Habu.

an increasing spatial density of columns along a ceremonial axis (Fig.101). In each of the six spaces, from the first courtyard to the sanctuary, the ratio of the area occupied by columns to that of interstitial space increases.

It must be noted that the above five principles apply only to perceptions of spatial segregation in *clearly defined spaces*. Such spaces possess the figural character of an enclosed shape, to which boundaries are generally subordinate, even when their character may be strong enough to challenge the predominance of the spatial figure. Furthermore, clearly defined spaces usually have strong, unequivocally positioned centers, which may be marked by objects that further accentuate and articulate the space.

By contrast, *partly defined spaces*, sometimes termed 'flowing' spaces, do not possess such unified character. Instead, they are characterized by spatial and corporeal shapes that compete, so that a viewer's sense of figural character changes depending on his position and direction of view. Mies van der Rohe's Barcelona Pavilion (Fig.102,103) provides a good example of such a space: its boundaries do not clearly separate its various subspaces from each other; its floor pattern does not follow the pattern of its spatial entities; and the transitions between its spaces are indistinct. Here, the boundaries of space clearly retain perceptual dominance over the spaces between, so that the walls form the figure,

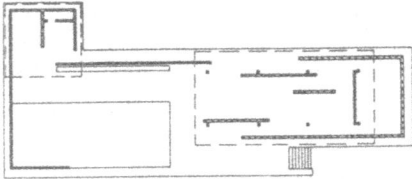

Fig.102 & 103. L. Mies v.d. Rohe, Barcelona Pavilion: plan & view.

and the space becomes the ground.

However, in cases where the enclosed space and its boundaries both possess strong figural character, but where the boundaries are still subordinate to the spatial figure, the overall perceived complexity of a design will be greater than when a volume has no perceivable shape, or when the boundaries are entirely uniform. Especially at the microstructural level of detail, the articulation of boundaries can deviate from principles which govern the boundary without resulting in a lack of unity.

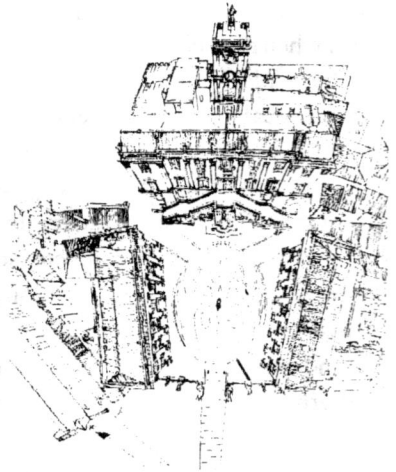

Fig.104 &105. Michelangelo: Piazza del Campidoglio, Rome.

Michelangelo's Campidoglio

In numerous laudations, the Piazza del Campidoglio in Rome has been described as the example *par excellence* of an urban stage set. This square, whose design incorporates the ideals of the Italian Renaissance to rare perfection, is able to provide a clearly defined sense of space and a self-contained spatial figure, even though it is only fully bounded on three sides. The complexity of the arrangement in perceptual terms is extraordinary: the elongated format of the piazza, the stairs at its end, and the tower atop the Palazzo del Senatori all indicate a strong north-south axis; yet, the shape of the piazza as a whole also manages to exhibit strong centricity.

The complete effect of the piazza results from a number of perceptual

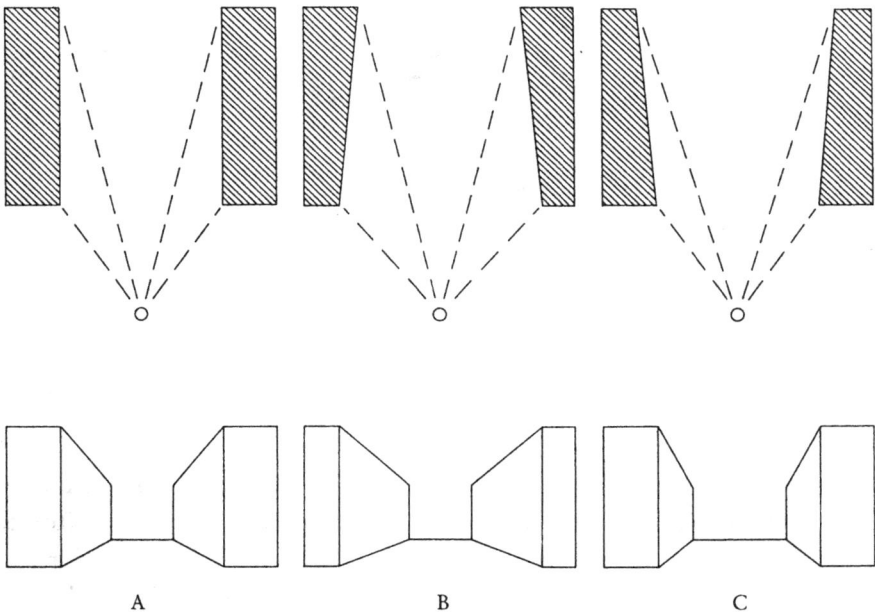

Fig.106. Effects of perspective distortion on the perception of apparent length.

factors. First, the lateral boundaries of the space are not parallel, resulting in a slight perspective distortion. Michelangelo here made use of a perspective trick that was well known during the Renaissance. This is that one does not often notice slight deviations from the parallel, even though the effect on the perceived length of a space can be considerable since boundaries will fill a larger or smaller area within one's field of vision than normal. (Fig.106a) represents the neutral case, where lateral boundaries are parallel and the dimension along the axis of symmetry is not distorted. But when the boundaries are closer at the viewer's end, as in (Fig.106b), the boundaries will appear shorter than they are in reality.

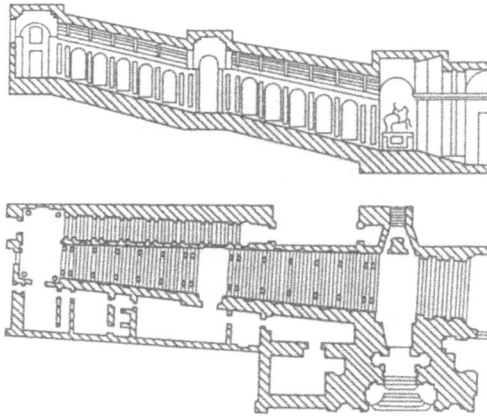

Fig.107,108. Gian Lorenzo Bernini: Scala Regia, Vatican.

When the boundaries are wider at the viewer's end, the illusion of a longer space will be produced. The Piazza Retta in St. Peter's Square in Rome, discussed earlier, provides a good example of such a visually shortened space. In the Retta the perspective distortion serves to bring the dome of St. Peter's perceptually closer to the viewer (Fig.66). One might compare this to the effect produced by Bernini's Scala Regia at the Vatican. Here, an illusion of increased depth leads to a viewer's sense of scale also being deceived, so that a person standing on the upper landing will be judged as being considerably larger than a person standing close by.

At the Campidoglio, the obliqueness of the boundaries creates a two-fold effect. The actual format of the piazza slightly exceeds that of a square. But when one approaches the space by way of the stairs ascending from the north, the converging boundaries on the east and west shorten the space so the piazza appears more square. When viewed from the south, however, the same device causes the space to appear lengthened. Such an effect helps achieve visual closure to the north. If the shape of the piazza were a true square (Fig. 109b),

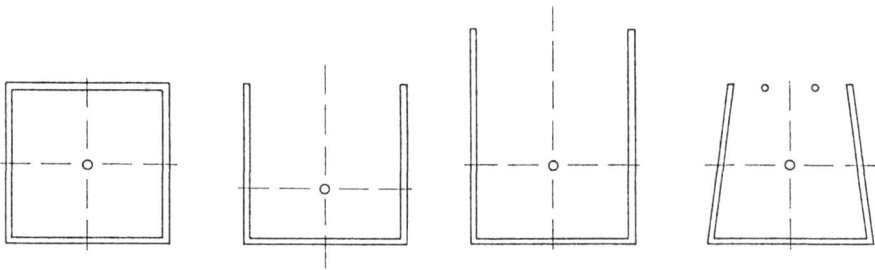

Fig.109. a. - d.

the effect of closure towards the north would be weak because of the low perceptual density of the northern boundary, marked only by a low balustrade and the statues of Castor and Pollux and their horses. However, the longer lateral boundaries, and their greater proximity to one another at the northern end of the piazza, strengthen the sense of enclosure there (Fig. 109d).

The sense of closure in the space and its perceived centricity are further enhanced by the centrally symmetrical position of the equestrian statue of Mark Aurel. The centricity of this figure is reinforced by a slight semispherical curve of the pavement. The surrounding paving pattern also mediates between an outer elliptical shape, which would create the sense of an ambiguous center, and an

163

Fig. 110 Piazza del Campidoglio Rome.

inner circular one, which provides a distinct center. A further effect of figural segregation in the space is provided by the three bounding *palazzi*. These three buildings are all fairly uniformly articulated, exhibiting horizontally oriented shapes with a vertical internal division. The format of the shapes created between the buildings' pilasters and the shapes of their windows are also proportional from building to building, though slightly varied in detail. An important additional effect in the space is the fact that surrounding balustrades are topped by statues. This gives visual strength to the top contour of the space, which is necessary to compensate for the lack of a top boundary.

However strongly these characteristics of the piazza establish a sense of centricity, the 'pull' of the central fulcrum will always be contested by the position of the Palazzo del Senatori and the articulation of its facade. Though the internal division and format of this building's main and subsidiary shapes

164

show congruities with features of the other *palazzi* bounding the space, its greater height and centrally located bell-tower break the uniformity of the spatial boundaries. This produces a strong secondary focus in the space that competes with the main center of attention in the square. However, when one ascends the steep stairs leading to the square, the axis induced by the tower is initially the stronger perceptual focus, an effect heightened by the location of the statues of the *dioskuri*. It is only when one arrives at the end of the ascent that this focus of attention loses its strength, and the centricity of the square abruptly unfolds to the eye. It is the uniqueness of Michelangelo's design that it combines the antagonisms of closure and openness, of centricity and directionality into a unified spatial appearance without ambiguity.

The Vocolo della Pace

Unlike the Campidoglio, where the shape of the space itself provides a clearly dominant figure, the small square which surrounds the facade of S. Maria della Pace in Rome is characterized by a strong figural rivalry between

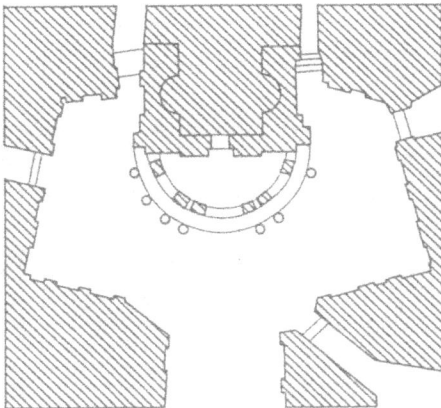

Fig.111. Vocolo della Pace, Rome: plan. Fig.112. View of S. Maria della Pace.

165

a concavely shaped space and a convexly protruding architectural element, the porch of the church. The original design of the square provided for a concave space into which the front of the church would protrude slightly. But in the seventeenth century a porch was added to the church which created a strong positive shape in itself. However, rather than asserting sole perceptual dominance in the space, the porch acts as a visual counterpoint enforcing the center of the spatial figure. Moreover, because there is ample space between the porch's pairs of columns, the columns do not form a strong boundary, allowing exterior and interior spaces to interlock visually.

The Campo in Siena

One of the most distinct urban spaces in the world, this great amphitheater of medieval city life formed in the shape of a shell displays a space where both enclosed space and contour assume nearly equal figural dominance, a condition where the boundary belongs to both positive and negative space. Although the plan of the Campo roughly approaches an irregular rectangle, its appearance is rather of a semicircle, an effect caused by the curved facades of surrounding buildings and the radial stripes set into its paving pattern. The main perceptual center of this space is induced by the semicircular northern boundary at the

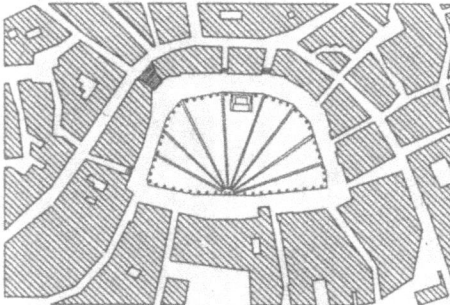

Fig.113 & 114. Campo, Siena.

location of the Palazzo Publico. Meanwhile, this building, with its dominating scale and vertical center risalite, breaks the uniformity of the spatial boundary, creating a focus of its own. However, since the perceptual center of the space coincides with the Palazzo, rather than competing, the two centers reinforce each other. A further complexity is provided by the location of the Fonte Gaia opposite the Palazzo, which counters the main spatial focus.

The strong centricity of the Campo is evident from all positions, because the curved surface of the pavement occupies such a large portion of one's field of vision and because the nine radii (which represent the 'government of nine', under whose rule the Campo was built) converge toward the visual center of the space. The radii also coincide with the entrances of streets leading into the space; and so, from wherever the Campo is entered, the dominant viewpoint is always the Palazzo Publico. Furthermore, even though the actual shape of the Campo is not a perfect semicircle, its ascending surface creates a perspective illusion by which the perceived distance to the facades opposite the Palazzo is lengthened, giving it a semicircular appearance. Although the height-width relation of the enclosed

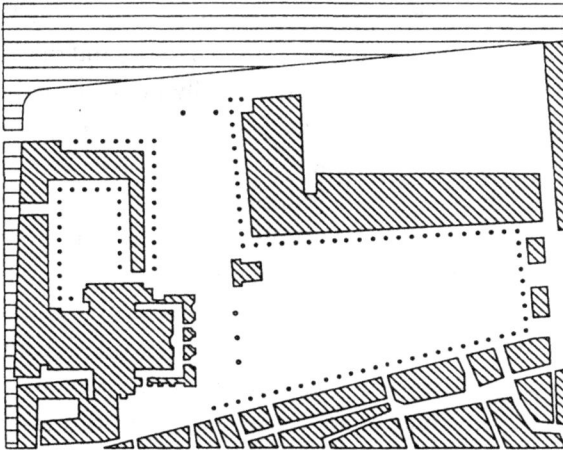

Fig.115. Piazza San Marco, Venice: plan.

space is roughly 1:6, indicating that the effect of enclosure in the Campo ought to be weak, the dominance of the ascending surface fills much of the clearest field of vision in the vertical (which, according to Schubert, is roughly 27 degrees[17]), allowing perceptual closure. By contrast, when looking back down from the top of the space, perceptual closure is achieved by means of the high center risalite of the Palazzo Publico and the enormously tall Torre del Mangia, which provide a powerful secondary center of attention.

The Piazza San Marco

The Piazza S. Marco provides a final example of an urban space in which the figural strength of an enclosed space varies with a viewer's position. This space, the stage for the glorious history of the city-state of Venice, has the form of a trapezoid with a ratio of approximately 1:2,5. Because of the perspective distortions resulting from the trapezoidal shape, the perceived length of the space is greater when it is seen from the end near the cathedral of San Marco than when viewed from its narrow end at the Ala Napoleonica. From this latter vantage point, due to perspective shortening, the cathedral appears to be visually pulled into the space and enlarged in size, and the piazza tends to appear as more central than its plan actually permits. Furthermore, the slight asymmetry of the plan towards the left is countered by the dominant shape of the campanile on the right.

When viewed from the cathedral, the effect of closure provided by the uniformly articulated facades of the Procuratii and the Ala Napoleonica provides the sense of a self-contained spatial figure whose boundaries are subordinate. However, when observed from the narrow end, the spatial figure of the square is challenged by the architectural forms of the cathedral and the campanile. Both these structures break the uniformity of the contour by virtue of their height and individual internal articulation. Here, indeed, the effect is theatrical: the space acts as subordinate ground for dominant buildings, which serve as symbols of a great city. From the narrow end the figural character of the space is further weakened by a decreasing sense of closure towards the church. This is caused by the opening of the trapezoidal shape of the square, which results in a decreasing height-width ratio in the piazza.

Fig.116. View at Napoleonica.

Fig.117. View at San Marco.

The final feature of the Piazza S. Marco is the Piazzetta, which opens toward the water. The campanile both functions as a pivot between the piazza and the Piazzetta and as a bounding object between them. Though the boundaries of the Piazzetta are not uniform (because of the different internal divisions in the facades of the Dogiana and the Libreria San Marco), its figural character is preserved by the bounding effect of the Duomo and the two columns of the Lion and San Theodor. However, because of the diaphanous character of this boundary and the vista over the water beyond, the figural strength of the Piazzetta is comparatively weak. Together, piazza and Piazzetta form a flowing space consisting of two interlocking spatial figures. It is the very controlled ambiguity between spatial and corporeal figures that makes these spaces such a distinctive setting.

WEBER

3. Complex Spatial Arrangements

In the last section I concentrated on architectural spaces that can be experienced in isolation from their surroundings. But most architectural spaces are not such clearly defined units, with strong figural definition and closure. A great many interiors and exteriors are experienced as parts of complex spatial systems. Such systems occur either as larger spaces *subdivided* into smaller units by semitransparent boundaries or space-accentuating objects, or as *sequences* of spaces that are more or less segregated from one another. Whereas the subdivided spatial type may still form a whole in terms of perceptual experience, the sequential type is experienced as a succession of individual perceptual units, which must be fused into a larger whole through a cognitive process.[18] Since perceptual criteria alone do not suffice to explain the experiences of complex spatial arrangements, I will not discuss them here. Instead, I will focus on exploring the effect of the two primary criteria of aesthetic experience I outlined at the end of Chapter Six: *orderliness* and *hierarchical organization*. The first can be analyzed as a matter of *topological* properties, that is, of *adjacencies* of spatial units; the second can be considered in terms of *congruities* of the shapes within a spatial system.

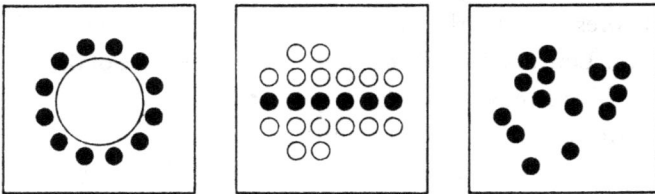

Fig.118. *Possible organization of parts within a whole: central, linear, free-form.*

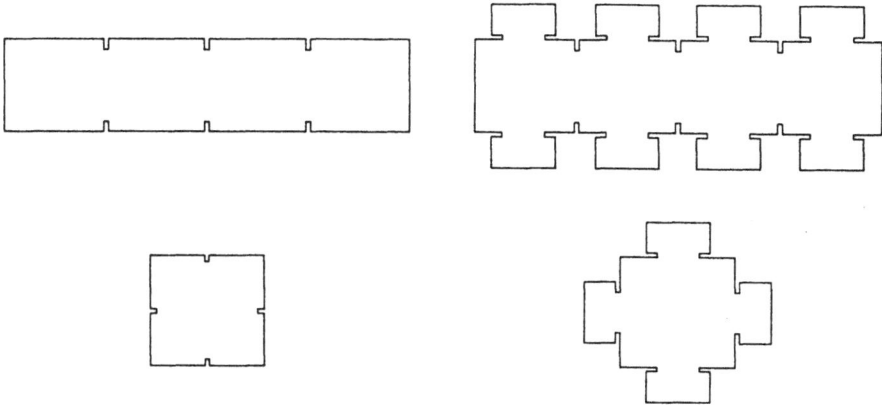

Fig.119. *Coordinated and subordinated arrangement of spaces.*

Spatial Hierarchy: Primary and Ancillary Space

The organization of individual spatial units within larger spatial wholes usually takes on a *central*, *linear*, or *free-form* arrangement. In each one of these cases the relationship of the units within the whole can be described as either *coordinate* or *subordinate*. Coordinate organizations are characterized by subspaces that are similar in size, shape and articulation, and which thus assume similar dominance. Subordinate organizations form hierarchical arrangements in which spatial parts of different size, format or articulation form themselves into groups, which in turn may become parts of larger assemblages. As discussed in Chapter Six, subordinate arrangements afford a higher absolute complexity than coordinate configurations, because perceptual redundancy increases with each level of subordination, preventing one's ability to perceive complex configurations from being overtaxed.

In subordinately arranged spatial systems, individual parts acquire different perceptual dominance, allowing a person to distinguish between *primary* and *ancillary* spaces. Ancillary spaces are subordinate to the main space of a

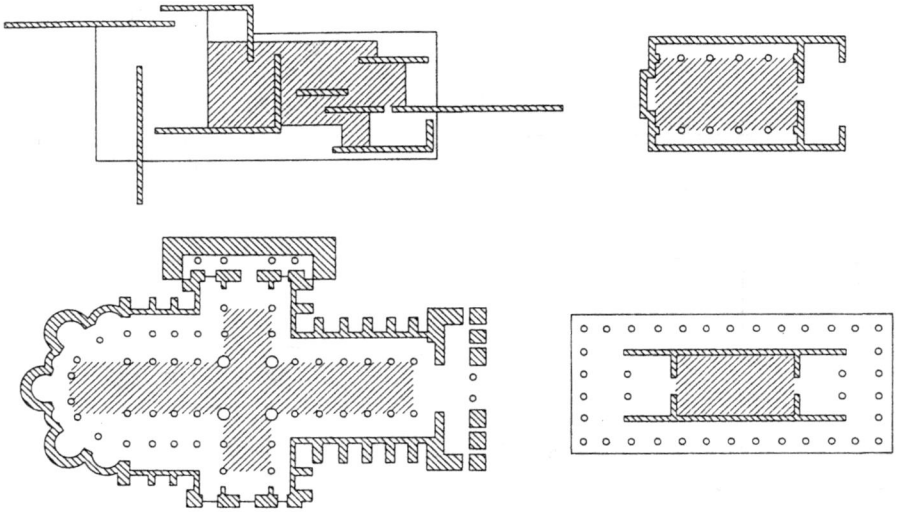

Fig. 120. Examples of primary and ancillary spaces (after Otto).

group, and at the same time enrich its experience. The distinction between primary and ancillary spaces is possible at every level of subordination. Hierarchical spatial organization of this nature can occur as single spatial appendixes, as groups or series, or as symmetrical or asymmetrical arrangements. It can be formed through addition, division, or interlocking of spaces. The simplest form

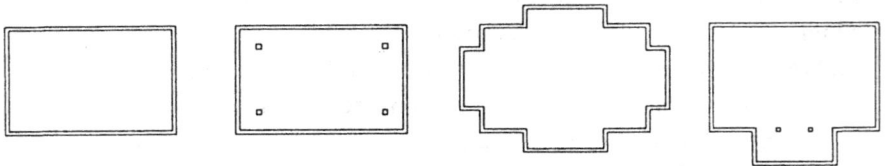

Fig. 121. Spatial appendixes.

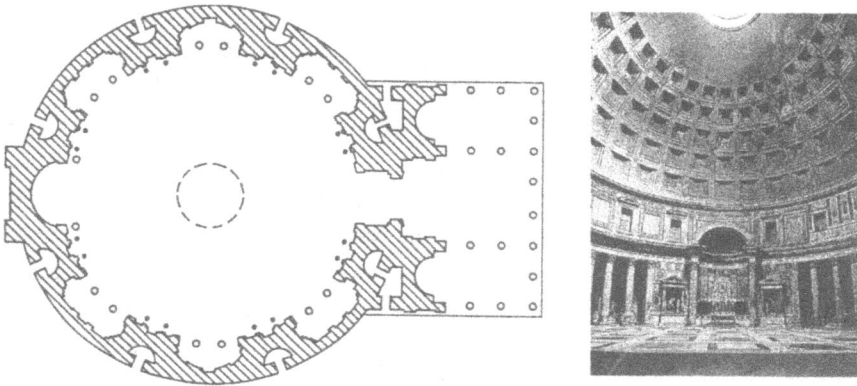

Fig.122. & Fig.123 Pantheon, Rome. Plan & Interior.

of hierarchical organization can be found in the subdivision of single spaces by means of articulating elements such as columns, or by the addition of small appendixes such as niches, alcoves, or bay windows. The appearance of a distinct spatial segregation can be further enhanced by boundaries created through differences in floor pattern, ceiling height, or texture.

Despite the addition of small appendixes, a main space can retain its figural character; in fact, spatial segregation often increases the overall sense of perceptual concavity. The addition of small appendixes can also cause the lateral

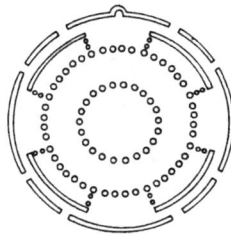

Fig.124. S. Stefano Rotondo, Rome

173

boundaries to become more dominant, because the boundaries themselves now contain spatial centers created by subordinate spaces. However, when symmetrically placed in relation to a main center, peripheral spatial subcenters often reinforce the main center. An example of this effect is in the Pantheon in Rome (Fig.122), where the dominance of the central interior space is not compromised by the various niches and chapels which rhythmically break its lateral boundaries. Normally, semicircular shapes such as that of the Pantheon exhibit low perceptual complexity because they possess such strong figural autonomy that their boundaries serve as little more than a perceptual ground for the spatial figure. However, the fact that the various concavities in the Pantheon's boundaries each attain distinct figural character creates a more complex and interesting spatial experience.

The effect of ancillary spatial centers can be even stronger when a primary central space is entirely surrounded by a secondary shape. The success of this

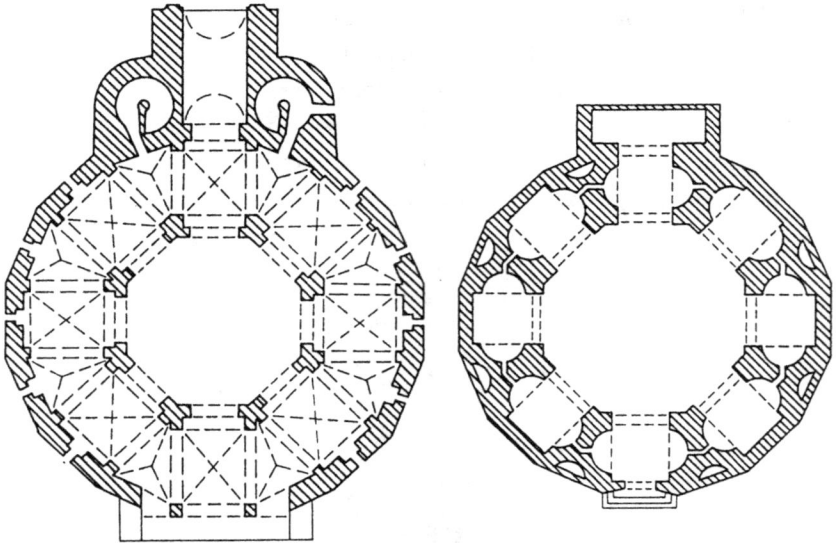

Fig.125. Palatine Chapel, Aachen. Fig.126. Sta. Maria degli Angeli. Florence

effect, however, is a matter of degree, and depends on the density of the elements separating the spatial entities. For instance, in the case of S. Stefano Rotondo in Rome (Fig. 124) the boundary formed by the columns of the inner space is of such low perceptual density that the surrounding spaces become visually annexed by the center. And because the surrounding space itself is encircled by one more spatial ring, the surrounding space is perceived as a separator between the center and the outer ring. From the center, this intermediary space is experienced as a multilayered, diaphanous boundary.

Spatial systems can be formed both by *subdivision* of a larger unit, as above, or by *addition* of similar or different parts. In his classification of Renaissance and Baroque architecture, Paul Frankl distinguishes between two principal types of spaces: *groups* and *series*. Groups are organized around main centers, while series are characterized by pronounced spatial direction. Frankl further distinguishes between simple groups and groups of higher order, those where the ancillary spaces themselves have further ancillary spaces attached to them.[19] Examples of simple groups might be said to include Sta. Maria degli Angeli in Florence (Fig. 126), and the Palatine Chapel in Aachen (Fig. 125). In both these cases the ancillary spaces form *coordinated* arrangements, i.e., they consist of

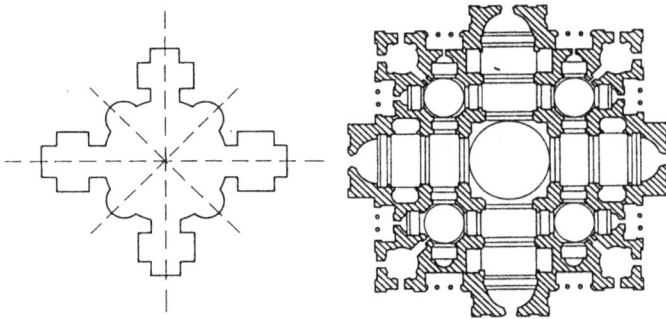

Fig. 127. Sta. Maria della Croce, Crema (left).
Fig. 128. St. Peter, Rome: Bramante's plan (right).

similar units. However, in the case of Sta. Maria the units are independent appendices that induce four pronounced axes within the central space, while in the Palatine Chapel the adjacent spaces are connected with the central space to form a single perceptual unit that is subdivided into different areas by pillars, arches, and differences in floor pattern.

The greater the number of subgroups in a spatial system, the higher its absolute complexity. But, due to the possibility of increasing redundancy at inferior levels of organization, the absolute complexity of such a configuration can be comparatively high without exceeding the brain's capacity to process complex orders. In such instances actual complexity may be considerably higher than perceptual complexity. However, a spatial system's actual complexity can be further increased when its ancillary spaces are *rhythmically*, rather than coordinately, arranged. Rhythms can be created by differences in format, size or articulation of spatial appendices. Frankl calls such cases "groups of second order with rhythmical ancillary centers."[20] Thus, in Sta. Maria della Croce in Crema (Fig.127), two different pairs of axes give primary and secondary orientation to a circular main space. And in Bramante's first design for St. Peter's (Fig.128), the

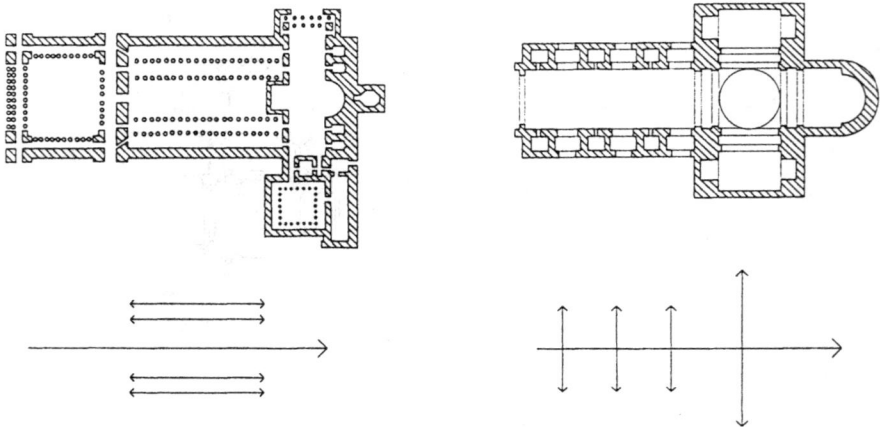

Fig.129. S. Paolo f.l.m., Rome. Fig.130. S. Andrea, Mantua.

basic shape of the plan in the form of a symmetrical cross retains its dominance over induced diagonal axes at the same time that each ancillary center possesses rhythmically arranged ancillary centers of its own, forming "a rhythmical group of a rhythmical group."[21] In both these examples primary spaces retain overall dominance because of their prominent location, which forms the pivot for other subordinate, centrally symmetrical arrangements. However, a clear hierarchy of scale also contributes to this dominance, as the redundancy of parts increases with their decreasing size within the entire arrangement.

A serial configuration can occur as a simple coordination or as a rhythmical arrangement of spaces. Simple, coordinated arrangement of similar spaces in a series results in a fairly static overall arrangement with a single, dominant direction. A serial configuration can occur as a simple coordination or a rhythmical arrangement of spaces. The simple coordinated arrangement of similar spaces without ancillary spaces results in static units with a dominant direction. Adding ancillary spaces with the same orientation as the main spatial units will not necessarily reinforce the directionality of the existing arrangement. Often the boundaries between primary and ancillary spaces attain a figural character that is strong enough to rival the main space. An example of such strong lateral attraction is found in the basilica of S. Paolo on the outskirts of Rome (Fig.129). Here the primary space retains its dominance due to its greater height and width. But in other places the strong directional pull of such long formats can be countered by ancillary spaces with a different orientation, as with S. Andrea in Mantua (Fig.130). Instead of being flanked by aisles, the nave of this church has laterally aligned chapels which induce a set of secondary axes perpendicular to the main axis. The dominance of the ancillary spaces in such an arrangement may be further enhanced when these are organized in a rhythmical fashion that breaks the uniformity of subdivisions within the lateral boundaries, and thus weakens the self-contained figural character of the space.

The less uniform the boundaries of a primary space become due to rhythmical spacing, the more these boundaries tend to assume a figural strength of their own and compete with the spatial figure. The pilgrimage church of Vierzehnheiligen

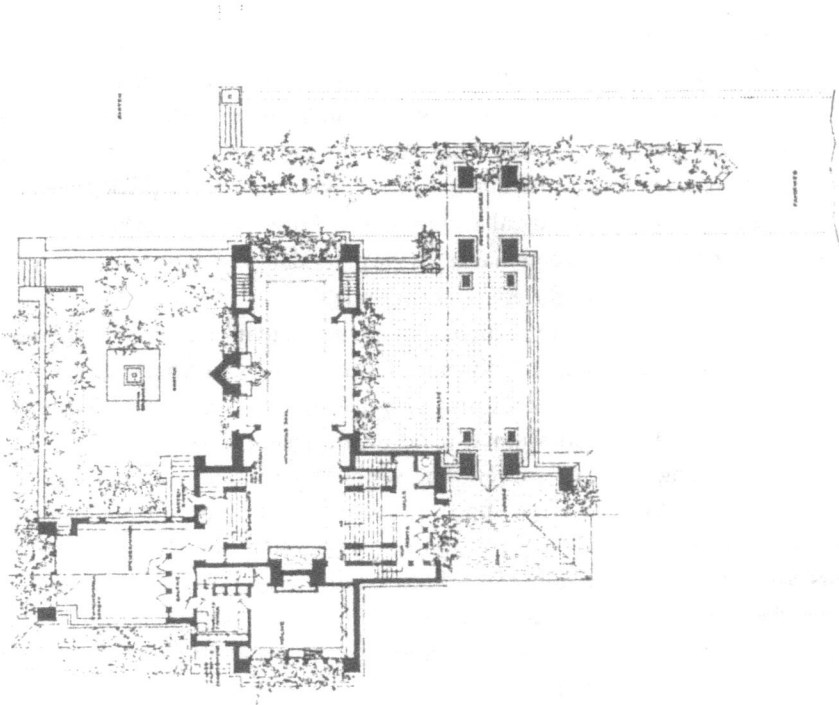

Fig.131. F.L. Wright, Clark Residence.

is imbued with such spatial structure to the point where its overall spatial form is hardly comprehensible (Fig.92,93). The church features five elliptical and two circular spaces formed by concave boundaries. None of these attain clear figural definition, however, and therefore they appear fragmentary. The main reason is that the uniformly articulated ceiling, with its ancillary lunettes, tends to create the sense of a larger shape incongruent with the spatial entities formed by the lateral boundaries. Whereas the plan indicates a spatial center formed by the crossing of the fragmented transept and the nave, three-dimensional reality contradicts this effect. In reality, the convex transepts merge with the rudimentary

178

concave aisles, and the centers of the vaults do not align with the center of the crossing. The figural character of the enclosed space is further weakened by the placement of the tabernacle in the middle of the main ellipse — a corporeal center that competes with the fulcrum of the cruciform space. The rivalry between interlocking spaces, and between spatial and corporeal form, is a perfect example of the intentional ambiguity of the late Southern German Baroque.

In the previously discussed examples, the distribution of spatial centers is always characterized by a symmetrical arrangement. All parts of a spatial system are thus organized in an orderly, balanced relationship. But when a spatial arrangement is asymmetrical, such as in Frank Lloyd Wright's Clark

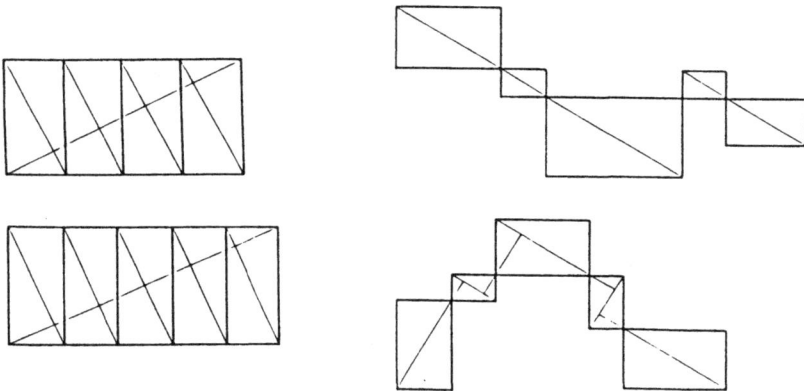

Fig.132. *Congruent shapes, same size.* **Fig.133.** *Congruent shapes of different size.*

Residence (Fig.131), the whole can still assume spatial balance — although this must be achieved using different sizes and formats of subspaces, each of which will attain a different perceptual dominance. In the Clark Residence, the primary space is not formed by a clearly bounded unit; rather, it functions as the pivot for various interpenetrating shapes. Such an area, which may not be clearly defined by lateral boundaries, can be segregated by, for example,

179

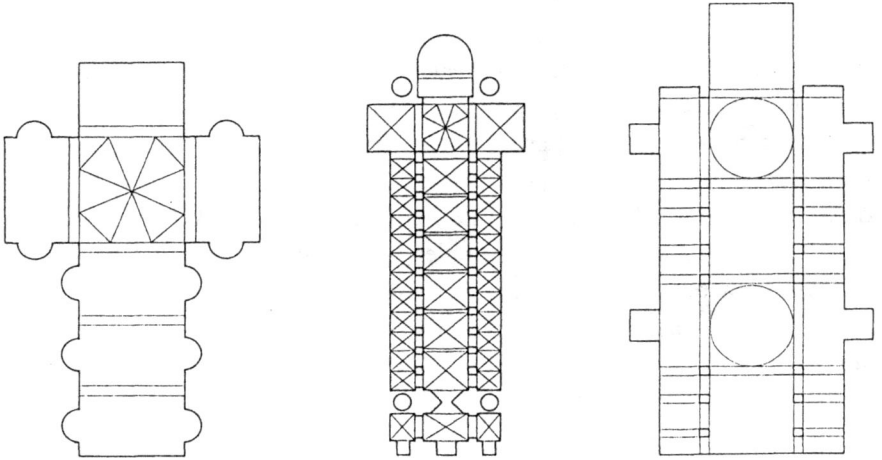

Fig.134. S. Maria del Caleinaio. Fig.135. Cathedral, Speyer.
Fig.136. SS. Flora e Lucilla, Arezzo.

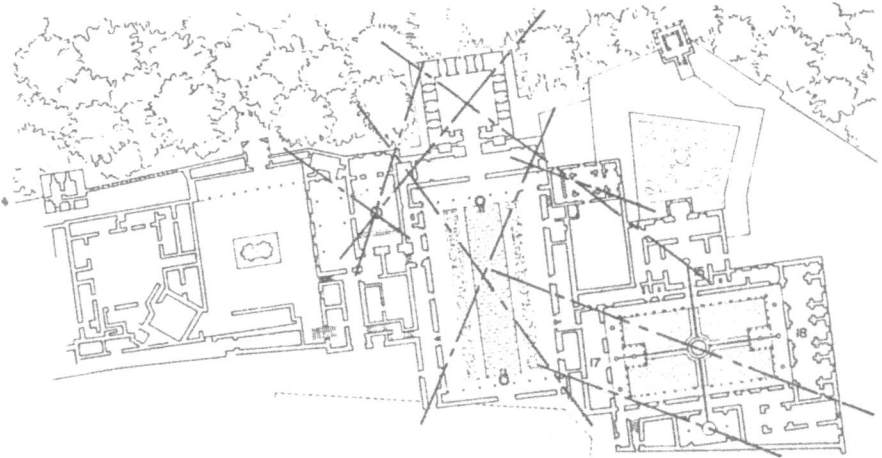

Fig.137. Alhambra, Granada. Principal proportional relationships

raising the ceilings, lowering the floor, or using differently textured materials. The figural definition, however, remains weak, for parts of both the spatial and the corporeal form tend to take on figural status.

Perceptual Congruity and Orderliness

Perceptual wholeness of a spatial system presupposes that its individual components share common, permeating orders with each other and with the organization of the system as a whole. Among the simpler ways of producing wholeness in complex spatial arrangements is the use of *congruities* among the spaces within an ensemble, or the use of an underlying *modular* system.

In strictly mathematical terms, congruent shapes are the same in all of their characteristics; in perceptual terms, however, one can speak of congruent shapes whenever one feels a family resemblance in the principal character of the shapes within a spatial group. Congruity is achieved most clearly when the individual spaces of a group are of the same or similar proportion. (Fig. 132) exemplifies the case of congruent spaces of the same size; (Fig. 133) shows congruent shapes of different size.

Spatial arrangements consisting of *additive groups* or *a series of congruent shapes* are comparatively rare in architecture. The diagrammatic plan of Sta. Maria del Calcinaio provides an example where all spaces except those in the crossing of the naves are of the same shape and size. A slightly more complex example involves the typical plan of a Romanesque church, such as that of the cathedral in Speyer, in which the cross vaults of the lateral aisles are congruent to those of the main aisle yet are a quarter of their size.

More common than the use of simple congruities is the rhythmical alternation of two or more different types of spaces within a larger system. In the example of SS. Flora e Lucilla in Arezzo (Fig. 136), spaces with barrel vaults and spaces with domes alternate rhythmically within the main aisle. This rhythm is also the permeating principle for the lateral axes of the church, where it is carried out with smaller shapes which are congruent to the larger

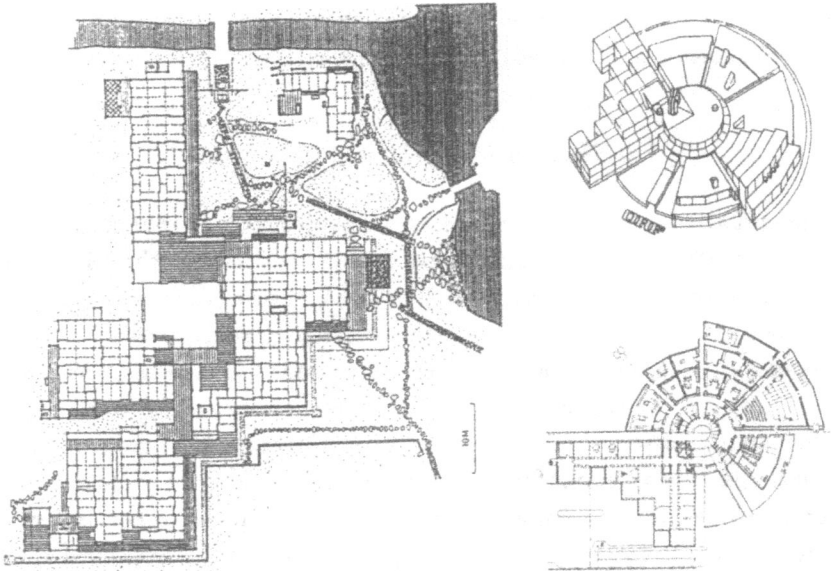

Fig. 138. Katsura Villa, Kyoto. Fig. 139. ORF Studio, Salzburg (G. Peichl).

spaces of the central aisle. Larger and smaller spaces are thus perceptually connected through a common order.

The Alhambra in Grenada is another example where a seemingly complex plan shows great simplicity of organization. The design of the major spaces is based on two types of shapes with similar proportions — squares and rectangles — in which the rectangles roughly approach the combined dimension of two squares. The shapes are arranged in a rectangular grid and positioned so that their lengthened diagonals almost precisely cut through the vertices of the diagonals of the other respective main shapes (Fig. 137). Perceptual congruity, however, does not necessarily demand such exactitude;

a mere family resemblance in the appearance of shapes will often suffice. For example, the Piazza S. Marco and the Piazzetta in Venice show nearly similar formats, thus being perceptually congruent.

In contrast to such systems of congruent shapes, ordering through an underlying modular system is often less apparent. Here, individual rooms may be of any proportion as long as their boundaries are placed on the lines and nodes of the common grid. Whereas in systems of congruent shapes there is an apparent order at the macrostructural level of the spatial units, in modular systems the order permeates at a microstuctural level.

A classical example of formal harmony achieved through the use of an underlying grid is the Katsura Villa in Kyoto (Fig.138). In such Japanese examples, it is the dimension of the tatami mat that defines a single increment whose multiples can determine a broad range of spatial sizes. The overall plan of the Katsura complex shows that each building has different proportion and size, and that only few of the interiors are congruent in shape. However, the tatami mats, as well as the panels that form the spatial boundaries, clearly determine an underlying order that permeates the system. Another case of an integrated system based on a modular order is Gustav Peichl's ORF broadcasting studio. Here, two modular grids, one rectilinear and the other radial, are combined. The result is a circular shape subdivided into concentric circles spaced at equal increments and partitioned into eight sectors. In two of the sectors the radial-concentric grid is replaced by a standard right-angle modular grid. In both cases, the Katsura Villa and the ORF Studio, standardization and prefabrication of building components go hand in hand with an harmonious design.

VIII

Corporeal Form

In moving through architectural space, either the form of an enclosed space or the form of its spatial boundaries can exert primary perceptual dominance. Yet even if the solids, planes and objects of architectural form seem perceptually secondary to a more dominant spatial figure they enclose, it is ultimately the organization of the tangible elements which determines the character of the visible form. While the previous chapter concentrated primarily on the form of enclosed space, this chapter will focus on the properties of space-bounding and space-accentuating elements. Specifically, the issue of visual harmony will be discussed. In this matter the concept of visual stability will be found to play a crucial role. Notions of visual balance and stability are prominently addressed in many theories of the visual arts and architecture, arguing that the composition of a drawing, a painting, or a building is judged as harmonious, balanced, or stable on intuitive grounds. Is the use of such a characterization merely metaphorical, or is there an actual physiological or psychological basis for such judgements? I begin with an analysis of the basic perceptual properties of shapes.

1. Shape, Mass and Center

Perceptually, a configuration is a network of relationships between interacting shapes. The appearance of the individual shape within the whole depends on its *dynamic properties*, its *location*, and its *perceptual mass*. In perceptual terms, a shape is not simply a face bounded by a contour; it is an entity whose parts have different visual impact. Dynamic properties operate in different directions and with different magnitudes, thus producing varying tensions at the contour and inducing a variety of perceptual centers. These nodes of attraction are the hubs around which perceptual forces come into balance. The distribution of dominant and subordinate centers represents the basic structure of simple shapes and larger compositions, and the different impact of these fulcrums is a major factor in the perception of order within a work of art. Perceptual centers can be thought of in a number of ways: as centers of balance between perceptual forces; as areas of high potential energy in the corresponding field of the visual cortex; or as centers of fixation for the eyes during the process of visual scanning.

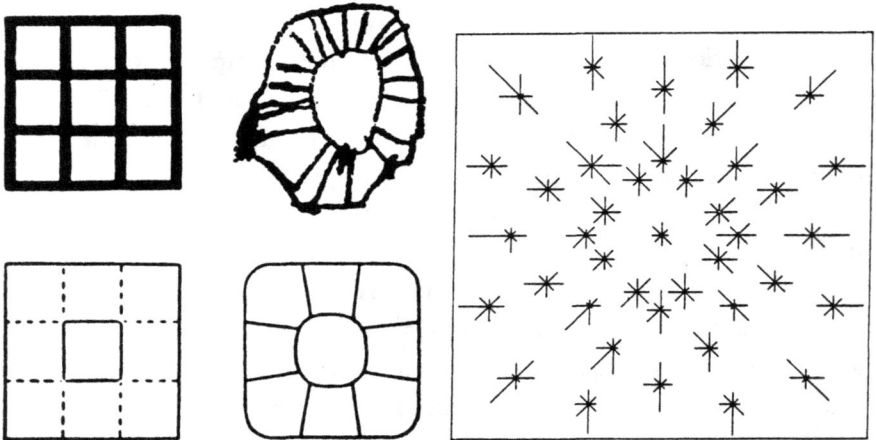

Fig.140. Induction of centers in Drawings of Homogeneous Patterns [after Metzger].
Fig.141. Relative perceptual stability is strongest at center [after Goude & Hjorzberg].

Arnheim[1] defines a visual balancing center as "the principal locus of attraction and repulsion," an area at which the "vectors constituting a visual pattern are in equilibrium."[2] To sustain this definition, he cites experiments by Goude and Hjorzberg[3] which suggest that the observed directional tendencies of various points distributed over a simple shape show both a relative stability around a principal midpoint and a strong radial orientation towards the periphery, especially along the principal axes of the shape (Fig. 141). The dominance of the center, even in homogeneously arranged patterns, has also been noted by Metzger,[4] who writes of a *law of the common middle*. He shows that people's drawings from memory after tachistoscopic presentations of grid-like patterns clearly overemphasize the midpoint. Children's drawings of the same patterns after longer exposure also display the same tendency (Fig. 140).

A similar explanation is offered by the field hypothesis of the Gestalt psychologists. Kurt Koffka described figural segregation as the result of the greater density of potential energy in a figure compared to the surrounding cortial field.[5] This assumption is further supported by the rule that the ground is always simpler than the figure — that is, that out of a given number of shapes of similar contour and size, those with the strongest textural articulation will always assume figural status.[6] If the amount of potential energy is assumed to decrease toward the ground, then it seems plausible that such energy must increase toward the center. Experiments have, in fact, shown a greater resistance by enclosed areas to the intrusion of shapes projected upon them. For example, it takes greater intensity to make a spot of light visible on a surface when the spot is projected in the center of a shape than when it is projected onto a surrounding area.[7]

However, the above explanations allow generalizations only about the location of perceptual fulcrums in simple, symmetrical shapes. A more promising explanation of the role of visual centers may come from the study of eye movements. These offer some possibility for locating visual centers in more complex configurations. Eye-movement studies may also help describe how the directional properties and masses of shapes influence the location of internal centers of interest, and the varying durations of eye fixations that they cause. The human eye is an extremely mobile organ; it can shift up to 250 times per minute (saccadic movement). But clear vision occurs only when the eye fixates, allowing the fovea, the point of clearest vision on the retina, to be directed toward a particular area. The fovea, an area which covers a cone of vision roughly two degrees in size, is characterized by a concentration of cones — receptor cells which operate at high illumination, allowing the perception of fine detail and differences in color.[8] Naturally, the fovea will be directed at areas of high articulation and contrast; and, when a shape is uniformly articulated, this area will normally be that where the visual forces converge, namely, the visual center.[9]

Indeed, as plot diagrams of eye movements indicate, the eyes do not follow the contours of shapes, but rather scan along the main directions induced by and around central concave areas.[10] Nor do the eyes move continuously: rather, they make short, fast jumps, called saccades, which cluster around targets of interest, as can be seen in a graph of fixations for Manet's *Olympia* (Fig. 142). In this example, the central area of the painting receives the greatest number of fixations, followed by the woman's and the servant's upper bodies. These three areas constitute the principal centers of interest.[11]

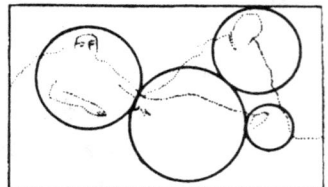

Fig. 142. Scanning diagram of Manet's Olympia (after Molnar).

Though eye-scanning patterns do not allow conclusions about such things as figural segregation, they do allow analysis of the relative perceptual interest aroused by the different stimuli in visual displays. It is evident from such analyses that fixations are not uniformly distributed over a visual display, but rather, as Mackworth and Morandi[12] have shown, that they cluster around angles, junctions, and areas of high contrast. The duration of fixations also varies over different points of interest, with highly contrasting and symmetrical areas showing repetitious fixations. And although different observers often exhibit similarities in their initial fixations on a display, scanning patterns may come to differ with prolonged exposure — especially when, as demonstrated by Noton and Stark,[13] the observers are asked to relate to the meaning of the display. Nevertheless, according to Molnar,[14] the statistical distribution of fixations between different people is nearly always identical. And Kaufmann and Richards[15] have shown that the most explored area in a display is the visual center of gravity, whose location is determined by the distribution of the principal centers and their perceptual masses.

Further evidence of the selectivity of visual attention is shown in Buswell's plot diagrams of paintings and photographs. These show a considerable density of fixation at areas of high contrast, along symmetry axes, and along the vertical axes of shapes and larger composite patterns. For example, when looking at a picture of a cathedral interior, subjects' fixations tended to cluster around the rose window, the organ, and the entryway (Fig. 143). A careful study of such plot diagrams further indicates that in simple shapes, fixations tend to cluster around the middle, and that a hierarchy of density of fixations develops from the more dominant to the more redundant features of a pattern. Additionally, the ground, or negative space, generally induces fewer fixations than the figural area, and regular shapes form stronger centers of attraction then irregular ones.

When scanning patterns are analyzed according to concentration and duration of fixations, it becomes apparent that the predominant targets of fixation are those whose figural character is strong, meaning that a correlation

Fig. 143. Scanning diagram of cathedral interior (after Buswell).

appears to exist between centers of attraction and the laws of figural segregation. Fixations are also more likely to occur in areas which are *concave* and *enclosed*, meaning that the area inside a contour dominates the area outside. Furthermore, foci are predominantly induced at the *radius point* of convex contours. *Heterogeneous* elements in otherwise homogeneous arrangements also trigger primary fixation reflexes, for these more readily assume figural character.[16] The same can be said for *contrasting* areas; to be able to perceive complex detail, the foveae have to be directed to these areas. The difference between perceived and measured distance in numerous visual illusions can be explained through the distance between eye movements. For instance, the Müller-Lyer illusion (Fig. 144) may be explained by the differences in the magnitude of eye movements between the two principal centers induced by the concave contours of the arrowheads.

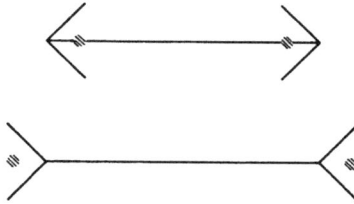

Fig.144. Eye-movement theory of the Müller-Lyer illusion.

Some generalizations about the location of fulcrums in simple shapes can be derived from the different approaches to defining perceptual centers. However, the concept of centers and their positions used in the following discussion remains an abstraction, locating perceptual centers where the likelihood of fixation clusters is relatively strong. Although Brandt[17] has found that the median location of the initial fixations in centrally symmetrical fields can be located roughly in the middle, it can be noted that, in the case of redundant features, fixations are not triggered for each of these. Thus, not all secondary centers provoke fixations.

Centrally symmetrical, concavely bounded shapes without a prominent orientation, such as circles, squares or pentagons, possess a single perceptual center whose location is identical with the geometric midpoint.[18] In centrally symmetrical shapes which possess boundaries that are both convex and concave, additional centers of secondary impact will be induced outside those

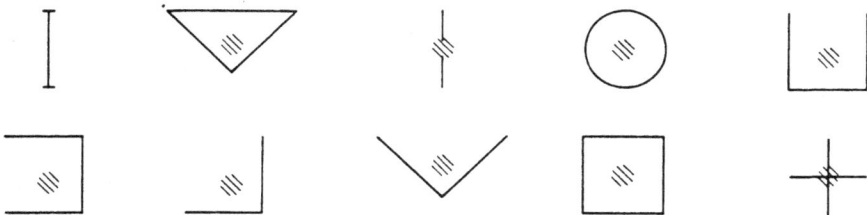

Fig.145. Median location of spontaneous fixation position in simple shapes.

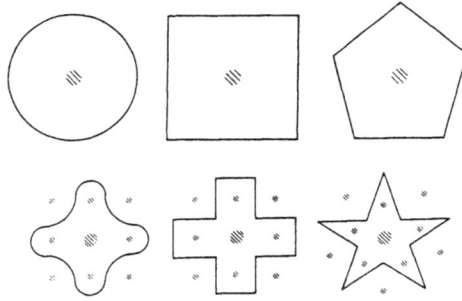

Fig.146. Location of perceptual centers in symmetrical shapes.

parts of the contour which are convex relative to the inside of the shape.

Whenever a shape possesses a dominant vertical axis, a dislocation of the perceptual center caused by an overestimation of the vertical takes place. I have already mentioned that Metzger assumes this overestimation to be around 28 percent. In *vertically elongated* shapes, this dislocation pulls the perceptual center upward. But the effect of the shape's concavity also creates a perceptual distortion, because the concavity in general induces perceptual centers at similar distances from the contour. Interestingly enough, rectangles of a proportion slightly less then the golden ratio seem to combine the two factors without rivalry. In such shapes, the center induced by the concavity of the lateral and the upper boundary occurs at a location roughly two-thirds of the way up the vertical axis, creating a single strong center. However, when the format of the shape exceeds a ratio of 1:2, no distinct perceptual center can be induced, because the center which results from concavity is incongruent with the perceived vertical midpoint. The effect of concavity is particularly strong when parts of the contour are semicircular and the radius point tends to induce a fulcrum.

The effect of a strong center is not common to all concave shapes. In *horizontally elongated* shapes, those which exceed the ratio of 1:2, no clear center is induced. Buswell's studies of the fixations of borders have shown zigzag shifts without particular dominant clusters of interest.[19] Complex visual patterns, as earlier maintained, may be thought of as hierarchically organized perceptual structures, in which centers of varying impact operate at every level. The centers of the subordinate levels group together with larger centers of the whole composition to form one or several main centers. Additionally, it may be noted that centers are not only induced by shapes. Arnheim[20] claims that in more complex patterns, perceptual nodes are generated by *clusters of shapes, sheaves of concentric radii, or crossings of axes.*

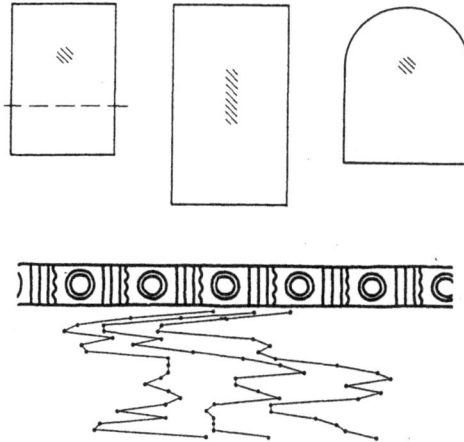

Fig.147. *Centers in elongated shapes.* Fig.148. *Fixations in borders.*

As much as the dynamic character of a pattern is a matter of the directional properties of shapes and the location and interaction of the various centers induced by contours, it is also a matter of the *perceived heaviness* of the various parts of the configuration. And among other factors, the perceptual intensity of a visual pattern will depend on the distribution of its principal masses. This concept of perceptual balance has only been explained in rudimentary form. For example, Kaufmann and Richards[21] have attempted calculations of the distribution of visual weights in patterns. But their work has only concerned simple patterns, because numerous factors influence perceived weight, and the interdependence between them has not yet been satisfactorily established. However, some principal factors leading to a determination of perceptual weight can be formulated, and they may suffice for the following consideration.

Three major factors of perceptual weight are *size, tone* and *articulation.* Thus, a larger shape appears heavier than a smaller one of the same type, a darker shape appears heavier than a lighter one, and an articulated shape appears heavier than one with an empty surface. In addition, *regularity* can also be assumed to contribute to the weight of a shape because of the effect of perceptual dominance. The example from the Graves test (Fig. 149) shows how a circle, which is the most regular shape, can counterbalance a rectangle and a triangle, even though the latter are comparably larger.[22]

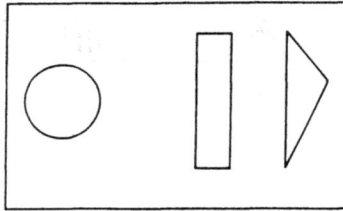

Fig.149. A small regular shape is able to balance two comparably larger shapes (pattern from Graves test).

Arnheim mentions several additional factors that must be considered when evaluating perceptual weight: *isolation, location* and *direction.*[23] For instance, a shape which is placed on an isolated ground assumes more weight than one which is located adjacent to other figures. It is interesting to note within this context that Brandt[24] found that the attention paid to a particular shape increases as the amount of emptiness on a surface around it increases.

It follows that the same shape can assume greater visual weight when it is placed in a peripheral position than when it is placed at the center or along one of the main axes of a larger shape. This implies that 'heavy' shapes in the center of a large configuration can be counterbalanced by 'lighter' shapes on the periphery. A final important determinant of relative weight is that vertically oriented shapes appear to be heavier than obliquely oriented ones.[25]

2. Perceptual Stability

The previous discussion of shape, mass and center allows a number of conclusions about the perceived stability of shapes and configurations. In architecture, the appearance of stability is an important factor because the 'gravitational pull' toward the horizontal plane on which a building is rooted relates to the viewer's kinesthetic frame of reference. That a building's appearance can be 'top-heavy', or 'stably rooted', can be understood as a result of the arrangement of the perceptual centers and the distribution of the shapes' perceptual masses.

Fig.150/151. Ledoux. Barriers, Paris. Top-heavy vs. Stable appearance.

A good example of a top-heavy versus a stable arrangement can be seen in the comparison of two of Ledoux' *Barriers* which use a similar formal pattern for the center and top part of the building, but a different base. In the case of the colonnade substituting for a wall, the main masses of the building are clearly located in the upper sectors of the facade: the light appearance of the columns and their interstices hardly indicate an ability to carry the visual mass above. In the second case, the central and upper parts of the building rest on a base which is visually heavy itself, thus leading to the appearance of a stably rooted building.

The perceived stability of a shape rests on three major factors: its *format* and *orientation* along principal directions induced by the contours of the shape; the *orientation* and *dominance of the axes* induced by the various primary and subordinate centers; and the *distribution of the perceptual mass* of the surface in relation to the main perceptual center.

For most traditional architecture, the first factor is of almost negligible importance. The main shapes of a building usually adhere to the Cartesian frame of reference, and any deviation from the principal horizontal and vertical axes of this system would violate the observer's kinesthetic sense of balance. More recently, however, an architectural style under the heading of 'Deconstruction' has made its mark by deviating from the Cartesian rectilinear system of order. Instead, oblique axes of orientation are used which are usually carefully counterbalanced by other oblique axes in different directions. Also, strong verticals or nearly vertically oriented axes elsewhere in the building can compensate for a possible feeling of instability. A good example is the design proposal for the First Media Tower in Hamburg by the group Co-Op Himmelblau (Fig.152).

This example also shows that a factor far more critical for the perceived stability of a shape is the distribution of principal masses. While traditional architecture relies more on a symmetrical arrangement of the major visual masses in facade, it has become quite common in examples of contemporary architecture to work with asymmetric yet balanced compositions, as shown in Morphosis' Sixth Street Project in Los Angeles (Fig.153). Here, the masses of the opening

196

Fig.152. Co-Op Himmelblau. First Media Tower, Hamburg.
Fig.153. Morphosis Sixth St. Project.

are balanced by the masses of the negative spaces of the facade.

Equally important is the orientation of the axes along which the various visual centers in a pattern or a facade are aligned. For instance, in Fig.154a, two sets of subordinate centers with different dominance are induced in addition to the main focus in the center of the star. The centers induced in the larger arms of the pattern exert a stronger impact due to their size   and the

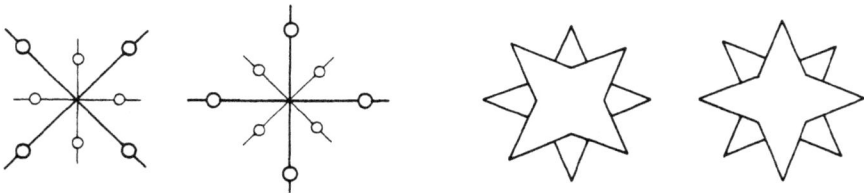

Fig.154 Perceptual stability as a result of distribution of visual centers.

uninterrupted contour, causing the appearance of one figure in front of the other.

The diagram in Fig.154c. shows an alignment of the stronger centers along the horizontal and the vertical and the weaker centers along the diagonals. In this case, the secondary centers enhance the stability of the whole because they balance around the main center. Yet, when the pattern is rotated by 45 degrees (Fig.154d), the axes of the principal orientation induced by the dominant centers are the diagonals, causing the figure to appear less stable. The reason for this is that the primary centers also produce two parallel sets of vertical and horizontal axes. Several axes are competing: the underlying structure is not as simple as in the former case.

The example of a cross inscribed in the square (Fig.155a,b) would seem to contradict these observations. Tests[26] have shown that when people were shown the figure in horizontal-vertical orientation, their later drawings from

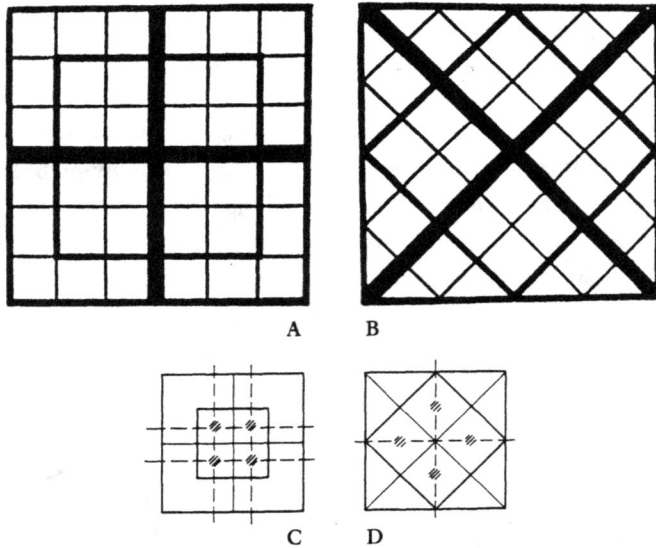

A B

C D

Fig. 155 Greater stability resulting from simplicity of distribution of axis of perceptual center.

memory showed it in an orientation, as in Fig.155b. When the distribution of the principal centers in the two patterns is accounted for, it becomes clear that Fig.155b is the simpler of the two. This is because the centers in each of the four squares of Fig.155b induce only one horizontal and one vertical axis each, whereas the pattern in Fig.155a also allows a diagonal alignment of the centers. Since the underlying grid has a strong horizontal-vertical orientation, two additional, yet less dominant, sets of horizontal and vertical axes are also

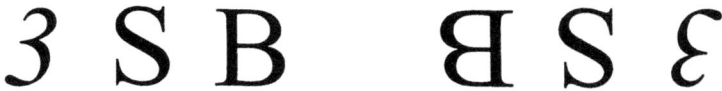

3 S B   B S Ɛ

Fig.156. Letters and numbers placed upside-down: top-heaviness results.

induced. Thus, in terms of horizontal-vertical alignment Fig.155b is simpler.

The perceived stability of a shape depends predominantly on the distribution of its surface weight in relation to its perceptual midpoint. As a rule, the more a figure's weight is located beneath its fulcrum the more it is perceived as being stable. This fact is quite familiar to typographers, who make the upper part of B's or S's shorter than the bottom part to avoid a macrocephalic appearance.

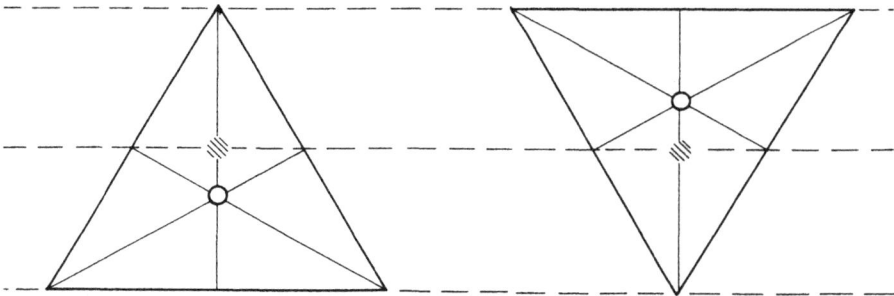

Fig.157. Equilateral triangle: location of center of gravity and perceptual center.

This principle of stability can be demonstrated by looking at an equilateral triangle in different orientations. When this figure rests on its base, it appears more stable then when it stands on its vertex. As an explanation I suggest the following: in the base-down case, the main weight of the shape is located beneath its perceptual center. When the triangle is turned upside down, the center of balance is located above the vertical midpoint, slightly above or coincident with the perceptual center of the shape. If it is true that the latter triangle appears perceptually less stable than the former, then it follows that for a shape to be in a perceptually stable position, its main weight must be located beneath its perceptual fulcrum. The fact that the distribution of perceptual weight is unisotropic must also be taken into account. The visual weight of a configuration increases with increasing distance from its base. In other words, the upper parts of a pattern appear to be heavier than the lower parts. This further adds to the visual instability of the upside-down triangle. A possible explanation of this phenomenon might be found in Brandt's[27] observation that the statistical distribution of the locations and duration of fixations is higher by two-thirds in the upper parts of empty shapes than it is in the lower parts, causing the upper parts to attain visual dominance.

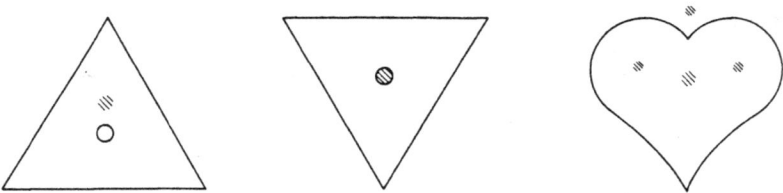

Fig.158. Distributions of centers of gravity and perceptual centers in different shapes.

However, when this principle is applied, why does, for example, a heart-shaped figure not appear to be unstable, even though its principal orientation is similar to that of the unstable triangle? One reason may be that the concavity of the top part of the contour induces two major foci inside the upper area of the shape and a third one of slightly less strength outside the contour. In addition, the abrupt change in the continuation of the contour produces an additional center. In the heart shape, again, all the major perceptual centers are located above the actual center of balance. This example also shows that the negative space, or *ground*, has to be taken into consideration. This is especially the case with articulated shapes which contain shapes within them, but it also applies to figures which produce strong negative spaces with rudimentary figural character at the outside of the contour.

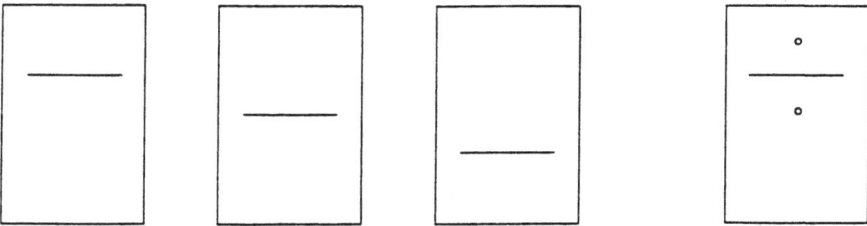

Fig.159. a - d

For articulated shapes the analysis of stability poses a slightly more complex problem. When stability is desired, the articulated area which adds a visual weight of its own does not necessarily need to be positioned at the lower part of the figure. Rather, the influence of this additional weight depends on the weight of the surrounding negative spaces and on the perceptual weight of the shape itself. This can be demonstrated with a simple rectangle divided by a horizontal line.

The reasons that the shape in Fig.159a appear stable may be twofold: first, the position of the inner shape roughly coincides with the main fulcrum of the rectangle; and, second, there is a noticeable relation of the symmetrical position of the smaller centers induced by the segregated spaces within the shape in relation to the main center. This second condition may be compared to the condition of the shape in Fig.159c, where the distribution of foci is asymmetrical. In the latter figure, the centers compete, creating a situation where there can be no balance of inferior centers around a main center; hence, the shape is not in equilibrium. (Tests[28] have shown a clear preference for Fig.159a, and it is tempting to assume a correlation between this preference and perceptual balance.) Theoretically, it should be possible to calculate the position of the line in order to arrive at a symmetrical position of the centers of the negative spaces. The example of the facade of the Villa Rotonda shows such a perfect position; in that case, the placement of windows laterally perfectly accompanies the Villa's porch.

With a triangular figure the case is different. In the upright position, Fig.160b was clearly preferred over Fig.160a and Fig.160c; but in the upside down version, Fig.160f was preferred over Fig.160d and Fig.160e.[29] Only when the black dot is placed in the center of the triangle are the negative spaces equal in size and thus of similar perceptual importance, allowing them to balance around the main center of the shape. When the dot is located at the bottom of the triangle, the impact of the negative space at the top of the triangle is stronger than that of the lateral ones, and it rivals the stronger center of the dot. In terms of the distribution of centers, the figure is not in equilibrium.

The situation is different when the triangle rests on its vertex. Here, Fig.160f is clearly preferred to Fig.160d or Fig.160e — although the triangle is also relatively stable with the dot in the central position. In Fig.160d, three perceptual centers are induced in the 'ground' of the triangle relative to the 'figure' of the central circular shape. The center which is located in the lower region is the strongest of these. Again, two principal centers located at the vertical axis are competing. And again, perceptual weight has to be taken into account. This means that the principal weights of the pattern are located in the upper region, that the dot as well as the larger area of the surface of the triangle are located above the perceptual center. All these factors lead to the triangle appearing unstable. In Fig.160f, the

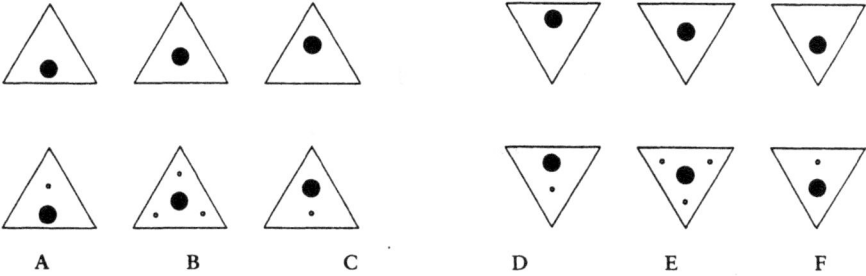

Fig.160.

weight of the dot compensates for the weight of the negative space above, and the
shape appears more stable than in Fig.160d. Furthermore, simplicity plays an
important role. Only in this case do all the perceptual centers align along the
main symmetry axis, thus adding to the stability of the configuration.

It is apparent that, in the design of facades, both positive and negative
spaces have to be accounted for in discussing stability. Whether or not these
shapes are bounded is particularly important. For example, the shapes of the

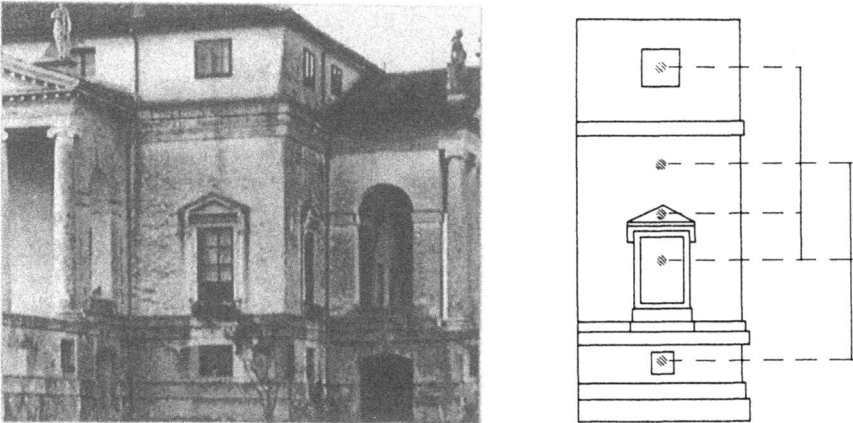

Fig.161a,b. Villa Rotonda, Vicenza. Effects of balanced centers.

lateral windows of the Villa Rotonda are connected to a horizontal ledge, causing the main center of the negative space to be induced above the shape of the window and allowing the center of the window, and the center of the negative space to balance symmetrically around the aedicula.

In comparison, when the lower sill is removed, an additional center is induced beneath the window, and the three centers can only be brought into balance when the shape of the window is shortened considerably. Thus, the lower sill is an important means for achieving local stability of windows within a facade. Furthermore, when windows are connected with sills, and when a stable appearance is desired, the sill ought to be connected to the bottom of the window rather than to the top. When windows are placed in an isolated location, stability is best achieved when they are placed slightly above the central position. However, this rule holds only for shapes that are nearly square; the more a window is elongated vertically, the lower it has to be placed in order for it to allow a symmetrical arrangement of vertically aligned centers.

Fig. 162, 163, 164 Placement of windows with and without sills

Vertical Accents

One of the most fundamental phenomena in the perception of space is the human body's tendency toward orthogonal localization.[30] The two cardinal dimensions, the horizontal and the vertical, provide the framework for stability as well as for the apparent dynamic properties of a building. The interplay between the vertical and the horizontal has been one of the most critical design tools in the history of architecture. One can see it in such stylistically separate examples as the tower of the Renaissance city hall in Leipzig and the twin towers of the Parliament in Brasilia — in both cases the

Fig.165/166. Interplay of horizontal and verticals. Parliament in Brasilia and City Hall, Leipzig.

vertical element is set dynamically in contrast to bold horizontal forms — colonnades and bands of windows in the former case, the saucer-like semicircular assembly structure in the latter. The effect in the case of the Leipzig city hall is heightened by the bold asymmetric placement of the tower according to the golden ratio.

Of the two cardinal dimensions, the vertical has much greater significance for figural segregation than the horizontal. For instance, so-called 'hidden figures' in visual puzzles can be perceived more easily when they possess a vertical axis of symmetry. But most important is the role of a vertical axis of symmetry in the perceived stability of a figure. The results of studies on perceived movements and phenomenal stability carried out by the psychologist Takala with abstract shapes[31] may be translated into some general principles for the perceptual stability of buildings. Takala found that shapes which possess a vertical symmetry axis show a higher perceptual stability than those with a horizontal axis of symmetry or without any distinct symmetry. In addition, he discovered that visual stability depends on the direction in which the main dimensions of a shape extends; in other words, when the main dimension of a figure stretches horizontally, the figure appears more stable than when it stretches vertically. The highest degree of perceived stability is attained when figures are both horizontally and vertically symmetrical and when their main dimension extends horizontally.[32] But this case is rare in architecture. Rather, the prototype of a stable building is one whose main dimension extends horizontally, while its main axis of symmetry is vertical. Takala's observations clearly support the previously stated hypothesis that the perceptual center of a stable shape is always located above its geometric center. Since the perceptual center of a vertical shape is always slightly above the actual midpoint, horizontally elongated shapes with vertical bilateral symmetry adhere to this condition of having the main mass located beneath the perceptual center. It follows that the perceptual stability of horizontally oriented shapes can be increased by interlocking them with vertical shapes placed at the axis of vertical symmetry. Such an effect is often produced by a high center risalite, or tower, which will move the main focus of a composition upwards.

The relationship between the orientation of the principal axis of symmetry of a shape and its format has yet another important implication. According to Takala, the impression of *apparent* or *phenomenal movement* generated in figural perception is stronger in those cases where the orientation of the shape's main dimension and its axis of symmetry coincide.[33] Such considerations show how such architectural expressions as 'the upward-moving tendency of a building' may be justified. Such a perception may also be explained by Buswell's observation that eye fixations move upward faster than they move downward.[34] Moreover, according to studies by Brandt, the initial fixations in a viewing sequence show a strong tendency to move upwards and a greater relative duration in the upper regions of a pattern than in the lower ones.[35] If it is true that the pattern of fixations and the perception of apparent movement are linked, then it ought to be possible to emphasize these *dynamic* tendencies of architectural shapes by locating a marked center

Fig.167. St. Mary's. Larger windows in upper region enhance visual upward movement.
Fig.168. Bath, Queen Square. Pediment atop building provides central focus and produces visual upward movement.

or a concentration of smaller foci in the upper regions of a vertical shape. Such an effect might, for example, be realized by windows or ornaments in the upper part of a tower, as, for example, on St. Mary's church in Stendal, or by a pediment atop a horizontal shape, as in the building on Queen Square in Bath (Fig.168). Findings such as these give sounder basis to the common distinction between *static* and *dynamic* appearances of buildings.

Four buildings may illustrate these principles of stability. The western facade of the cathedral in Ulm (Fig.169a) provides an example of a compo-

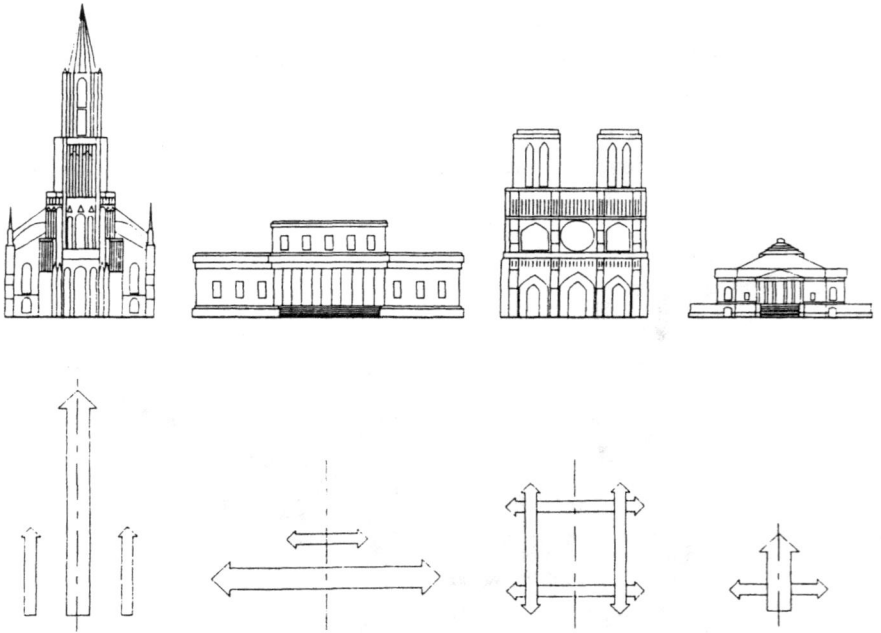

Fig.169. Comparison of apparent movement and stability.
Ulm Cathedral; Glyptothek, Munich ; Notre Dame, Paris; Villa Rotunda.

sition in which strong apparent upward movements are induced by the coincidence of the main dimensions of the building and the axis of vertical symmetry. At the same time, the perceptual stability of the facade is not in danger because of the distribution of visual weights in the lower half of the shape.

By contrast, Klenze's design for the Glyptothek in Munich (Fig. 169b) appears rather static and stable in itself because its main dimension extends horizontally while its main axis of symmetry extends vertically. This effect is enhanced by the vertical orientation of the central colonnade, since it induces a main center which is virtually aligned along the horizontal and subordinate centers of the windows. The building appears static because its center of balance and its main fulcrum coincide.

The case of Notre Dame in Paris is more ambiguous (Fig. 169c). The main dimensions of the facade extend vertically, but the internal division of the galleries and the sills is decidedly horizontal. Neither the horizontal nor the vertical can be said to dominate the facade. The centrally symmetrical rose window dominates the middle part, but the towers are too short to induce a strong vertical axis of symmetry in between. Thus, rudimentary upward thrust is held in check by an overall static appearance, an ambiguity which might have been avoided had the towers been completed.

Palladio's Villa Rotonda (Fig.169d) combines the principles of stasis and dynamism without ambiguity in a facade of great harmony. Its main shape clearly stretches horizontally, an effect which is enforced by the visibility of the flanking *pronaos*. And the static appearance of the whole is further supported by the division of the facade through the sills, which segregates horizontal shapes at the upper and the lower periphery, producing an axis of horizontal symmetry along which are placed the centers of the *ædicula* windows. However, the porch, the dome, and the flight of steps form a vertically oriented figure which interlocks with the horizontal figure. The upward thrust of the vertical is further enhanced by the statues on the *acroteria* and by a diminishing interval in the sizes of shapes toward the dome.

In general, it is the contrast between vertical and horizontal elements in a design that produces perceptual dynamics. When all of a facade's main centers are aligned on one horizontal axis, the design will appear static. But perceptual dynamics and stability are closely related, and the perceptual stability of a configuration will increase when the main perceptual center is located above the actual center of balance. Moreover, according to Buswell,[36] vertical elements trigger stronger fixation reflexes than horizontal elements. However, the principle of verticality does not necessarily require a vertical format for a building, only a strong vertical accent at the position of the main focus. Important, too, is the vertical orientation of the various axes along which the individual centers of the pattern are aligned.

The above point can be illustrated with a number of diagrams. In Fig.170a the nonhierarchical arrangement of the parts allows no focus to be established. Both the format of the shape and the alignment of the centers stress a horizontal

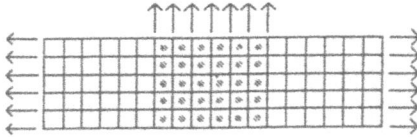

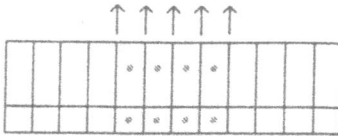

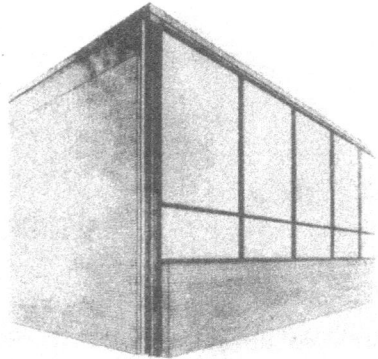

Fig.170a
Fig.170b

Fig.171. Fiat workshops, Turin.
Fig.172. M.v.d.Rohe, Libary &
Adm.Bldg. I.I.T Chicago.

210

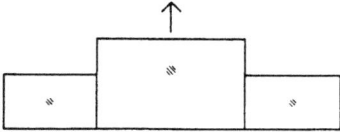

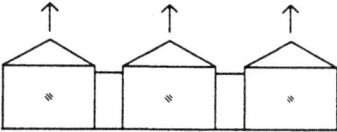

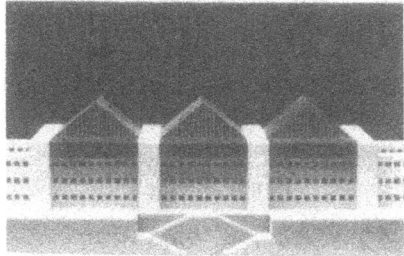

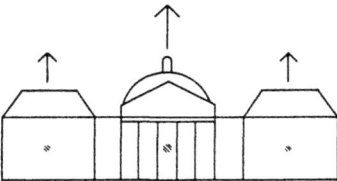

Fig 170c
Fig.170dFig.170e.

Fig.173. Klenze. Ministry of War
Fig.174. Rossi,A. Regional
administration center
Fig.175. Vaux-le-Vicomte.

in Turin. By contrast, in Fig.170b (as in Mies v.d. Rohe's project for a Library in Chicago), the different formats of the internal shapes produce minor vertical axes. However, the dominant center may also be located above the main horizontal, as in Fig.170c, with its high central shape. Such an arrangement will create a stronger sense of horizontal-vertical contrast than that in either Fig.170a and Fig.170b.

Additional shapes, such as roofs, may, of course, enhance the vertical tendency of the individual parts, as in Fig.170d, where the separation of shapes also enhances the individual vertical axes of symmetry of the main parts of the building.

And the dominance of the main vertical can be further strengthened by heterogeneous elements in the middle, as in Fig.170e. The prototype of this kind of construction is the castle Vaux-le-Vicomte. When the individual perceptual centers are connected to form a symmetrical graph, it becomes apparent that visual tension is a matter of vertical distance between the various centers of a configuration.

3. Hierarchical Composition

I have previously suggested that one of the main conditions of aesthetic value is a hierarchical organization of architectural elements into subordinate groups and subgroups. Hierarchical arrangements best allow sustained perceptual arousal without overtaxing perceptual capacity because they can permit a comparatively high absolute complexity while at the same time maintaining a relatively moderate level of perceptual complexity.

An especially important role in attaining hierarchy in a facade is played by the arrangement of its perceptual centers. In this regard, two main factors are crucial: the facade must possess a *distinct overall fulcrum* as well as distinct centers for each of their component groups at the subordinate levels; and it must be based on an *organization of a subordinate type* at the highest levels, while coordinate arrangement may govern at lower levels.

Distinct Foci

Perceptual hierarchy demands that each of the various groups and subgroups of shapes in a facade should be identifiable as discrete perceptual wholes. One quality that allows a perceptual whole to be well demarcated from other shapes is a clear compositional center. This center of a visual display is the area where perceptual forces compensate for each other and where the perceptual masses are in equilibrium. Ideally, this point of balance is identical with the perceptual focus of a configuration (that area which is most attractive to the eye during the initial stages of the scanning sequence). According to Molnar, good compositions produce a distribution of eye movements that follow a process in which a final state of equilibrium can be reached after only few transitory states. The more balanced a composition, the fewer transitory states will be required to reach this final equilibrium. "This equilibrium will be such that all the important parts [of the display] will be successively explored following a strict hierarchic probability".[37] Molnar calls this process *ergodic*. However, when two or more main foci of the same intensity compete, a case of *periodic* rather than ergodic modality is reached: *the eye oscillates and equilibrium cannot be achieved*. Moreover, when the composition is such that certain areas are difficult for the eye to explore, final equilibrium may take a long time to be achieved.[38]

It becomes clear from these studies that a distinct focus and an overall hierarchical organization are very important in terms of the intelligibility of a visual pattern. Depending on the organization of the inferior levels of scale in the composition, the lack of distinct overall centers may result either in a *monotonous* or a *restless* appearance. Homogeneously arranged patterns like in the ORTF building in Paris, (Fig. 176), which are composed of repetitive elements, do not permit the differentiation of a distinct center which can attract the viewer's eye. Here, the appearance is monotonous because both the absolute and the perceptual complexity of the facade are of a similarly low degree.

213

Alternatively, a heterogeneous, nonhierachical arrangement of elements of only slightly different size but varying shape and articulation, such as Lucian Kroll's *Maison Medicale* in Brussels (Fig.177), may result in a state of restless disequilibrium. Again, because of a lack of hierarchy in this case, absolute and perceived complexity are again of roughly equal degree, only

Fig.176. ORTF Building, Paris.

Fig.177. Maison Medicale,

greater in comparison to the previous example. However, as stated before, for such a high level of perceptual arousal to avoid overtaxing the information-processing capacity of the brain, a high degree of absolute complexity must be coupled with a relatively lower perceptual complexity of the pattern, a condition which can only be fulfilled when there is a hierarchical organization of component parts into groups with increasing redundancy at the inferior levels.

As stated above, in order to clearly and easily identify the various subdivisions of the overall composition, each of the subgroups of shapes ought to have distinct visual foci. Distinct foci can be created by various means such as by *heterogeneous shapes*, difference in *size*, *rhythm*, *symmetry*, by *dilatation* or *gradients*, or by contrast in *tone*, *color* or *texture*.

Fig.169a shows the case of an undivided horizontally extended facade. Arne Jacobsen's City Hall at Copenhagen Fig.179 is an example of such an

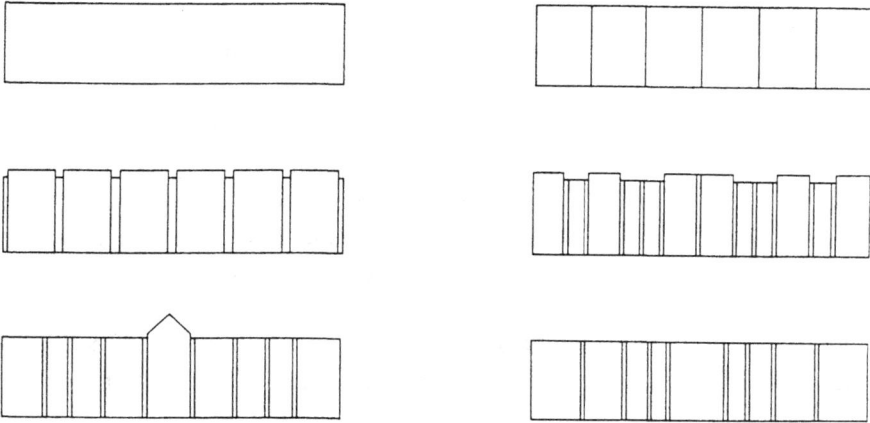

Fig.178a-d. *Divisions of facades in order to produce distinct visual foci.*

internal division, where the weak center induced by the boundaries of the shape is not even compensated for by the position of the entry. Fig.169b shows a coordinate arrangement of centers of similar impact, yet a clear focus is lacking, even though an axis of symmetry is latently induced. Particularly, then, when the number of similar parts exceeds the maximum number of elements which can be perceived at once — according to Miller this is between five and seven[39] — a monotonous appearance results. Sverre Fehn's Home for the Elderly follows this scheme.

A rhythmical alternation of different elements (Fig.178c) only leads to a strong overall center when one uncontested central vertical symmetry axis is induced. Such is the case in the example of the Chateau Chambord (Fig.184), in which the articulated roof of the center risalite strengthens the perceptual dominance of the middle of the composition. By contrast, it is apparent that the arrangement in Fig.178c does not produce a strong central symmetry, but results, rather, in a number of subordinate symmetries which enhance the dominance of the larger shapes but do not produce a strong overall center.

The division of de Klerk's housing project in Amsterdam is an example of this kind, yet here strong centers are produced within the shapes of the individual houses because of their internal division.

The monotony of the arrangement is further reduced in Fig.178d by a change of rhythm. The remaining illustrations show how rhythms, which are organized on both sides of an axis of vertical symmetry, can produce a strong central focus. They demonstrate how the dominance of the main symmetry axis can be enhanced when the shapes on either side of it are organized in gradients or dilatations of size, as in the case of Niemeyer's office building in Segrate. If, as so claimed by Ross,[40] the eye indeed moves in the direction of diminishing intervals, then dilatations produce a decrescendo effect towards

Fig.179. Jacobsen City Hall, Copenhagen.   *Fig.180. Sverre Fehn, Home for Elderly*

the smaller elements (Fig.178d).

Conversely, when the size of the elements increases toward the lateral peripheries (Fig.178e), additional foci compete with the main center. An example is St. Peter's in Rome, where the lateral risalites compete for attention with the center which offers a counterpoint through the portico roof. When this ambiguous effect is undesired, it can be countered by a larger or more heterogeneous shape in the middle, as, for instance, in the central cupola of the Karlskirche in Vienna (Fig.185).

In a composition of similar elements, a strong focus can also be produced

Fig.181. De Klerk, Amsterdam.

Fig.182. Niemeyer. Office building. Segrate.

by articulating one of the shapes using tone, texture or color. But the simplest way of creating a strong overall focus exists in the use of a heterogeneous shape, or a shape of distinctively different scale (Fig.178g,h), especially when it is placed at the main axis of symmetry. The typical example of this is the rose window of a cathedral, whose placement usually coincides with the center of balance of the facade. In the case of the Villa Rotonda (Fig.161), this strong heterogeneous accent is supplied by the different articulation of the central porches protruding from each of the facades. The effect of a single heterogeneous element is normally so strong that it can easily center an otherwise homogeneous arrangement, catalyzing an otherwise monotonous appearance. For instance, the tympanum above the main facade of a typical Greek temple or the Quadriga atop the redundant arrangement of columns of the Brandenburg Gate provide each composition with a strong central focus, which pulls the main

Fig.183. St. Peters, Rome. Main façade.

Fig.184. Chateau Chambord.

Fig.185. Karlskirche, Vienna.

fulcrum upward, enhancing overall perceptual stability (Fig.187).

Subordinate Organization

Ideally, the arrangement of the various centers of attraction in the facade of a building ought to be hierarchical; that is, the relationships of shapes should be such that they allow the formation of subgroups of shapes which form segregated perceptual units — which themselves become subgroups of larger

Effects of a shape placed in top symmetrical position (a-c):
Fig.186. Glyptothek, Munich, with and without tympanon (a,b).
Fig.187. Brandenburg Gate (c).

groups, and so on — there are several reasons for this. First, only a subordinate arrangement of the parts of a facade will allow the visual segregation of a distinct fulcrum, whereas a coordinate arrangement results in similar, and competing perceptual dominance.

Second, compared to nonhierarchical organization, a hierarchical arrangement permits greater absolute complexity without leading to an equally high degree of perceptual complexity. The reason is that similar groups of shapes at each level of perceptual dominance may form into *supersigns* which, due to an increased redundancy, can be perceived with less perceptual information processing. Such arrangements, therefore, allow a greater variety of constituent parts of a pattern without overtaxing a viewer's perceptual capacity.

Third, the organization of parts into groups complies more readily with the demands of wholeness in a complex configuration, thus allowing a more complicated arrangement of shapes to emerge. When each group forms a whole its compositional order can be different from that of other groups within the large configuration without resulting in a conflict of uncoordinated orders. Within the overall whole, groups can be treated as parts, that is, parts which form *confederate structures* with other groups without thus loosing their identity.

Fourth, in an hierarchical organization, there is a clear difference between various levels of scale, that is, between the sizes of the individual entities in relation to the whole. Consequently, there can be a greater number of levels without resulting in visual chaos. Moreover, in an hierarchical organization the macrostructural and the microstructural levels of scale — that is, the larger building parts and the smaller shapes of ornaments and textures — become linked more clearly than in a nonhierarchical set.

Fifth, hierarchical organization allows similar elements to be grouped into larger shapes instead of simply fusing with the overall pattern. These should be arranged in groups not to exceed more than five to seven elements of the same type, because the maximum perceptual comprehension of single parts is about seven.[41]

219

Finally, in terms of the previously described ergodic modality of eye-fixation patterns, it has been found that equilibrium of fixations can more easily be achieved when there is a hierarchical succession for the eye to follow when exploring perceptual centers. When foci of similar dominance are competing, it is harder to realize equilibrium.

A comparison between an hierarchically and a nonhierarchically organized facade will illustrate these principles further. The curtain-wall facade in Fig.189 exemplifies nonhierarchical subdivision, in which a multitude of similar shapes induce many perceptual centers of low impact but at only one principal level of scale and perceptual dominance. The distribution of contrast throughout the facade is thus homogeneous, and a main fulcrum is latently induced only by the boundaries of the overall shape.

Fig.188/189. *Hierarchical vs. non-hierarchical arrangement of a facade. Reed House, Curtain Wall Facade.*

In comparison, the Sudanese reed house clearly shows the impact of an hierarchical organization. The overall shape is subdivided into two areas whose horizontal orientation contrasts with the verticality of the main shape. Each of these areas is differently articulated: the upper one shows little internal division; the lower one shows a lot. At the third level of scale redundancy increases: four elements, whose vertical orientation contrasts with the horizontal division of the second level, connect two horizontal shapes. Again, the vertical orientation of the four elements is horizontally subdivided into parts whose height is based on the same module of internal division as that of the lower area and of the diamond shapes in the upper area. At the fourth level of dominance — that is, the internal division of the lower areas — the vertical grid structure is again horizontally divided, and each of the grids is differently oriented. This example clearly shows an increasing redundancy at the inferior levels of organization. It also illustrates the previous considerations of stability and horizontal-vertical contrast. The highly articulated shapes in the lower area assume stronger perceptual weight than the void in the upper part, and so the building appears stable. At the same time, the vertical divisions can cause upward progression of fixations counteracting the bottom-heaviness of the overall shape. Due to their isolated position, the two diamond shapes at the top assume a strong perceptual dominance which pulls the main fulcrum upwards.

Another important aspect of hierarchical organization is also apparent in this facade, namely, that decreases in scale at various levels of organization should follow some kind of order. Many medieval and Renaissance buildings used strict ratios derived from proportion systems that often followed arithmetic or geometric progressions. Though such strictness is not required in perceptual terms, the lack of orderly digression can easily lead to an appearance of either monotony or restlessness. The previously discussed curtain-wall facade shows an abrupt jump from the large size of the overall shape to the comparatively small size of the shapes that make up the vertical dividers, and to the windows, and to the sills that separate them. Such a gap in the ratio of digression leads to a monotonous appearance because too many elements of equal dominance are coordinately arranged, rather then forming groups. The absolute complexity of this facade is approximately the same as its relative complexity, causing a low level of perceptual stimulation.

Low stimulus levels are also characteristic of those facades whose division is hierarchical, yet which lack a complexity of subordinate levels — specifically the lack of detail and textural articulation. In other words, the lack of microstructure leads to poverty of information. For example, many Neoclassical buildings show comparatively less detail than their Classical models, and

Fig.190. Speer. Reichskanzlei, Berlin. Fig.191. Santa Maria Novella, Florence: Façade.

so their appearance is somewhat stark and sterile. Often Neoclassical buildings adopt only the macrostructural level of their Classical model, leaving behind the important microstructural level of detail.

By contrast, the facade of Santa Maria Novella in Florence serves as a good example of complete hierarchical organization from an overall macrostructure to a microstructural level of increasingly redundant detail. The originally Gothic facade, whose upper part was completed by Alberti one hundred years after it was begun, displays a clearly marked fulcrum two-thirds of the way up from the ground. Here, the circular window functions as a hub for the secondary centers of the circular shapes in the volutes, the pediment, and the portal. (An underlying graph derived from the position of these centers would form a rhomboid whose center is identical with the main fulcrum.) The three square shapes which form the second level of scale have three subdivisions at the upper part and four subdivisions at the lower parts of the facade, respectively. Each of these shapes is further subdivided into six parts in the upper region of the building and four parts in the lower area. The lower region thus has 32 redundant parts, each formed into groups of four. The number of similar elements increases even further in the bands separating the main parts of the facade, and is highest in the circular patterns in the volutes. Here, then, redundancy clearly increases as the size of the elements decreases, and also as the subordination of the elements within the whole increases. In fact, the increase of similar elements at each main level of scale follows a clear progression of 1,2,(3),4,8,16,32.

An Example of Perceptual Balance: The Laon Cathedral

Perceptually, a whole is characterized by equilibrium, that is, by a balance of the visual forces that determine the composition. As noted above, in a complex visual pattern, equilibrium is more easily achieved when the overall organization is hierarchical. This is because in such arrangements each group of parts can operate as a simple part within the next higher level of perceptual organization, and thus the perceptual complexity can be kept at a relatively low level compared with coordinated arrangements.

For a balanced arrangement, the distribution of perceptual centers and their levels of dominance within a composition is of major importance. The most critical factors are the perceptual weights and locations of the constituent parts of the composition. While actual calculations of balance do not seem to be feasible in the design process, and would, at any rate, be possible only for very simple shapes of similar contour, articulation and size, the principle of balancing can be applied intuitively.

The most elementary way of creating balance is through symmetry, that is, by locating similar parts at similar distance from the main center. But in asymmetrical arrangements — when the distances are different, or when parts with different degrees of dominance are used — perceptual balance can be thought to operate according to the lever principle: a shape of strong perceptual impact can be balanced by a less dominant one when the second is located closer to the center. Likewise, two shapes of lesser dominance can be counterbalanced by a more dominant shape at equal distance from a balancing center. As discussed earlier, the more *regular, concave, articulated,* or *contrasting* a shape is, the more perceptually dominant it will be. Accordingly, in a symmetrical arrangement of parts of similar impact, the distribution of the centers should form regular or semiregular graphs. A good example of this principle in a symmetrical arrangement is the main facade of the cathedral in Laon. When each of the shapes of similar size in this facade is assigned a level of importance on a scale, it becomes evident that each high-level center is supported by a number of low-level centers, implying that the vertex of the graph formed by the latter is at the position of the former.

Further inspection of the facade reveals that these balancing relationships operate not only between adjacent levels, but between the main center and the secondary, tertiary and quartiery centers. Similarly, the secondary centers are supported by other secondary centers and by tertiary centers; and some tertiary centers are supported by other tertiary centers, and by secondary and quartiery centers. The relationships between these centers can be illustrated in diagrammatic form by distinguishing four basic levels of scale. These are as follows: first, the main fulcrum of the circular window; second, the centers of the portals, the large windows of the naves, and the large double windows at the towers; third, the centers of the galleries, the small windows at the towers, and the small pyramidal towers atop the portals; and fourth, the parts of the central window. In the diagrams the centers are marked according to

Fig.192. Laon Cathedral: west facade. Arrangement of main centers.
Fig.193a. main center supported by secondary centers. Fig.193b. main centers
supported by tertiary centers. Fig.193c. main centers supported by quartiary centers.

the principles discussed earlier — principally the two-thirds position in vertical shapes and the radius point in concave shapes.

Because of the symmetries operating around various horizontal and vertical axes, the facade of the cathedral shows a relatively simple organization of centers at the main levels of scale. However, the total web of relations between centers is rather intricate. For instance, many of the tertiary centers are located at the vertices of the graph pattern which is formed by connecting all the secondary centers of the facade (Fig.196).

Of course, the result is less astounding when the graph derived from a

Fig.194 a. Secondary centers supported by secondary centers
Fig.194 b. Secondary centers supported by tertiary centers
Fig.195 a. Tertiary centers supported by secondary centers
Fig.195 b. Tertiary centers supported by tertiary centers

Fig.196. Laon Cathedral, west facade, Graphs derived from connections of centers.

diagonal connection of the centers is considered. This shows a typical triangulation, quite commonly used by the Gothic masterbuilders. Even though an awareness of perceptual centers may not have played a role in the construction of the facade, there is little mystery why these principles nevertheless apply: in circular and semicircular shapes, the perceptual center lies at the radius point where it is coincident with the geometric center of the shape accounted for in a proportion system. While such analysis seems rather complete some questions do remain. For instance, if the perceptual centers in the vertically elongated windows of the towers are placed at the two-thirds position and still fit into the triangular proportion system, no geometric reasons can be accounted for. Is the increasing elongation of the upper shapes of the towers and the increasing slimness of the windows a result of an 'intuitive decision' in terms of a desired perceptual balance? According to the theory of form which I have already proposed, this is a definite possibility.

A much more complex case of organization exists when there is no basic vertical axis of symmetry. Here the simple unisotropy of perceived space has to be taken into account. When there is no symmetry strong enough to cancel this factor, then the left side of a composition can assume a heavier weight than the right.[42] A good example is the facade of the residential building in Muttenz (Fig.197). Though the area left of the main vertical provided by the gable is 'heavier' than the area to the right (because it is larger, and because of the skewing impact of the horizontal shape at the bottom and the triangular shape of the gable), the building does not appear imbalanced. Moreover, since vertically extended shapes assume stronger perceptual dominance than horizontal ones, the vertical shape at the right is quite capable of balancing the horizontal shapes on the left.

4. Figure and Ground Articulation

For an analysis of the perceptual impact of corporeal form, a factor equally important as the distribution of visual weight and mass, is the internal articulation of the spatial boundaries. It is their appearance, which is crucial to

Fig.197. Residential Building, Muttenz.

228

the sense of a building's 'character'. Of the many properties of a facade's articulation, its textural appearance and the organization of component elements into figure and ground are of predominant importance. Of these two, the completeness of figure-ground organization largely determines the perceived orderliness of a facade, whereas the distribution of contrast endows the shape with heterogeneous structure. Both factors are also closely interrelated with regard to the strength of figural segregation of shapes or groups of shapes; that is, the degree of contrast of an articulated boundary determines, among other things, the autonomy of the figure in its surroundings.

Although the facade of a building can be treated in simplified terms as a two-dimensional plane, perceptually it is by no means flat. The reason is that its parts possess different visual dominance, and thus they appear to advance or to recede farther, resulting in a number of 'depth-levels'. The effect, as we have seen in other instances, is due to the perceptual organization of stimulus patterns into figure and ground. Though various areas in a field of stimuli are equally reflected on the retina, their relative importance in the resulting image is not at all equal, different features will attain perceptual dominance or subordinance. Perception is a process of selecting stimuli and unifying them into perceptual figures that segregate themselves from a surrounding ground. Visually, the figure always dominates the ground, which can be seen either as forming a series of subordinate shapes or as providing a continuous background extending behind the figure. In fact, the term 'ground' may be somewhat misleading, because the spaces between dominant figures can form perceptual shapes in their own right. Thus, areas that are not part of a figure are frequently called 'negative space' — in contrast to the principal figures which form 'positive spaces'.

The conditions under which figures and ground segregate have been extensively described in the pioneering works of Rubin and Koffka,[43] and they are illustrated in every major textbook in perception.[44] In the following I shall describe them briefly, inasmuch as they are important for the perception of spatial boundaries.

Most important for the formation of perceptual units is the function of the contour. Whenever an area is surrounded by a contour, the contour will function as a boundary for the enclosed area. In such a case the contour ceases to be an entity in its own right, but becomes an integral part of the bounded unit. This so-called 'asymmetry', or one-sided function,[45] of the contour will cause the *inside* but not the outside of an object to appear shaped. Because the contour is monopolized by the figure it bounds, the ground must necessarily become perceptually boundless. According to Arnheim: "The ground stops at the figure. The figure prevents the ground from advancing farther, but it has no own demarcation: ergo it appears to continue behind the figure."[46]

Whenever a contour is common to shapes of equal dominance, the situation becomes perceptually ambiguous, a situation which is inherently 'unstable'. In fact, when people are asked to draw figures after having them tachistoscopically presented, they often 'improve' them by separating equally dominant shapes by drawing a separate contour for each; such is often the case with honeycomb patterns.[47] The only exception to this rule of perceptual instability is provided by coordinated arrangements of similar shapes that share straight contours — for instance, a band of rectangles. Here the contour operates as an axis of symmetry, and its function becomes 'double-sided'. However, when shapes of similar dominance with partly concave contours border or interlock each other, the resulting pattern approaches a state of 'multistability'.[48] This is the well-known effect of reversible patterns, where ground and figure oscillate because the figural segregation of one pattern momentarily cancels the segregation of the other.

Other conditions being equal, segregation into figure and ground is governed by the following laws.[49] (1) *Orientation*: shapes whose dominant orientation extends along the cardinal axes will form figures more easily than shapes with divergent orientations. Fig.198a shows how a horizontal-vertical cross shape perceptually dominates a diagonal one. (2) *Proximity*: small areas will dominate larger ones, with the larger areas tending to assume the role of ground (Fig.198b). An example here might be the way pilasters perceptually dominate a wall. (3) *Closure*: fully enclosed areas will segregate more easily than

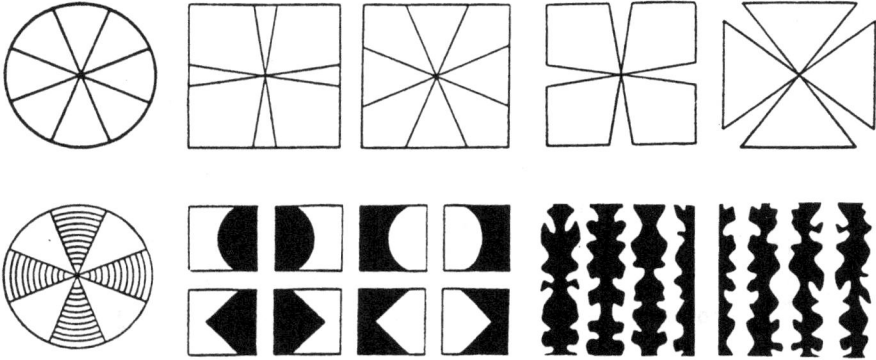

Fig. 198 a-f. Principles of figural segregation (after Metzger).

partially enclosed ones (Fig.198c). Thus, windows usually form primary figures in relation to the surfaces they appear in. (4) *Articulation*: by definition, the ground is always simpler than the figure, and areas with greater internal articulation will form figures more easily than areas with little articulation (Fig.198d). This effect may be seen in ornamental window frames and friezes. (5) *Concavity*: the concave side of a contour will induce shapes more readily than the convex side (Fig.198e). Arches and circular shapes thus form dominant features of a facade. (In fact, concavity is such a strong factor that contours need not be complete to induce shapes.) (6) *Brightness and color*: so-called 'hard' articulations will resist fusion with the ground more strongly than soft ones. Thus, brighter tones and 'hard' colors like red segregate into figures more strongly than do 'soft' colors like blue, which tend to be less autonomous. (7) *Symmetry*: of a given number of shapes, the more symmetrical will tend to form figures (Fig.198f).

The importance of these laws in terms of the overall appearance of a building becomes apparent if one considers the case of windows. That windows, which are but 'holes' in a wall, in most cases form the principal figures in a facade is primarily due to the laws of proximity and concavity. There are, however, additional issues that must be considered. Because contours belong to figures (in this case, the windows), the ground (in this case, the wall) will appear borderless if it is large and not further subdivided; the result may be a somewhat 'naked' appearance (Fig.199a). If this effect is undesired, a second contour added around the shape of the window (Fig.199b) and the principal shape of the ground (Fig.199c) may help. Because the ground can now claim a contour of its own, it can also assume figural character, but this character (according to the law of proximity) will be secondary to that of the windows.

How autonomous a shape will appear on a ground will further depend on its regularity and contrast in relation to adjacent shapes. In this regard, it must be remembered that regular shapes segregate more strongly from a ground than irregular ones. A circular shape is the most autonomous shape, and will, accordingly, assume a particularly strong perceptual dominance. However, such figural autonomy can be reduced by adding a parallel contour. Such a compositional device may be especially effective when the second contour is articulated with ornament or when it is strongly contrasting in tone, color and texture (for example, in the case of an aedicula window). The parallel contour can also serve to enhance figural segregation from adjacent figures that may be similar in size, tone and color.

Arnheim[50] has pointed out that the effect of a boundless ground can also be countered by enlarging the windows relative to the ground. In such a case the ground will be reduced to narrow strips which can, due to their

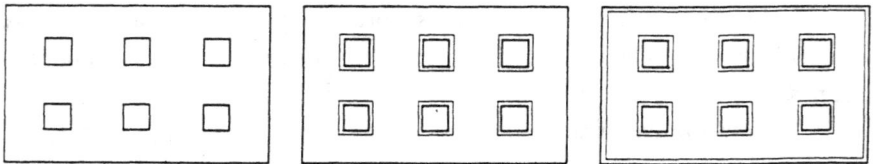

Fig. 199. Effect of window boundaries on figure-ground segregation in facades.

proximity, more easily take on figural character (Fig.200). Such a case also shows the compositional importance of complete organization of figure and ground — that is, the ability of both positive and negative spaces to assume figural character.

But many facades cannot be described as a simple layer of figures in front

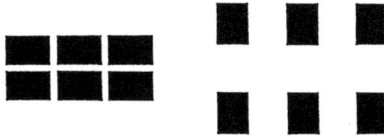

Fig. 200 Effect of size of shapes on figuredness of background.

of a ground. Rather facades form complex, multilyered configurations. Schumacher has demonstrated such a case in the analysis of the various figural layers of Palladio's Palazzo Valmarana. The cut-out of the windows form one simple figure ground layer, the architraphs separate three horizontally oriented shapes; Frames around the windows, series of small pilasters around the ground floor windows and the large pilasters extending over two stories each add a figural layer to the facade of the building. The individual figural layers tend to form a perceptual ground for the next layer 'on top', resulting in an increased perceptual complexity of the facade.

The various possibilities the figure-ground organization in a facade may take can be summarized through the following categories, which quite frequently occur in combination.

A. Unified ground — intervening spaces do not form figures. This is the simplest possible form of figure-ground organization. Here the negative spaces between or surrounding the primary shapes will possess no, or only a weak, figural character of their own. When the negative spaces are similarly articulated (for instance, by use of a similar material, texture or color), then

Fig. 201. Palladio. Palazzo Valmarana, Vicenza. Complex layers of figure and ground

they will tend to be perceived as one larger shape providing a continuous ground 'behind' the figures. In architecture the typical example is the non subdivided wall with 'cut-out' windows, producing a composition of two principal planes. A more complex organization into layers of planes, however, may be achieved by subdividing the wall with pilasters, sills, and so on. In this case areas between and around the windows will function as figures within the larger ground bounded by the overall shape of the building. Even when the spaces between primary figures do not become segregated as figures in this way, as mentioned above, the entire ground may acquire secondary figural character.

Fig.202. Castle Heddingham. Continuous ground: Interstices do not form figures.
203. Rossi, Ossuary Modena Cemetery. Continuous Ground: weak figure
segregation of spaces between windows..

B. Unified ground—intervening spaces form figures. In this case the
negative spaces between the principal shapes assume their own figural
character, and when all the negative spaces are similarly articulated, they
group together into a larger shape that will be perceived as a continuous,
unified ground, which itself may form a larger perceptual figure. To form
figures of secondary perceptual dominance, the shapes of negative spaces
need to be fully bounded, or they must have a concave character. The more
the negative spaces approach figural 'goodness' (as described in Chapter Six),
the stronger will be their perceptual prominence. In the extreme case, this
will lead to a multistable pattern, in which adjacent shapes vie for a common
contour and appear restless. This effect can be avoided by separating
competing shapes using parallel boundaries, or by similarly articulating
negative spaces so that they may be more easily perceived as forming a group
and serving as a ground. Organization of this kind is quite common in the
facades of Northern Baroque buildings, in Islamic decorative tilework, and in

Greek meander patterns. The Ossuary in the Modena cemetery exempifies a case where a larger perceptual ground stretches between the windows. Yet, at the same time, the viewer is able to see perceptual figures when focusing on the spaces between four windows each. However, since these figures are not bounded the effect is weak. The case where the intervening figures form individual shapes but do not counter the effect of the ground as continuing is

Fig.204. Palazzo della Chancelleria. Rome.
Fig.205 Appartment Buildings. Chicago. Mies v.d.Rohe.

shown in the example of the Palazzo della Cancelleria. (Fig 204)

C. *Nonunified ground—duo-formation of shapes.* This kind of organization occurs frequently in curtain-wall facades like Mies' Chicago Apartment Buildings (Fig.205), in which equal or similar shapes are coordinately added. Here no distinction into figure and ground is possible, and all shapes assume equal dominance. Though such patterns lack a clear focus, the restlessness appearance discussed above may be minimized if the contours are straight lines. In this case they will function as axes of symmetry between adjacent shapes, and constitute the only exception to the rule of contour rivalry. However, the effect of restlessness may still be produced when the shapes are differently articulated — for instance, in checkerboard patterns. Here, a clear separation into figure and ground is not possible, and figure and ground become multistable, or reversible.

D. *Nonunified ground—intervening spaces form figures.* In this case, negative spaces form figures in their own right but do not result in duo-formations. The figural character of the negative spaces will here be weaker than the figural character of the main facade components. However, when negative spaces in such an arrangement are not similarly articulated, a con-

Fig. 206. Palazzo Farnese.

Fig. 207. North Dade Courthouse.

237

tinuous ground cannot be formed. In this case the negative spaces will either be grouped according to similarities in size or orientation. This organization is often found in the main facades of Gothic cathedrals, for instance, in Strassburg and Cologne, but is also typical of the complex layering of Renaissance facades such as the Palazzo Farnese. (Fig. 206)

E. *Nonunified ground — intervening spaces do not form figures*. When intervening spaces do not assume figural character (or when such character is weak), and when these spaces are articulated to form a continuous ground, the resulting orderliness will be low. In such a case the negative spaces cannot group themselves together and the overall pattern will appear restless. An example of this kind of composition is Kroll's Maison Medicale (Fig. 177).

The figure-ground principle is an extremely important principle in the design of facades. For example, even though the spaces intervening between the principal architectural elements of a facade may be perceptually subordinate (and one may, so to speak, even be oblivious to them if they are part of a uniform ground), these negative spaces should not be given merely secondary importance in the design process. Overall considerations of appropriateness of form demand that designers pay as much attention to them in their work as to the form of principal shapes. Perceptual organization is always a matter of relations: the dimensions, orientations, and 'weights' of negative spaces will thus directly effect the appearance of primary forms. In the facade of the North Dade Courthouse the negative spaces do not form strong individual figures, but it is obvious that the windows are placed within the ground with great visual care (Fig. 207)

As Koffka[51] has stated, the characteristics of a figure always depend "upon the characteristics of the ground on which it appears. The ground serves as a framework in which the figure is suspended and thereby determines the figure." A clearly ordered figure-ground organization is thus an indispensable condition for overall orderliness of a configuration of shapes. When there is no clear distinction between the principal shapes and the ground, or when the permeating order of the organization is locally violated, the result is perceptual ambiguity.

As a general rule, in regard to the wholeness of a pattern, those forms of organization described under A, B and D above ought to be preferred. In other words, facades should either present a uniform ground (or various layers of these), or an interlocking arrangement of positive and negative spaces in which the former dominate the latter. In either case the ground will come to possess figural qualities of its own. In perceptual terms such an overall composition will present no unorganized parts, and therefore be in a position to comply with the conditions of wholeness as described in Chapter Six.

In addition, the choice of a type of figure-ground organization has implications for the perceived complexity of the pattern. A unified ground which takes on figural status as a whole but not in terms of the individual shapes intervening between principal architectural elements will result in a lower perceived complexity than if the intervening spaces do attain figural character. But an even higher level of perceived complexity may emerge from an organization in which the figural character of the negative spaces approaches the figural strength of the primary elements, without appearing to form a continuous ground (assuming, of course, that such an arrangement avoids multistability). In such a case the ground may be organized hierarchically into 'layers'. As noted in Chapter Six, such hierarchical organization will allow the perceived complexity of the pattern to be lower than its absolute complexity, resulting in a condition of sustained perceptual arousal.

However, the perceived complexity of a surface can also be a matter of internal contrast and 'texturing'. And a key principle in the regard is that the distribution of areas of contrast ought not to run counter to the hierarchical organization of perceptual centers. This is because areas with a high concentration of contrast will trigger strong fixation reflexes. To be most effective, a hierarchical distribution of contrast should be made in support of the segregation of shapes into figure and ground. In other words, larger areas should be less (and preferably homogeneously) articulated in terms of texture and ornament to avoid competing perceptually with figures.

The figure-ground organization of a facade also has important implications for the perceived stability of a building. When a facade is subdivided into horizontal bands with dissimilar systems of figure-ground organization, a certain effect of ambiguity in terms of the whole will result. For instance, the palace of the Doge in Venice (Fig. 208) owes its top-heavy appearance to the different organizations of figure and ground on its upper and lower levels. The facade of this building is clearly divided into two horizontally elongated areas, the lower of these is further divided into two galleries. On the lower level, the columns and the spatial figures between them rival each other for dominance because of a competition between 'the law of proximity' and 'the law of concavity'. However, since the latter is stronger, the concavity of the shapes between the columns in the end is the stronger perceptual effect. In the upper part of the facade, however, the large, individually placed windows assume primary figural character since the effects of proximity and concavity operate in unison. However, on the upper part, the area of the ground is articulated

Fig.208. Doge's Palace, Venice.

by intarsia. This allows it to establish a perceptual dominance of its own. Moreover, this area of ground is extremely large in comparison to the area of the ground in the lower region — the columns. As a result, the dominant perceptual weight of the ground on the upper level causes the building to appear top-heavy, an effect which was further enhanced by the fact that the level of Saint Mark's square was raised because of the frequent floods in this city, thus shortening the columns even further and so enhancing the dominance of the visual weight of the upper floors of the building.

I X

Summary and Outlook

At this point, proper conduct asks for a conclusion. For two reasons, however, I feel this is inappropriate. The first is that I consider it an accomplishment of my investigation that I have not found anything new concerning what 'good form' ought to be. Had the result been otherwise, not only would two millennia of architecture stand against such claims, but my primary contention, advanced in the first section of this book, namely, that good form is nothing but perceptually appropriate form, would have been groundless. The second reason is that, instead of displaying a fully developed theory of the perception of architectural form and a method of its analysis, this approach forms a start for further investigations from which conclusions for architectural design can be, and, indeed, if well developed, should be drawn.

It was not the intent of my inquiry to explain what is, or what makes, good, successful or beautiful architecture: such an examination would have been entirely different for it would have meant exploring the formation of value concepts. These frames of reference, by which one's world attains significance and value, and on grounds of which such preferences are established, are not, according to the position I have presented, based on the sensory-motor internalization of the stimulus pattern, but on individual learning through the internalization of manipulations with objects and on socio-cultural conventions. Whereas the former process was assumed to be organismically determined and thus must be assumed to be similar for all, the latter is an act largely individually determined; hence, attempts at generalization would be futile. Nevertheless, quite a number of the buildings and spaces which I have used as examples of being appropriate to perceptual organization might as well, in my personal opinion, be called beautiful examples of their kind.

What I have done is this: I have argued that experiences of, and, consequently, judgements about, architecture must in part be determined by the composition of the sensory stimulus pattern, that is, by the form of architecture — its shapes, their articulation in texture and color, and their organization into larger units. Adopting an organizational-organismic position in regard to perception, I have maintained that the internalization of form is organismically determined and thus highly similar among different individuals. In discussing perceptual organization, I have argued that certain constellations of environmental stimuli are more appropriate for perceptual organization than others, and I have suggested a number of conditions for perceptually appropriate form, which I have illustrated with examples of buildings and urban spaces.

Though I have claimed that the lack of perceptual appropriateness results in a dissatisfaction of the organism in the process of internalizing the stimulus pattern, and that, therefore, appropriate form may be taken as one of the causes for preferences for specific buildings in impromptu judgements, the criterion is insufficient to explain the fact of aesthetic preferences in general. When discussing cognitive organization — that is, the transformation of the sensory-motor internalization of perceived instances into forms of knowledge that facilitate abstract mental manipulations — I have proposed a model of information-processing which shows that preferences are established on grounds of the fusion of both morphic and extramorphic schemes, or concepts. But since it appears impossible to find out to what extent each of these schemes participates in the formation of the cognitive image of an object, the impact of form upon generating specific experiences and judgements cannot be clearly demarcated.

Where, then, lies the value of my project? It is first in having proposed an epistemology which may provide a somewhat sounder basis for discussing architectural form than presently exists in architectural circles, where form is treated as the enigma par excellence. The explanations which I have suggested for some of the issues designers frequently reckon with — for instance, the stability, balance, or 'dynamic' properties of shapes — might be useful when taken into consideration during the design process. Whether there is agreement on what a desirable design is, the criteria which I have proposed and their explanations may aid in objectifying one's goals. Provided that one wants to arrive at the kinds of architectural forms which I have called appropriate to perception (and one might just as well opt for other appearances of architecture), the awareness of the properties by which such forms are characterized might prove helpful. The formulation of criteria for design, against which, often for good reasons, skepticism has arisen, does not need to imprison the architect's 'creativity'; rather, being cognizant of that which makes harmonious and ordered form may liberate him from indecision.

On the other hand, these criteria cannot constitute principles for design which will automatically result in good architectural form. Not the least of the reasons why is the multitude of possibilities of combining individual parts into different configurations of which many can comply with the requirements for order. But it is also crucial to note that design decisions are never exclusively about form. First of all, the decisions which lead to the initiation of a building's design are rarely of an exclusively aesthetic nature but rather much more commonly concern some utilitarian end. Second, the desired performance of a building and a host of context variables outside the immediate control of the designer limit the range of design variables in a given case and, therefore, choices of form from the start. Third, recalling the suggested model of information-processing, it must be pointed out once more that decisions about form cannot exclude any meaning or significance that form possesses in the eye of the individual designer. I have maintained that the sequence of reception is an inclusive one in which the cognitive image of an object includes its morphic representation, whereas the morphic structure is internalized independently of any meanings which are assigned after the sensory-motor process of perception. In other words, operative knowledge includes figurative knowledge, but not vice versa. However, because design is a matter of operative knowledge, any forms handled are, intended or not, laden with meanings previously acquired. A fourth reason why design decisions do not concern form exclusively involves the fact of style and the history of the design profession: in other words, forms often develop by virtue of forms previously used, which are adopted or rearranged in the new designs. Hence, the architecture of different cultures and times has led to different styles of combining shapes to form buildings. That there are timeless forms in architecture is not just an unlucky metaphor: the notion itself is incorrect.

Aside from its contributing to the discussion about design, the worthiness of this investigation is to be found in its potential as a basis for further examinations, that is, specifically through experimental research and through the further exploration of the criteria of perceptually appropriate form. In terms of experimental research there are two possible paths. The first is to look at individual preferences of selected groups for particular buildings, and relate them to individual aspects of form. The other direction leads into the provision of more experimental evidence for some of the criteria of form. Though I have based my discussion on experiments in the laboratories of perception, many of my conclusions and generalizations have been of a logical nature. Here, a collaboration between architects and psychologists can be fruitful—the architects providing the specific questions and the psychologists the methods of investigation. Many of the conclusions which I have drawn from experimental research on perception can themselves be tested. Especially promising in this respect appear to be specific studies in eye-movement patterns in the observation of buildings[1]: for instance, the comparison of actual three-dimensional displays with two-dimensional representations, the study of single shapes and the influence of different articulation, contrast and location of these at the perceived balance and stability of simple configurations. Also of interest is the issue of how to measure the 'phenomenal complexity' of a configuration: I suggest that the approaches of information aesthetics can be further developed when geometric properties are substituted by perceptual ones, such as the figure-ground organizations in a pattern. Moreover, there are a number of criteria which I have not discussed here, but which are equally important for this approach as the described ones. There is, for instance, the consideration of the effect of microstructure — that is, the articulation, material and color of the individual shapes, as these add to the perceived complexity of a configuration — and the discussion of the effect of varying sizes of one and the same pattern.

Finally, I would like to make it clear once more, that although my discussion has focused exclusively on the form of architecture, I do by no means suggest that architectural design is predominantly a matter of form. To detach form from what it is for, to separate architecture from function and meaning, is formalism — empty and meaningless. Even though a building ultimately exists by virtue of its form, it is the adaptation of the physical boundaries to the ends within it, that makes architecture a suitable habitat.

Notes

Preface

1   P. Feyerabend, *Wissenschaft und Kunst* (35).

Chapter I

1   H. Rittel, *On the Planning Crisis* (121), p.390.

2   For the distinction between deliberated and off-hand judgments, see H. Rittel, *Some Principles for the Design of an Educational System for Design* (122), p.26.

Chapter II

1   L. Sullivan, *Kindergarten Chats* (133).

2   J.F. Blondel, *Cours d'architecture* (27), p.229.

3   Plato, *The Dialogues of Plato* (116), Timaeus 32.

4   The overview of different concepts of proportion is a paraphrased summary of Rudolf Wittkower, *The Changing Concept of Proportion* (155), who gives a comprehensive account of the various concepts of proportion throughout history.

5   The Bible, *The Book of Solomon* XII, 20.

6   E. de Bruyne, *Éthudes d'esthéthiquie médiévale* (30), p.255 ff.

7   Aristotle, *Poetics* (8), Sextus Empiricus VII, 106. Similar to this is Aristotle's view that beauty is a matter of magnitude and ordered arrangement, 1450b, 38.

8   Vitruvius Pollo, *Ten Books of Architecture* (142), I, 2, 1.

9   L.B. Alberti, *Ten Books of Architecture* (1), VI,2.

10   G. Birkhoff, *A Mathematical Theory of Aesthetics* (26), pp. 189-342. Birkhoff defines the aesthetic measure M as a function of order and complexity: $M=O/C$. Instead of using order and complexity, both Bense and Moles describe aesthetic stimulation as a matter of information and redundancy. See M. Bense, *Aesthetica* (19); and A. Moles, *Information theory and Aesthetics* (106).

11   *Geometric progressions*: the ratio of two consecutive terms is the same ($a/b = b/c$), when the 1st is to the 2nd as the 2nd is to the 3rd (e.g., 1:2 = 2:4).

Arithmetic progressions: the difference between two consecutive terms is the same (b-a = c-b), when the 2nd exceeds the 1st by the same amount as the 3rd exceeds the 2nd (e.g., 2:3 = 3:4). *Harmonic progressions*: the reciprocals of the terms form an arithmetic progression [(b-a)/a = (c-b)/c], when the distance between two extremes from the mean is the same fraction of their quantity (e.g., 6:8 = 8:12).

12   R. Lawlor, *sacred geometrie* (87).

13   The numerical equivalent of the 'golden ratio'is 1:1.618.

14   Vitruvius Pollo (142), book III, chpt.I.

15   E. Burke *A Philosophical Enquiry into the Origin of Our Ideas of the Sublime and the Beautiful* (31).

16   J. Hambidge, *Dynamic Symmetry: The Greek Vase* (59) relates the logarithmic spiral to right-angle spiral. He claims that rational proportions result in 'static symmetry', and incommensurable ratios in 'dynamic symmetry'.

17   D'Arcy Thompson, *On Growth and Form* (138).

18   H. Kayser, *Harmonica* (78).

19   O. Schubert, *Optik in Architektur und Städtebau* (125).

20   N.L. Prak, *The Language of Architecture: A Contribution to Architectural Theory* (117); and C. Jencks, *The Language of Post-Modern Architecture* (74). While these authors actually consider architecture a language, C. Alexander uses the term 'Pattern Language' in somewhat metaphorical form to describe the making of buildings as a process of arranging functional patterns into a whole. See C. Alexander et al., *A Pattern Language: Towns, Buildings, Construction* (2).

21   Attempts to define architecture as a language can be found in U. Eco, *A Theory of Semiotics* (39); and, most notably, in G.K. Koenig, *Analisi del linguaggio architettonico* (83), and *Archittetura e communicazione* (84)).

22   J.J. Gibson, *The Ecological Approach to Visual Perception* (49).

23   The theory of empathy was developed in the 19th century by Vischer and Lipps. The classical sources are R. Vischer, *Das Optische Formgefühl* (141); and Th. Lipps, *Aesthetik* (90).

24   R. Arnheim, *The Gestalt Theory of Expression* (10), in: *Toward a Psychology of Art* (14), p.6

25   *Ibid*, p.64.

26   C. Jencks, *Meaning in Architecture* (74), for example, claims that there are masculine or feminine styles of architecture and maintains that architecture possesses syntactical systems like languages.

27   G. Frege, *The Philosophical Writings of Gottlob Frege* (46). Frege's argument is further expounded in R. Scruton, *The Aesthetics of Architecture* (127).

Chapter III

1   I. Kant, *Critique of Judgement* (75)

2   D. Hume, *Of the Standard of Taste* (69)

3   H. Osborne, *Aesthetics and Art Theory* (109), p.154.

4   For Bullough's approach, see Sh. Dawson, *Distancing as an Aesthetic Principle* (36), pp.155-74. For a critical account of this theory, see G. Dickie, *The Myth of the Aesthetic Attitude* (32), pp.29-45.

5   J. Stolnitz, *The Aesthetic Attitude* (132), in J. Hospers, *Introductory Readings in Aesthetics* (65), p.19.

6   *Ibid.*, p.20.

7   *Ibid.*, p.21.

8   R. Wollheim, *Art and its Objects* (158), pp.70-71.

9   Hume, (69).

10   A. Danto, *The Artworld* (35), in Margolis (101), pp.132-144.

11   Rittel (lectures on *Design Methods and Theories* delivered at UC Berkeley, 1980) defines planning as an activity which leads to the production of a plan, which, when implemented, yields the desired results and no unforeseen side- or aftereffects.

12   T. Binkley, *Contra Aesthetics* (24), in Margolis (101), pp. 25-44.

Chapter IV

1   For a comprehensive discussion of the various positions in the debate between nativists and empiricists, see F.H. Allport, *Theories of Perception and the Concept of Structure* (3); P. Machenauer and R. Turnbull, *Studies in Perception, Interrelations in the History of Philosophy and Science* (97); N. Pastore, *Selective History of Visual Perception 1650-1950* (112); and M. Mandelbaum, *Philosophy, Science & Sense Perception, Historical & Critical Studies* (100).

2   G. Berkeley, *Three Dialogues between Hylas and Philonous* (20).

3   W.H. Ittelson, et al., *Introduction to Environmental Psychology* (72), p.66.

4   A. Ames, *Visual perception and the rotating trapezoidal window* (4).

5   W. Köhler, *Gestalt Psychology* (82).

6   H. Wallach, *Brightness constancy and the nature of achromatic colors* (143), pp.310-24.

7   C. Zuckerman and I. Rock, *A Reappraisal of the Roles of Past Experience and Innate Organizing Processes in Visual Perception* (160), pp.277-78.

8   *Ibid.*, p.278.

9   J.J. Gibson, *The Senses considered a Perceptual System* (51), p.275.

10 *Ibid.*, chpt.12.

11 *Ibid.*, p.5.

12 *Ibid.*, p.5.

13 *Ibid.*, p.5.

14 *Ibid.*, p.253.

15 I. Kant, Introduction to *The Critique of Pure Reason*.

16 Quoted in P. Machenauer and R. Turnbull (97), p.467.

17 A good account of the arguments on which the organizational position was originally developed can be found in the introduction to W. Metzger, *Gesetze des Sehens* (102), chpts.I-IV.

18 W. Köhler, *Die Physischen Gestalten in Ruhe und im stationaeren Zustand* (83).

19 For a comprehensible discussion of research on visual perception, see W. Metzger (102).

20 M. Wertheimer, *Untersuchungen zur Lehre von der Gestalt* (152), pp.301-50.

21 E. Rubin, *Visuell wahrgenommene Figuren* (123).

22 K.S. Lashley, *Persistent problems in the evolution of mind* (86), p.35.

23 M. Banissoni and E. Ponzo, *Percezione strutturata e trasposizione di forme nelle prime esperience vivise di un cieco dai primi mesi di vita operato in eta adulta di osteo-odonto-cheratoprotesi di Strampelli* (17); further explicated in Metzger (102), pp.685-87.

24 C. Zuckerman and I. Rock (160); and N.S. Sutherland, *Object Recognition* (134).

25 E. Siro, *Über die Autonomie des Seelischen im Lichte des Phi-Phenomaens* (130).

26 V. v. Weizsäcker, *Die Gestaltkreislehre* (150), pp.103-9.

27 E.H. Gombrich maintains in *Art and Illusion* (53) that the history of visual representation is a history of formulating and testing hypotheses about representation that match environmental perception.

28 M.H. Segall and D.T. Campbell and M.J. Herskovits, *The Influence of Culture on Perception* (128).

29 J.J. Gibson, *The Ecological Approach to Visual Perception* (49), p.278ff.

30 *Ibid.*, p.209.

31 E. Cassirer, p.46, as quoted in R.A Hart and G.T. Moore, *The Development of Spatial Cognition: A Review* (60), p.253.

32 B. Inhelder, *Some Aspects of Piaget's Genetic Approach to Cognition* (71), in H. Furth, *Piaget and Knowledge* (42), p.23.

33 *Ibid.*, p.12.

34 H. Furth, (42), p.134.

35 J. Piaget, *Structuralism* (115), pp.3-17.

36 *Ibid.*, p.18.

37 *Ibid.*, p.134.

38 *Ibid.*, p.13.

39 Inhelder (71), in Furth (42), p.29.
40 Hart and Moore (60), p.255.
41 *Ibid.*, p.27.
42 Ontogenetic development: development of an individual organism. Phylogenetic development: evolutionary development.
43 Hart and Moore (60), p.2.
44 For processes of adaptation see H. Furth (42), p.44.
45 J. Piaget, *Assimilation and Sensory-motor Knowledge* (113), p.56.
46 Hart and Moore (60), p.261.
47 *Ibid.*, p.57.
48 For the construction of operational knowledge through processes of classification and generalization, see Furth (42), p.56.
49 When classifying concepts, there are obviously also forms of concepts, or internal representations, other than the ones discussed here — namely, representations of instances without morphic character. Among these might be mentioned, for example, such concepts as democracy or freedom, which, however, are not immediately relevant to this discussion.

Chapter V

1 For a discussion of IRMs, see I. Eibl-Eibesfeld, *Der vorprogrammierte Mensch* (40); K. Lorenz, *Gesammelte Abhandlungen*, Bd.1 & 2 (93); and M. Schuster and H. Beisl, *Kunst-Psychologie: Wodurch Kunstwerke wirken* (126).
2 A similar distinction is made by J.J. Gibson in *The Senses Considered a Perceptual System* (51), p.244. Here Gibson distinguishes between perceptual and verbal meaning.
3 A. Moles, *Information Theory and Aesthetic Perception* (106).
4 For the distinction between denotative and connotative signifiers, see U. Eco, *Die aesthetische Botschaft,* in Henrich and W. Iser (62), pp.404-29. Based on a model of Bense's, Eco distinguishes six layers of information, which together form the "idolect" of a work of art.

Chapter VI

1 M. Beardsley, *Theories of Beauty since the Mid-Nineteenth Century* (20), in Ph. Wiener, ed., *Dictionary of the History of Ideas* (156), p.209.
2 K. Lorenz, *Über die Bildung des Instinktbegriffs* (94). Also *Die angeborenen Formen möglicher Erfahrung* (95).

3   A. Gehlen, *Über einige Kategorien des entlastenden, zumal des ästhetischen Verhaltens* (47).

4   The principle of simplicity and its various interpretations in perceptual organization are well summarized in W. Metzger, *Gesetze des Sehens* (102), chpts.II,VII; see also R. Arnheim, *Entropy and Art* (11), in which a contrast is made between a tendency toward simplicity and a tendency toward higher geometric order.

5   W. Köhler, *Die Physischen Gestalten in Ruhe und im stationären Zustand* (83).

6   K. Koffka, *Principles of Gestalt Psychology* (81), chpt.II. The most complete summary of the research on perceptual organization and its bibliographical references up to 1975 is to be found in W. Metzger (102).

7   A.R.Granit, *A study on the perception of form* (56); E.Lindemann, *Experimentelle Untersuchungen über das Entstehen und Vergehen von Gestalten* (89); and K. Koffka (81).

8   E. Wohlfahrt, *Der Auffassungsvorgang an kleinsten Gestalten* (157); or in displays of shapes at the periphery of the field of vision; O. Graefe, *Analyse des inneren Aufbaus einer im peripheren Gesichtfeld wahrgenommenen Figur* (57)

9   These 'laws of grouping' are explicated in most standard works on visual perception; fairly complete listings of such principles can be found in M. Wertheimer, *Untersuchungen zur Lehre von der Gestalt* (152); W. Metzger (102); and K. Koffka (81).

10 For figural 'goodness', see M.B. Hubbel, *Configurational Properties Considered "Good" by Naive Subjects* (66); and K.M. Michels and L. Zusne, *Metrics of Visual Form* (103).

11 For principles of praegnanz see M. Wertheimer, (152); W. Metzger, (102) chpt.7; and E. Rausch, *Das Eigenschaftproblem in der Gestalttheorie der Wahrnehmung* (119).

12 Aristotle, *The Metaphysics* (7), p.1024a.

13 Alberti, *On Painting*, quoted in Osborne (109), p.287.

14 St. Augustine, quoted in *ibid.*, p.286.

15 F.H. Allport, *Theories of Perception and the Concept of Structure* (3), p.113.

16 K. Lewin, *Principles of topological psychology* (88).

17 K. Lynch, *The Image of the City* (96).

18 J. Piaget, *Structuralism* (115). According to Piaget, a structure is a whole, closed under transformations and being self-regulated.

19 M. Plank, *Eight Lectures on Theoretical Physics*, p.50, as quoted in Arnheim (9), p.8.

20 W. Köhler, *Die physischen Gestalten in Ruhe und im stationären Zustand (83)*.

21 Heron, B.K. Doane and T.H. Scott, *Visual disturbances after prolonged perceptual isolation* (63), pp.13-18.

22 J.W. Osborne, *The relationship between aesthetic preference and visual complexity in abstract art* (110), pp.69-70.

23 D.E.Berlyne, *Aesthetics and Psychobiology* (22).

24 H. Frank, *Über grundlegende Sätze der Informationspsychology* (44).

25   G.A. Miller, J.S. Bruner and L. Postman, *Familiarity of letter sequences and tachisto-scopic identification* (105), p.50.

26   H.W. Franke, *Phänomen Kunst* (44).

27   The two major sources in which information theory is applied to aesthetics are A. Moles, *Information theory and esthetic perception* (106); and M. Bense, *Aesthetica* (19). More specific applications to aesthetic measures can be found in R. Gunzenhauser, *Ästhetisches Maß und ästhetische Information* (58).

28   See Frank (44) and Miller et al. (105).

29   H. Heckhausen, *Complexity in perception: Phenomenal criteria and information theoretic calculus - a note on D.E. Berlynes 'complexity effects'* (61), pp.168-73 chpt.2.

30   E. Raab, *Bildkomplexität, Farbe, und ästhetischer Eindruck* (118), p.100 ff.

31   H. Frank *Informationsasthetik: Grundlagenprobleme und erste Anwendung auf die Mime Pure* (44).

Chapter VII

1   K. Koffka, *Principles of Gestalt Psychology* (75), p.119.

2   D.H. Hubel, *The visual cortex in the brain*, in Atkinson (13), pp.3-27.

3   See W. Metzger, *Gesetze des Sehens* (93), chpt.VI.; and E. Rausch, *Zur Theorie der soge-nannten Vertikalentäuschung* (108).

4   E.H. Gombrich, *Art and Illusion* (48), p.64.

5   K. Koffka, *Gestaltpsychology*. (48), p.125 ff.

6   R. Arnheim, *The Dynamics of Architectural Form* (11), p.19.

7   K. Koffka, *Principles of Gestalt Psychology* (75), p.125.

8   For figure ground organization, see Koffka ibid., chapt.VI.

9   R. Arnheim, *Art and Visual Perception* (8), pp.223-27.

10   R. Arnheim, Speaks of shapes as beeing endowed with "perceptual forces."(8), p.11.

11   E. Rubin, *Visuell wahrgenommene Figuren* (123).

12   Theory of perception of spatial depth through the reflection of light by surfaces in the visual array is described both in J.J. Gibson,*The Perception of the Visual World* (45), and *The Ecological Approach to Visual Perception* (44).

13   For a discussion of cognitive contours, see G. Kanizsa, *The Role of Regularity in Perceptual Organization* (70).

14   Institut für Städtebau Publikationen, *Prinzipien der Stadtgestaltung*. Universität Stuttgart, 1974.

15   For an attempt to link the various cones of clear vision and chromatic color perception with

the perception of architectural space, see O. Schubert, *Optik in Architektur und Städtebau* (114); and R. Weber, *An Approach to the Definition of the Architectural Term 'Scale'* (131).

16 For a discussion of good continuation, see W. Metzger, (93), chpt.I.

17 For a discussion of the law of proximity, see Metzger, *ibid.* chpt.I.

18 For the various cones of clear vision see O. Schubert, opcit., chpt.1.

19 Theories of cognitive mapping and sequential notation in urban spaces have been developed by K. Lynch, *The Image of the City* (87); and M. Trieb, *Stadtgestaltung, Theory und Praxis* (127).

20 P. Frankl, *Principles of Architectural History* (40), chpt.I.

21 *Ibid.*, pp.8-10.

22 *Ibid.*, p.10.

Chapter VIII

1 Arnheim, R. *Art and Visual Perception* (9), p.13.

2 Arnheim, R. *The Power of the Center* (1012), p.237.

3 G.Goude and I. Hjorzberg, *An Experimentell Provning* (55); discussed by Arnheim (8), p.15.

4 W. Metzger, *Gesetze des Sehens* (102), p.116.

5 K. Koffka, *Principles of Gestalt Psychology* (81), p.193.

6 *Ibid.*, p.197.

7 See Koffka's interpretation (*ibid.*, p.187) of the experiment of A. Gelband and R. Granit, *Die Bedeutung von Figur und Grund für die Farbenschwelle* (56).

8 For the function of the fovea, see G.D. Cumming, *"Eye Movements and Visual Perception,"* in C. Charterette and M. Friedman, *Handbook of Perception*, Vol.IX (33), pp.221-50.

9 Comprehensive bibliographies of recent studies of eye movement are in: R.A. Monty and J.W. Senders, eds., *Eye Movement and Psychological Processes*; and F. Molnar, *About the Role of Visual Exploration in Aesthetics* (107).

10 G. Buswell, *How People Look at Pictures* (32).

11 Example from Molnar (107), p.401.

12 N.H. Mackworth and A.Y. Morandi, *The Gaze Selects Informative Details within Pictures* (98), pp.574-582.

13 D. Noton and L. Stark, *Eye Movement and Visual Perception* (108), pp.34-52.

14 Example from Molnar (107), p.409.

15 L. Kaufmann and W. Richards, *Spontaneous Fixation Tendencies for Visual Forms* (77), pp.85-88.

16 According to Metzger (102), p.54, here the 'figure ground principle of the second order'

operates.

17 H.F. Brandt, *The Psychology of Seeing* (28), p.30.

18 The slight overestimation of the vertical can be neglected in these cases, although, for example, a square, in order to be seen as one, has to be a little wider than higher.

19 Buswell (32), p.109 ff.,fig.78.

20 Arnheim (8), pp.155-58. welches Buch?

21 Kaufmann and Richards (77), see reference 15.

22 This example is taken from Arnheim (8), p.25.

23 Ibid.,p 29.

24 Brandt (28), p.78.

25 *op cit.*, p.24-25.

26 J.C. Brengelmann, *Preferences for Upright Structure in Memory Traces* (29), discussed in Metzger (102), p.212.

27 Brandt (28), p.30.

28 R. Weber, *Focalcenters* (145), p.47-50.

29 *Ibid.*, p.48.

30 The tendency towards orthogonal localization is discussed in J. Jarvinen, *Orthogonal Localization of Visual Objects — Some Experiments on Space Perception* (73).

.31 The influence of the cardinal dimensions and of the orientation of shapes on perceived stability is discussed in M. Takala, *Asymmetries of Visual Space* (135).

32 *Ibid.*, p.57.

33 *Ibid.*, p.67.

34 G.T. Buswell, *Cathedral Displays*(32).

35 Brandt (28), pp.30-33.

36 Buswell (32), *Cathedral Displays*.

37 Molnar (107), pp.408-11.

38 *Ibid.*, p.408.

39 G.A. Miller, *The magical number Seven, plus or minus two: Some limits on our capacity for information processing* (104), pp.81-87.

40 D.W. Ross, *A Theory of Pure Design* (120), p.26, discussed in Arnheim (8), p.39.

41 According to Miller (104), seven is the maximum of parts which can be comprehended as a whole. Also, interestingly enough, Molnar (107), p.304-5, found that the velocity of the initial fixations abruptly reduces between the fifth and the tenth fixation.

42 Arnheim (8), p.102.

43 For an extensive description of the various laws of figural segregation these two studies are still the most valid ones: E. Rubin, *Visuell Wahrgenommene Figuren* (123); and K. Koffka, *Principles of Gestalt Psychology* (81), specifically chapt.V.

44 For a comprehensive bibliography of recent studies of figure-ground segregation see W. Metzger, *Gesetze des Sehens* (102), chapt.I & III.

45 Koffka (81), p.187.

46 R. Arnheim, *Art and Visual Perception* (9), p.223.

47 H. Rupp, *Über optische Analyse* (124), quoted in W. Metzger (102), p.35. Piaget has shown a similar tendency for children's drawings (114), pp.72ff., discussed by Arnheim (8) p.224.

48 F. Attneave, *"Multistability in Perception,"* In: R.L. Atkinson and R.C. Atkinson, eds., *Mind and Behavior* (15), pp.107-16.

49 For a more detailed discussion see the above mentioned Metzger, Koffka and Rubin.

50 Arnheim (8), p.241.

51 Koffka (81), p.184.

Summary and Outlook

1 First studies in this direction have been undertaken by Weber, R. Choi, Y. and Stark, L. at the Telerobotics Unit at the University of California, Berkeley through an NEA funded project On the Impact of Geometry on the Perception of Architecture (1993).

Bibliography

1   Alberti, L.B. *Ten Books of Architecture*. Translated into English by James Leoni. New York, 1966.

2   Alexander, C. et.al. A *Pattern Language: Towns, Buildings Construction* . New York: Oxford University Press, 1977

3   Allport, F.H.. *Theories of Perception and the Concept of Structure*. N ew York, 1955.

4   Allport, G. and P.E. Vernon, *Studies in Expressive Movement*. New York, 1933.

5   Ames, A., *Visual Perception and the Rotating Trapezoidal Window*. Psychol. Monogr.,1951. vol. 5, #7, (Whole #324).

6   Aquinas. Thomas St., *Summa Theologiae*. London, 1989.

7   Aristotle. *The Metaphysics*. Transl. by Hugh Tredennick, Cambridge, Mass., 1956.

8   Aristotle. *Poetics*. Transl. by S. H. Butcher, New York, 1961.

9   Arnheim, R. *Art and Visual Perception*. Berkeley and Los Angeles, 1954.

10   _____. *The Gestalt Theory of Expression*. In: (14)

11   _____. *Entropy and Art: an Essay on Disorder and Order*. Berkeley and Los Angeles, 1954.

12   _____. *The Power of the Center: a Study of Composition in the Visual Arts* . Berkeley and LosAngeles, 1985.

13   _____. *The Dynamics of Architectural Form: based on the 1975 Mary Duke Biddle Lectures at Cooper Union*. Berkeley and Los Angeles, 1977.

14   _____. *Toward a Psychology of Art: Collected Essays* . Berkeley and Los Angeles. 1966.

15   Atkinson, R. L., and R.C. Atkinson. *Mind and Behavior: Readings from Scientific American*. San Francisco, 1980.

16   Attneave, F. *Multistability in Perception*. In: Atkinson (15) pp. 107-116.

17   Banissoni, M. and E. Ponzo. Pe*rcezione strutturata e trasposizione di forme nelle prime esperienze vivise di un cieco dai primi mesi di vita operato in eta adulta di osteo-odonto-cheratoprotesi di Strampelli*. Riv. di Psicol,1968, vol. 62, pp. 685-687.

18   Beardsley, M. *Theories of Beauty since the Mid-Nineteenth Century* . In: Ph. Wiener, ed., D*ictionary of the History of Ideas* , p.209.

19   Bense, M. *Aesthetica: Einführung in die neue Aesthetik* . Baden-Baden, 1965.

20   Berkeley, G. T*hree Dialogues Between Hylas and Philonous*. Chicago, 1929.

21   Berlyne, D.E. *Conflict, Arousal and Curiosity*. New York, 1960.

22   _____. *Aesthetics and Psychobiology*. New York, 1972.
23   Berlyne, D. E. and A. Oostendorp. *Dimensions in the Perception Architecture*. Scand. J. Psychol. 1978, vol. 19, pp. 83-89.
24   Binkley, T. *Piece: Contra Aesthetics*. In: Margolis, (101), pp. 25-44.
25   Birkhoff, G.D. *Aesthetic Measure*. Cambridge, Mass., 1933.
26   Brikhoff, G.D. A *Mathematical Theory of Aethestics*. The Rice Institute Pamphlet, 1932.
27   Blondel, J.F. *Cours d'architecture enseigné dans l'Académie Royale d'Architecture* . Paris, 1675 (2.ed. Hildesheim - New York, 1982), p.229.
28   Brandt, H. F. *The Psychology of Seeing*. New York, 1945.
29   Brengelmann, J.C. *Preference for Upright Structure in Memory Traces*. Psychol. Forsch. vol. 30,1967.
30   de Bruyne, E. Éthudes d'esthéthiquie médiévale. II. Brugge, 1946.
31   Burke, E. *A Philosophical Enquiry into the Origin of Our Ideas of the Sublime and Beautiful*. London, 1958.
32   Buswell, G. T. *How People Look at Pictures*. New York, 1935.
33   Carterette, E. C. and M. P. Friedman *Handbook of Perception*. San Francisco, vol. 9. 1978.
34   Cumming, G. D. *Eye Movements and Visual Perception* . In: Carterette (33) pp. 221-256.
35   Danto, A. *The Artworld*. In: Margolis (101) pp. 132-144.
36   Dawson, Sh. *Distancing as an Aesthetic Principle* . Hospers (65) pp. 155-174.
37   Dickie, G. *The Myth of the Aesthetic Attitude* . Am. philosoph. Q.. 1964, vol.I, pp. 56-66.
38   Downs, R.M. and D. Stea, eds. I*mage and Environment: Cognitive Mapping and Spatial Behavior*. Chicago, 1973.
39   Eco,Umberto. *A Theory of Semiotics* . University of Indiana Press, Bloomington1976.
40   Eibl-Eibesfeldt, I. D*er Vorprogrammierte Mensch: Das Ererbte als bestimmender Faktor im menschlichen Verhalten*. Wien, 1973.
41   Espe, H. *Differences in the Perception of National Socialist and Classicist Architecture* . J. of environ. Psychol., vol.1,1981, pp. 33-42.
42   Furth, H. G. P*iaget and Knowledge: Theoretical Foundations*. Chicago and London, 1981.
43   Frank, H. *Informationsasthetik: Grundlagenprobleme und erste Anwendung auf die Mime Pure*. Quickborn, 1968.
44   _____. Über Grundlegende Sät*ze der Informationspsychologie* . In: Franke, H. W. *Phänomen Kunst*. Köln, 1974.

45   Frankl, P. Die Entwicklungsphasen der neueren Baukunst. Leipzig, 1914. (Principles of Architectural History; translated and edited by James F. Gorman. Cambridge, Mass. and London, 1968.)

46   Frege, G. The Philosophical Writings of Gottlob Frege. Oxford, 1952.

47   Gehlen, A. Über einige Kategorien des Entlastenden, zumal des Aesthetischen Verhaltens . In: Henrich E. and W. Iser (62) pp. 237-260.

48   Gelb, A. and A. R. Granit. Die Bedeutung von 'Figur' und 'Grund' für die Farbenschwelle. Zts. f. Psych. 1921, 93.

49   Gibson, J.J. The Ecological Approach to Visual Perception. Boston, 1979.

50   _____. The Perception of the Visual World. Boston, 1950.

51   _____. The Senses Considered a Perceptual System. London, 1968.

52   v. Goethe, J.W. Dichtung und Wahrheit. Bergen II, 1947.

53   Gombrich, E. H. Art and Illusion: A Study in the Psychology of Pictorial Representation. London and New York, 1960.

54   _____. The Sense of Order: A Study in the Psychology of Decorative Art. Ithaca, New York, 1984.

55   Goude, G. and I. Hjortzberg. An Experimental Prövning, etc. University of Stockholm, 1967.

56   Granit, A. R. A Study on the Perception of Form. Brt. j. Psychol.1921, 12.

57   Graefe, O. Analyse des inneren Aufbaus einer im Peripheren Gesichtfeld wahrgenommenen Figur. Zeitschr. f. exp. und ang. Psychol. no.4, 1957.

58   Gunzenhäuser, R. Aesthetisches Mass und Aesthetische Information: Einführung in die Theorie G.D. Birkhoffs und die Redundanztheorie asthetischer Prozesse. Quickborn, 1962.

59   Hambidge, J. Dynamic Symmetry: The Greek Vase. New Haven, 1920.

60   Hart, R.E., and G.T. Moore. The Development of Spatial Cognition: A Review. In: Downs, R.M. and Stea, D. (38)

61   Heckhausen, D. Complexity in Perception: Phenomenal Criteria and Information Theoretic Calculus - a note on D. E. Berlynes 'complexity effects' . " In: Can. j. Psychol. vol. 18,1964, pp. 168-173.

62   Henrich, D. and W. Iser (ed.). Theorien der Kunst. Frankfurt am Main, 1982.

63   Heron, W.; B. K. Doane and T. H. Scott. Visual Disturbances after Prolonged Perceptual Isolation. Can. j. Psychol. vol. 10, 1956. pp. 1-22.

64   Hochberg, J. and E. McAlister. A Quantitative Approach to Figural 'Goodness'. J. exper. Psychology. vol. 46,1953. p.361.

65   Hospers, J. Introductory Readings in Aesthetics. New York and London, 1969.

66   Hubbel, M. B. Configurational Properties Cons idered "Good" by Naive Subjects.

Amer. j. Psychology. 1940. vol. 53, pp. 46-69.

67   Hubel, D. H. The Visual Cortex of the Brain. In: Psychology in Progress. R. C. Atkinson
      ed. New York, 1975.

68   Hubel, D. H., and T. N. Wiesel. Brain Mechanisms of Vision. In: Atkinson (15) pp.
      32-44.

69   Hume, D. *Essays, Moral, Political and Literary* . London, 1741.

70   ____. Of the Standard of Taste. In: *Critical Theory Since Plato*. New York, 1971.

71   Inhelder, B. Some Aspects of Piaget's *Genetic Approach to Cognition*. In: Furth (42)
      pp. 22-23.

72   Ittelson, W. H. et al. *An Introduction to Environmental Psychology*. New York, 1974.

73   Jaervinen, J. *Orthogonal Localization of Visual Objects - Some Experiments on Space
      Perception.* Annales Academiae Scientarum Fennicae. Helsinki, 1969.

74   Jencks, Charles. *The Language of Post-Modern Architecture* . New York, Rizzoli,
      1987.

75   Kant, I. *Critique of Judgment.* Translated with analytical indexes by James Creed
      Meredith. New York, 1951.

76   Kanizsa, G. The Role of Regula *rity in Perceptual Organization* . In: Studies in
      Perception . hrsg.v.G.B. Flores d'Arcais. Mailand, 1975.

77   Kaufman, L. and W. Richards. Spontaneous Fixat *ion Tendencies for Visual Forms.* Per
      ception and Psychophysics. 1969. vol. 5, pp. 85-88.

78   Kayser, H. *Harmonica.* Bern.

79   Kiemle, M. *Asthetische Probleme der Architektur unter dem Aspekt der
      Informationsästhethetik.* Quickborn, 1967.

80   Klaus, M. *Wörterbuch der Kybernetik.* Berlin, 1967.

81   Koffka, K. *Principles of Gestalt Psychology.* New York, 1935.

82   Köhler, W. *Gestalt Psychology.* New York, 1929.

83   ____. *Die physischen Gestalten in Ruhe und im stationären Zustand.* Braunschweig,
      1920.

84   Koenig, G.K. *Archittetura e communicazione* .(Firenze: Liberia editrice fiorentina,
      1970).

85   Koenig, G.K. *Analisi del linguaggio architettonico* .(Firenze: Liberia editrice fiorentina,
      1964).

86   Lashley, K. S. Persistent Pro *blems in the Evolution of Mind* . In: Quart. Rev. Biol. 1949,
      vol. 24, p. 93.

87   Lawlor, R. *Sacred Geometry* . London 1982

88   Lewin, K. *Principles of Topological Psychology.* Translated by F. Heider et al. New
      York, 1936.

89   Lindemann, E. *Experimentelle Untersuchungen über das Entstehen und Vergehen von Gestalten.* Psychol. Forsch. 1922, 2.

90   Lipps, T. *Aesthetik: Psychologie des Schönen und der Kunst*. Berlin, 1907.

91   _____. *Einheiten und Relationen - Eine Skizze zur Psychologie der Apperzeption.* Leipzig, 1902.

92   _____. *Raumaesthetik und geometrisch-optische Täuschungen.* Leipzig, 1897.

93   Lorenz, K. *Gesammelte Abhandlungen* . Bd. 1 und 2, München, 1966.

94   _____. *Über die Bildung des Instinktbegriffs.* In: (93).

95   _____. *Die Angeborenen Formen Möglicher Erfahrung.* In: (93).

96   Lynch, K. *The Image of the City.* Cambridge, Mass., 1960.

97   Machenauer, P. K. and R. G. Turnbull (ed.). *Studies in Perception: Interrelations in the History of Philosophy and Science.* Columbus, Ohio, 1978.

98   Mackworth, N. H. and A. Y. Morandi. *The Gaze Selects Informative Details Within Pictures.* Perception and Psychophysics. 1967, vol. 2.

99   Maertens, H. *Der optische Maßstab oder die Theorie und Praxis des ästhetischen Sehens in den Bildenden Künsten.* Berlin, 1884.

100 Mandelbaum, M. *Philosophy, Science and Sense Perception: Historical and Critical Studies.* Baltimore, 1964.

101 Margolis, J. *Philosophy Looks at the Arts.* Philadelphia, 1978.

102 Metzger, W. *Gesetze des Sehens.* Frankfurt, 1975.

103 Michels, K. M. and L. Zusne. *Metrics of Visual Form.* Psychol. Bull. 1965, vol. 63.

104 Miller, G. A.. *The Magical Number Seven, Plus or Minus Two: Some Limits on our Capacity for Processing Information.* Perception and Psychophysics 1967, vol. 63, pp. 81-87.

105 Miller, G. A., J. S. Bruner, and L. Postman. *Familiarity of Letter Sequences and Tachistoscopic Identification.* J. gen. Psychol. 1954, vol. 50.

106 Moles, A. A. *Information Theory and Esthetic Perception.* Translated by Joel F. Cohen. Urbana and London, 1966.

107 Molnar, F. *About the Role of Visual Exploration in Aesthetics.* In: Advances in Intrinsic Motivation and Aesthetics. New York. 1981.

108 Noton, D. and L. Stark. *Eye Movements and Visual Perception.* Scientific American 1971, vol. 244, pp. 34-53.

109 Osborne, H. *Aesthetics and Art Theory.* New York, 1968.

110 Osborne, J. W. *The Relationship between Aesthetic Preference and Visual Complexity in Abstract Art.* Psychonomic Science 1970, vol. 19, pp. 69-70.

111 Otto, W.T. *Der Raumsatz: Neue Gestaltungsprobleme der Architektur.* Stuttgart, 1959.

112 Pastore, N. *Selective History of Theories of Visual Perception: 1650-1950*. London, 1971.

113 Piaget, J. *Assimilation and Sensory-Motor Knowledge*. In: Furth (42) pp. 52-54.

114 Piaget, J. and B. Inhelder. *The Child's Conception of Space*. New York, 1967.

115 _____. *Structuralism*. New York, 1970.

116 Plato *The Dialoges of Plato*. Timaeus 32, trans. B. Jowett. Berkeley, 1978.

117 Prak, N.L. *The Language of Architecture: A Contribution to Architectural Theory* The Hague, 1968.

118 Raab, E. *Bildkomplexität. Farbe und ästhetischer Eindruck*. Graz, 1976.

119 Rausch, E. *Das Eigenschaftsproblem in der Gestalttheorie der Wahrnehmung* . Hdb. d. Psychol. 1966, vol. 71.

120 Ross, D. W. *A Theory of Pure Design*. New York. 1933.

121 Rittel, H. *On the Planning Crisis: Systems Analysis of the 'First and Second Generations'*. Bedrifts Okonomen 1972, vol. 8, p. 390.

122 _____. *Some Principles for the Design of an Educational System for Design*. In: Education for Architectural Technology. Berkeley, 1966.

123 Rubin, E. *Visuell wahrgenomene Figuren*. Copenhagen, 1921.

124 Rupp, H. *Über Optische Analyse*. Psychol. Forschung 1923, vol. 4.

125 Schubert, O. *Optik in Architektur und Städtebau*. Berlin, 1965.

126 Schuster, M. and H. Beisl. *Kunst-Psychologie: Wodurch Kunstwerke wirken*. Köln, 1978.

127 Scruton, R. *The Aesthetics of Architecture*. Princeton, 1979.

128 Segall, M. H., D. T. Campbell and M. J. Herskovits. *The Influence of Culture on Visual Perception*. New York, 1966.

129 Sibley, F. N. *Aesthetic Concepts*. In: Margolis (101) pp. 64-88.

130 Siro, E. *Über die Autonomie des Seelischen im Lichte des Phi-Phanomens*. Annales Academiae Scientarum Fennicae, Helsinki, 1969.

131 Skinner, B. F. *Science and Human Behavior*. New York, 1953.

132 Stolnitz, J. *The Aesthetic Attitude*. In: Hospers (65) pp. 17-27.

133 Sullivan, L. *Kindergarden Chats*, New York, 1947.

134 Sutherland, N. S. *Shape Discrimination and Receptive Fields*. Nature 1963, vol. 197.

135 Takala, M. *Asymmetries of Visual Space*. Annales Academiae Scientarum Fennicae, Helsinki, 1951.

136 Tatarkiewicz, W. *Form in the History of Aesthetics*. In: Dictionary of the History of Ideas: Studies of Selected Pivotal Ideas. New York, 1973.

137 The Bible, *The Book of Solomon*

138 Thompson, D'Arcy. *On Growth and Form*. Cambridge, Eng. 1969.

139 Tootell, R. B. H., et.al. *Deoxyglucose Analysis of Retinotopic Organization in Primate*

Striate Cortex. Science 1982, vol.218. pp. 902-904.

140   Trieb, M. *Stadtgestaltung: Theorie und Praxis.* Düsseldorf, 1974.

141   Vischer, R. *Das Optische Formgefühl.* Reprinted in: Drei Schriften zum asthetischen Formproblem. Halle, 1927.

142   Vitruvius Pollo. *The Ten Books of Architecture.* New York, 1960.

143   Wallach, H. *Brightness Constancy and the Nature of Achromatic Colors.* J. exp. Psychol. 1948, vol. 38, pp. 310-324.

144   Weber, R. *Approach to a Definition of the Architectural Term Scale.* (working paper) U.C. Berkeley, 1979.

145   _____. *Focal Centers: An Approach to Link the Geometrical Structure of Buildings to the Order of Visual Perception. (working paper)* U.C.Berkeley, 1980.

146   _____. *On the Structure and the Order of Perceived Architectural Space: Towards a Psychological Based Approach on the Aesthetics of Architecture.* Stuttgart, 1982.

147   _____. *Some Thoughts About Structures in Architectural Design.* (working paper) U.C. Berkeley, 1980.

148   _____. Systematology of Space - Structural Criteria. (working paper) U.C. Berkeley, 1980.

149   _____. *The Myth of Meanigful Forms.* Traditional Dwellings and Settlements Vol. 3, No. 1

150   v. Weizsäcker, V. *Die Gestaltkreislehre.* Stuttgart, 1947.

151   Werner, H. *Comparative Psychology of Mental Development.* New York. 1940.

152   Wertheimer, M. *Untersuchungen zur Lehre von der Gestalt .* Psychol. Forschung Bd. 1923, vol. 4.

153   _____. *Über Gestalttheorie.* Symposium Bd. 1925, vol. 1, pp. 1-24.

154   Weyl, H. *Symmetry.* Princeton, 1952.

155   Wittkower, R. *The Changing Concept of Proportion.* Daedalus, Winter 1960, pp. 201ff.

156   Wiener, Ph., ed. *Dictionary of the History of Ideas.* New York 1968, vol.1

157   Wohlfahrt, E. *Der Auffassungsvorgang an kleinsten Gestalten. Ein Beitrag zur Psychologie des Vorgestalterlebnisses.* Neue Psychol. Stud. 1928, 4.

158   Wollheim, R. *Art and its Objects.* New York, 1960.

159   Yarbus, A. L. *Eye Movements and Vison.* Translated from Russian by Basil Haigh, translation ed. Lorrin A. Riggs. New York, 1967.

160   Zuckerman, C. B. and I. Rock. *A Reappraisal of the Roles of Past Experience and Innate Organization Processes in Visual Perception.* Psychol. Bull. 1957, vol. 54, pp. 269-296.

List of Figures

Chapter II

Chapter IV

Chapter VII

Fig. 75.   Amalienburg Square, Copenhagen.
             Author's material.
Fig. 76.   Square with streets entering at corners.
             Author's material.
Fig. 77.   Niches and appendixes enhance perceived concavity.
             Author's material.
Fig. 78.   Illusionist painting.
             E. H. Gombrich. *The Story of Art.* Garden City, New York. 1968, p. 332.
Fig. 79.   Piazza S. Ignazio, Rome.
             Portoghesi, Paulo. Roma Barocca, Cambridge, Mass. 1970, p. 374.
Fig. 80.   S. Ivo, Rome: (plan)
             Frankl, P. *Die Entwicklungsphasen der neueren Baukunst.* Leipzig, 1914. (Principles
             of Architectural History; translated and edited by James F. Gorman. Cambridge,
             Mass. and London, 1968, p. 50.)
Fig. 81.   S. Ivo, Rome. (interior)
             Ibid. p. 50.
Fig. 82.   Effect of 'cognitive contours': Protruding elements produce perceptual closure.
             Author's material.
Fig. 83.   Ravensburger Tor Square, Wangen.
             Alte Deutsche Baukunst. Langewiesche. Leipzig. p. 80.
Fig. 84.   Via degli Angeli, Ferrara.
             Kostof, S. *A History of Architecture.* New York, 1985, p. 429.
Fig. 85.   Medieval street, Siena.
             Kostof, S. *A History of Architecture.* New York, 1985, p. 365.
Fig. 86.   Friedrichstrasse, Berlin. during Baroque period
             Kostof, S. *A History of Architecture.* New York, 1985, p. 587.
Fig. 87.   Dvortsovaia Square, St. Petersburg.
             Kostof, S. *A History of Architecture.* New York, 1985, p. 585.
Fig. 88.   Piazza S. Marco, Venice.(plan).
             Author's material.
Fig. 89.   Piazza S. Marco, Venice.View towards S. Giorgio Maggiore
             University of California, Berkeley. Slide Library.
Fig. 90.   Karlsruhe. Weinbrenner's design, Germany.
             Giedion, Sigfried. *Spätbrocker und Romantischer Klassizismus,* München 1922, p.228
Fig. 91   Street in Castelfranco, Italy.
             Author's material.

Fig. 110. Piazza del Campidoglio, Rome.
Author's material.

Fig. 111. Vocolo della Pace, Rome. (plan)
Author's material.

Fig. 112. View of Santa Maria della Pace, Rome.
Trachtenburg, Marvin. *Architecture: From Prehistory to Post-Modernism.* New York, 1986, p. 352.

Fig. 113. The Campo, Siena.
Author's material.

Fig. 114. The Campo, Siena.
Author's material.

Fig. 115. Piazza S. Marco, Venice. (plan)
Author's material.

Fig. 116. View at Nopoleonica, Venice.
Pescio, Claudio. *Vollständiger Führer für die Stadtbesichtigung,* Firenze, 1980, p. 38-39.

Fig. 117. View at San Marco, Venice.
Ibid. p. 40-41.

Fig. 118. Possible organization of parts with a whole: central, linear, free-form.
Author's material.

Fig. 119. Coordinated and subordinated arrangement of spaces.
Author's material.

Fig. 120. Primary and auxillary spaces.
Author's material after Otto, W.T. *Der Raumsatz. Neue Gestaltungsprobleme der Architektur.* Stuttgart, 1959.

Fig. 121. Spatial appendixes.
Author's material.

Fig. 122. Pantheon, Rome. (plan)
Author's material.

Fig. 123. Pantheon, Rome. (interior)
University of California, Berkeley. Slide Library

Fig. 124. S. Stefano Rotondo, Rome.
Deichmann, F. Frühchristliche Kirchen in Rom. Basel, 1948, plan 9.

Fig. 125. Palatine Chapel, Aachen.
Line drawings by author.

Fig. 126. Sta. Maria degli Angeli.
Line drawings by author.

Fig. 127.   Sta. Maria della Croce, Crema.

After Frankl, P. Die *Entwicklungsphasen der neueren Baukunst*. Leipzig, 1914, p. 8. Line drawings by author.

Fig. 128.   St. Peter's, Rome. Bramante's plan.

Ibid., p.10. Line drawings by author.

Fig. 129.   S. Paolo f.l.m., Rome.

After Beny, R. & P. Gunn. *The Churches of Rome*. New York, 1981, p. 86. Line drawings by author.

Fig. 130.   S. Andrea, Mantua.

Frankl, P. *Die Entwicklungsphasen der neueren Baukunst*. Leipzig, 1914, p. 26. Line drawings Author's material.

Fig. 131.   F.L. Wright. Clark Residence, Illinois.

Drawings and Plans of Frank Lloyd Wright. Dover Publications. New York, 1983, pl. 39.

Fig. 132.   Congruent shapes, same size.

Proportion. A Measure of Order. Carpenter Center for Visual Arts, Harvard University, Spring and Summer 1965, p. 40.

Fig. 133.   Congruent shapes of different size.

Proportion. A Measure of Order. Carpenter Center for Visual Arts, Harvard University, Spring and Summer 1965, p. 41.

Fig. 134.   S. Maria del Calcinaio.

Frankl, P. Die Entwicklungsphasen der neueren Baukunst. p. 27.

Fig. 135.   Cathedral, Speyer.

Author's material.

Fig. 136.   SS. Flora e Lucilla, Arezzo.

Frankl, P. *Die Entwicklungsphasen der neueren Baukunst*. p. 25.

Fig. 137.   Alhambra, Granada. Principal proportional relationships.

Kostof, S. *A History of Architecture*. New York, 1985, p. 400.

Fig. 138.   Katsura Villa, Kyoto.

Grütter, Jörg. *Ästhetik der Architektur: Grundlagen der Architektur-Wahrnehmung*. Stuttgart, 1987, p. 116.

Fig. 139.   Peichl, G. ORF Studio.

Salzburg. Fonatti, F. *Principles of Architectural Composition*. Wien, 1982, p. 27.

WEBER

Chapter VIII

Fig. 177. Maison Medicale, Brussels.
          Author's material.
Fig. 178. Divisions of facades in order to produce distinct visual foci.
          Author's material.
Fig. 179. Jacobsen. City Hall, Copenhagen.
          Sharp, Dennis. *A Visual History of Twentieth Century Architecture.* Munich,
          1973, p. 210.
Fig. 180. Fehn, S. Home for the Elderly.
          Sverre Fehn: *The Thought of Construction.* New York, 1983, p. 89.
Fig. 181. de Klerk Housing, Amsterdam.
          Sharp, Dennis. A *Visual History of Twentieth Century Architecture.* Munich, 1973,
          p. 68.
Fig. 182   Niemeyer, O. Office building, Segrate.
          Tafuri, *Modern Architecture.* New York, 1976, p. 355.
Fig. 183. St. Peter's, Rome. Main facade.
          Kostof, S. *A History of Architecture.* New York, 1985, p. 506.
Fig. 184. Chateau Chambord.
          Trachtenburg, Marvin. *Architecture: From Prehistory to Post-Modernism.* New York,
          1986, p. 328.
Fig. 185. Karlskirche, Vienna.
          Ibid., p. 371.
Fig. 186. Effects of a shape placed in top symmetrical position(a-c)
          (a & b) Klenze. Glyptothek, München.
          Piltz, Georg. *Deutsche Baukunst.* Berlin, 1959, p. 343.
Fig. 187. (c) Brandenburg Gate, Berlin.
          Piltz, Georg. *Deutsche Baukunst.* Berlin, 1959, p. 335.
Fig. 188. Hierarchial vs. non-hierarchial arrangement of a facade. Reed House.
          Duly, Colin. *The Houses of Mankind.* London, 1979, pl. 86.
Fig. 189. Hierarchial vs. non-hierarchial arrangement of a facade. Curtain Wall Facade.
          Author's material.
Fig. 190. Speer. Reichskanzlei, Berlin.
          Albert Speer: Architecture 1932-1942. Bruxelles, 1985, p.159.
Fig. 191. Santa Maria Novella, Florence. (facade)
          Kostof, S. *A History of Architecture.* New York, 1985, p. 412.
Fig. 192. Laon Cathedral. West facade. Arrangement of main centers.Overlays by author.
          Jantzen, Hans. *High Gothic: The Classic Cathedrals of Chartres, Reims, Amiens.*
          Princeton, 1962, p. 105.

Fig. 193a-c.Main center supported by: secondary, tertiary, quartiary centers.
Author's material.
Fig. 194a,b.Secondary centers supported by: secondary, tertiary centers.
Author's material.
Fig. 195a,bTertiary centers supported by: secondary, tertiary centers.
Author's material.
Fig. 196. Laon Cathedral. west facade. Graphs derived from connections of centers.
Author's material.
Fig. 197. Residential Building, Muttenz.
Author's material
Fig. 198. Principles of figural segregation.
Metzger, W. *Gesetze des Sehens*. Frankfurt, 1975. Chpt. 1.
Fig. 199. Effect of window boundaries on figure-ground segregation in facades.
Author's material.
Fig. 200. Effect of size of shapes on figuredness of background.
Metzger, W. *Gesetze des Sehens*. Frankfurt, 1975, b,c: p. 39.
Fig. 201 Palladio. Palazzo Valmarana, Vicenza. Complex layers of figure and ground.
Schumacher, Thomas. *The Palladio Variations*. Cornell Journal of Architecture, Fall 1987, pp. 25-28.
Fig. 202. Castle Heddingham, Essex. Continuous ground: Interstices do not form figures.
Kostof, S. *A History of Architecture*. New York, 1985, p. 297.
Fig. 203. Rossi, A. Ossuary, Modena Cemetary.
Aldo Rossi Architect. New York, p.1985, p.100.
Fig. 204. Palazzo della Cancelleria, Rome.
Fusco, Renato de. L'architettura del Quattrocento. Torino, 1984, p.64.
Fig. 205 Apartment Buildings. Chicago.Mies v.d. Rohe.
Johnson, Philip. *Mies van der Rohe*. New York, 1978, p.139.
Fig. 206. Palazzo Farnese, Rome.
Fusco, Renato de. *L'architettura del Cinquecento*. Torino, 1984, p. 169.
Fig. 207. Arquitectonica. North Dade Courthouse.
A.D. *Deconstruction in Architecture*. London, 1988, p. 21.
Fig. 208. Doge's Palace, Venice.
Gombrich, E.H. *The Story of Art*. Garden City, New York, 1968, p. 150.

For Product Safety Concerns and Information please contact our EU
representative GPSR@taylorandfrancis.com
Taylor & Francis Verlag GmbH, Kaufingerstraße 24, 80331 München, Germany

www.ingramcontent.com/pod-product-compliance
Lightning Source LLC
Chambersburg PA
CBHW050704280326
41926CB00088B/2446

* 9 7 8 1 0 3 2 8 2 0 9 1 0 *